Chords & Cards: The Music of Tarot

By Liz Halat, with heartfelt thanks to Sharon Ostrov, Jonas Manashowitz, James Ceribello and Byron John Moore

Introduction

Tarot and music are both ancient forms of art, deeply rooted in the human experience, and both serve as tools for expression, reflection, and connection. While tarot cards offer visual symbols and archetypes to explore the mysteries of life, music provides soundscapes and rhythms that evoke emotions and tell stories. When these two mediums intersect, they create a unique synergy, offering musicians profound insights into their creative processes, emotional landscapes, and professional journeys. Tarot for musicians is not just about seeking answers; it is about deepening the connection to one's art, fostering inspiration, and navigating the complexities of a musical career with clarity and intention.

At its essence, tarot is a system of archetypes and symbols that reflect universal themes and narratives. Each card in the deck represents an aspect of the human experience, from challenges and triumphs to transformation and introspection. Musicians, as storytellers and creators, often draw upon these same themes in their music, making tarot a natural complement to their craft. The process of interpreting tarot cards mirrors the creative process itself as both involve intuition, imagination, and the ability to find meaning in patterns. Whether used as a tool for sparking inspiration, exploring emotions, or making career decisions, tarot offers musicians a new lens through which to view their artistry and their lives.

For many musicians, inspiration is both a gift and a mystery. The creative process can feel elusive, with moments of flow interspersed with periods of stagnation or doubt. Tarot can serve as a bridge between these moments, helping musicians reconnect with their inner muse and uncover new sources of inspiration. The imagery and symbolism of the tarot cards invite musicians to step into a world of imagination and storytelling, offering fresh perspectives on their creative projects. For example, a musician working on lyrics might draw the

Moon card, which symbolizes intuition, mystery, and the subconscious. This could prompt them to explore themes of dreams or hidden truths in their songwriting, opening up new lyrical directions they might not have considered before.

In addition to inspiring creativity, tarot can also help musicians navigate the emotional challenges that come with a life in music. The path of a musician is rarely straightforward, often marked by uncertainty, rejection, and self-doubt. Tarot provides a safe space for reflection, allowing musicians to process their emotions and gain clarity on their personal and professional struggles. A musician experiencing burnout, for instance, might draw the Hermit, which encourages introspection and solitude. This card could serve as a reminder to take a step back, recharge, and reconnect with their purpose. By offering insights into the emotional and psychological aspects of their journey, tarot helps musicians find balance and resilience in the face of challenges.

The practical applications of tarot for musicians extend beyond creativity and emotional well-being. The music industry is complex and often unpredictable, requiring musicians to make important decisions about collaborations, contracts, and career paths. Tarot can be a valuable tool for navigating these decisions, offering guidance and clarity when faced with uncertainty. For example, a musician considering whether to join a new band might use a tarot spread to explore the potential outcomes of the decision, as well as their own motivations and concerns. By providing a structured way to reflect on these factors, tarot helps musicians make more informed and intuitive choices that align with their goals and values.

Another significant aspect of tarot for musicians is its ability to enhance self-awareness and personal growth. Music is deeply personal, often reflecting the artist's own experiences and emotions. Tarot encourages musicians to explore their inner worlds, uncovering hidden fears, desires, and strengths that can inform their music. This process of self-discovery not only enriches their artistry but also helps them grow as individuals. A musician working through a difficult period in their life might draw the Tower, which represents upheaval and transformation. While initially unsettling, this card could inspire them to write a song about resilience and rebuilding, turning a personal struggle into a powerful artistic statement.

Tarot can also foster a deeper connection between musicians and their audience. Both tarot and music are about communication such as sharing stories, emotions, and experiences in a way that resonates with others. By engaging with the archetypes and themes of the tarot, musicians can create work that speaks to universal truths, forging a stronger emotional bond with their listeners. A musician inspired by the Lovers card, for example, might write a song about connection, duality, or choice, themes that are likely to resonate with their audience on a profound level. Through this process, tarot becomes a tool not only for personal reflection but also for creating art that touches the hearts of others.

For musicians who perform live, tarot can also serve as a grounding ritual before stepping on stage. The act of drawing a card and reflecting on its message can help calm pre-show nerves, set an intention for the performance, or even inspire a new approach to connecting with the audience. A performer who draws the Star, symbolizing hope and inspiration, might take it as a sign to focus on uplifting their audience and channeling positivity into their performance. In this way, tarot becomes a source of strength and confidence, helping musicians bring their best selves to the stage.

The use of tarot in a musician's life is not limited to individuals; it can also be a collaborative tool. Bands and ensembles can use tarot to explore group dynamics, address conflicts, or set collective intentions for their work. By using tarot as a shared language, musicians can deepen their understanding of one another and foster a greater sense of unity and purpose within the group. This collaborative aspect of tarot can be particularly valuable in creative projects, helping musicians align their visions and work together more harmoniously.

Ultimately, tarot for musicians is about connection to oneself, to one's art, and to the larger narrative of life. It is a tool that encourages introspection, sparks creativity, and provides guidance in times of uncertainty. Whether used as a source of inspiration, a means of emotional support, or a guide for decision-making, tarot offers musicians a unique way to navigate the complexities of their craft and their careers. By incorporating tarot into their lives, musicians can deepen their connection to their music, their audience and themselves, unlocking new levels of creativity and self-awareness along the way.

The Intersection of Tarot and Music

The intersection of tarot and music is a rich, evocative terrain where symbolism, emotion, and intuition coalesce. Both are ancient forms of storytelling, interpretation, and expression, drawing deeply from human consciousness to convey meaning beyond the reach of mere words. This connection thrives not only in their capacity to provoke emotion but in their ability to serve as mirrors for the psyche, offering pathways to introspection, creativity, and transcendence.

Tarot, with its seventy-eight cards, unfolds as a visual symphony of archetypes. Each card represents a note in a greater melody of existence, resonating with themes that span the human condition: love, loss, triumph, transformation, and mystery. Similarly, music employs rhythm, melody, and harmony to articulate the inarticulable, channeling energy in ways that can uplift, console, or challenge. When the two are brought together, tarot and music create an interplay that deepens the experience of both, weaving visual and auditory textures into an immersive act of divination and artistry.

Consider the way a tarot reading unfolds. The cards, whether drawn from the Major Arcana with their universal, mythic resonance, or the Minor Arcana with their earthly, nuanced tones, invite interpretation through an interplay of imagery and intuition. When paired with music, this act of interpretation gains an additional layer of depth. Music serves as a medium to amplify the emotional current of a reading. A mournful cello might underscore the sorrow of the Five of Cups, while an upbeat acoustic guitar could mirror the joyful energy of the Three of Cups. The pairing transforms the act of reading into a synesthetic experience, where meaning emerges not just from the cards but from the way their energies dance with sound.

This interplay is not limited to readings alone. Composers and musicians have long drawn inspiration from tarot's archetypal language. The enigmatic Fool, the alchemical Magician, the serene High Priestess each offer a wealth of symbolism to translate into melody. Some artists craft entire albums based on tarot, using the cards as a creative framework to explore themes of fate, free will, and the cycles of life. In these works, music becomes a form of divination in itself, each note and lyric an invocation of the card it seeks to embody. For instance, the enigmatic Fool might inspire a wandering melody, a song of curiosity and risk, full of open intervals and playful rhythms. The Tower, with its dramatic upheaval, might find its sonic counterpart in discordant chords and sudden shifts in tempo. In this sense, music becomes a living tarot deck, an auditory pathway through the landscapes of the soul.

The relationship between music and tarot is not merely one of translation. Music can also be used as a tool for meditation during tarot readings, setting the emotional tone and guiding the reader into a more receptive state. Just as certain songs can transport us to specific moments or moods, carefully chosen music can evoke the qualities of a particular card or spread, making the reading feel more alive and resonant. The intuitive mind, already attuned to the symbols of the cards, becomes even more open under the influence of sound, allowing for interpretations that are richer and more nuanced.

At its core, the intersection of tarot and music is an invitation to expand our modes of understanding. It is a call to see, hear, and feel the world in new ways, to let the cards guide our hands on the piano keys or the strings of a guitar, and to let the music whisper the secrets of the cards back to us. It is an exploration of harmony, not only between sight and sound but between the inner and outer worlds, the known and the unknown. And in this exploration, we find not just art, but a glimpse of the divine.

Overview of Tarot and Its Symbolism

Tarot is a profound symbolic system that has captivated minds for centuries, a deck of seventy-eight cards that weaves together imagery, archetypes, and intuition. At its core, the tarot is a tool for exploration of the self, of the psyche, and of the forces that shape human existence. Its symbolism speaks to universal truths, transcending cultures and eras to offer insights into the cycles of life, the nature of change, and the mysteries of the unknown. Despite its origins being veiled in historical uncertainty, the tarot has evolved into a multifaceted practice that continues to inspire and guide those who seek its wisdom.

The structure of the tarot deck itself is significant. Divided into two main sections, it forms a complete representation of the journey of life. The Major Arcana, comprising twenty-two cards, is the heart of the deck, its images representing archetypal themes and stages of spiritual development. These are not mere pictures but mirrors reflecting universal experiences: innocence and risk in the Fool, mastery and creation in the Magician, mystery and intuition in the High Priestess. Each card is a world unto itself, a reservoir of meaning that invites interpretation through layers of myth, history, and personal reflection.

The Major Arcana begins with the Fool, the numberless card, a figure poised at the edge of a precipice. The Fool represents beginnings, the potential of the unknown, and the courage to embark on a journey without guarantees. This journey unfolds through the remaining cards of the Major Arcana, tracing a path of growth and transformation. The symbolism of these cards is richly layered: the Empress embodies fertility and creativity, while the Emperor represents structure and authority. The Lovers explore choice and union, while the Hermit seeks solitude and inner truth. Each card holds a dual nature, its meaning shifting with the context of a reading or the perspective of the querent. They are not static images but living symbols, capable of speaking to countless scenarios and emotional landscapes.

The journey of the Major Arcana culminates with the World, a card of completion, unity, and harmony. Here, the Fool's path is resolved, suggesting the fulfillment of a cycle and the promise of new beginnings. This cyclical nature of the Major Arcana echoes the rhythms of life itself, with its constant interplay of beginnings and endings, triumphs and trials. In this way, the cards offer a framework for understanding the complexities of human experience, providing both guidance and reassurance in times of uncertainty.

The Minor Arcana, with its fifty-six cards, delves into the details of daily life and practical concerns. It is divided into four suits: Wands, Cups, Swords, and Pentacles, each corresponding to an element and an aspect of existence. Wands, associated with fire, represent passion, creativity, and action. Cups, aligned with water, symbolize emotions, relationships, and intuition. Swords, tied to air, signify intellect, conflict, and communication. Pentacles, connected to earth, embody material matters, stability, and the physical world. Together, these suits form a mosaic of human experience, addressing both the tangible and the intangible facets of life.

Each suit progresses from Ace to Ten, followed by four court cards: Page, Knight, Queen, and King. The numbered cards reflect specific situations and emotions, from the joy of the Three of Cups to the disappointment of the Three of Swords. The court cards add another layer of complexity, representing people, roles, or aspects of the self. The interplay of these cards in a reading creates a dynamic narrative, a snapshot of the querent's life or a glimpse into possibilities yet to unfold.

Central to the tarot is its reliance on symbolism. The images on the cards are imbued with meaning, drawing from mythological, astrological, and esoteric traditions. These symbols are not fixed but fluid, open to interpretation based on context and intuition. A serpent might signify wisdom in one reading and deception in another. The sun might represent clarity or the promise of a new dawn, depending on its placement and surrounding cards. This fluidity is what makes the tarot so powerful; it adapts to the individual, offering a unique and deeply personal perspective with each use.

Beyond the cards themselves, the act of reading tarot is an art of synthesis. It requires the reader to weave together the symbolism of the cards, the question or situation at hand, and their intuitive understanding. The spread, or the arrangement of cards in a reading, further shapes the interpretation. A three-card spread might illuminate the past, present, and future of a situation, while the Celtic Cross offers a more detailed exploration of influences, challenges, and outcomes. Each reading is a dialogue between the cards and the querent, a co-creative process that draws from both the external imagery and the internal landscape of the mind.

The tarot's symbolism is deeply psychological, resonating with the ideas of Carl Jung and the concept of archetypes. Jung recognized the tarot as a tool for accessing the collective unconscious, a repository of shared human experiences and motifs. The cards, with their rich imagery, tap into this reservoir, allowing the querent to uncover hidden truths and gain clarity. In this way, the tarot functions not only as a means of divination but as a mirror for self-reflection, offering insights into one's desires, fears, and potential.

Despite its mystical associations, the tarot is not confined to the realm of the supernatural. It can be approached as a philosophical or psychological tool, a way of exploring possibilities rather than predicting certainties. Its symbols are not prescriptive but suggestive, guiding the querent toward their own interpretations and decisions. This flexibility is part of its enduring appeal, allowing it to adapt to the needs and beliefs of those who use it.

In essence, the tarot is a language of symbols, a bridge between the conscious and unconscious, the visible and invisible. Its power lies in its ability to evoke meaning and connection, to transform abstract concepts into tangible images that can be explored and understood. It is a tool for storytelling, a mirror for the soul, and a guide for navigating the complexities of life. Whether approached as an art, a science, or a spiritual practice, the tarot continues to inspire and empower those who seek its wisdom, offering a timeless testament to the richness of the human experience.

Tarot and Music Fusion

Tarot and music share a deep connection rooted in their capacity to express and explore the indescribable. Both are mediums through which the unseen becomes tangible, channels for emotions, stories, and archetypes that defy the limitations of language. For musicians, tarot serves as an extraordinary complement to the creative and emotional processes, offering inspiration, introspection, and a sense of connection to something larger than oneself. Through its rich symbolic language and intuitive nature, tarot becomes a tool for unlocking creative potential and navigating the emotional currents that often drive artistic expression.

Musicians are natural storytellers, weaving narratives and emotions into melodies, harmonies, and rhythms. Tarot, with its visual and symbolic richness, offers a complementary framework for this storytelling. Each card in the tarot deck is a story in itself, a snapshot of a particular moment or archetypal theme. For musicians, these stories can serve as starting points for songs, compositions, or improvisations, sparking ideas that might otherwise remain hidden. A single card, the Fool for example, can inspire a song about embarking on a new journey, filled with hope and uncertainty. The Tower might lead to a composition that captures the chaos and liberation of upheaval. The cards act as prompts, opening doors to narratives and emotions that resonate deeply with both the artist and their audience.

Beyond its narrative potential, tarot also engages the emotional core of music-making. Each card carries an emotional resonance, a tone or mood that can be translated into sound. The serene introspection of the High Priestess might find its musical counterpart in a delicate piano piece, while the fiery passion of the Knight of Wands could inspire an energetic guitar riff. By meditating on the imagery and feeling of a card, a musician can tap into emotions that might be difficult to articulate in words but come alive in music. This process is deeply intuitive, allowing the musician to move beyond intellectual analysis and connect directly with the heart of their creativity.

Tarot also serves as a mirror for the musician's own inner landscape, reflecting their emotions, challenges, and aspirations. In moments of creative block or emotional turmoil, the cards can provide clarity and guidance, helping the artist to understand and work through their experiences. A reading might reveal underlying fears or desires that are influencing the creative process, offering a new perspective that leads to artistic breakthroughs. For instance, a musician struggling with self-doubt might draw the Strength card, a reminder of their inner resilience and the power of vulnerability. This insight can fuel not only their emotional growth but also their artistic expression, leading to music that is more authentic and deeply felt.

The ritualistic aspect of tarot can also enhance the creative process. For many musicians, creating music is a sacred act, a way of connecting with the divine, the universe, or the depths of their own soul. Incorporating tarot into this process can heighten its sense of magic and intention. A musician might begin a songwriting session by drawing a card, using its imagery and symbolism as a guide for the themes or emotions they wish to explore. The act of shuffling the deck, focusing on a question or intention, and interpreting the cards becomes a meditative practice, grounding the artist in the present moment and opening them to inspiration.

In collaborative settings, tarot can foster connection and creativity among musicians. A group might draw cards together, using the collective interpretation of the spread to shape the direction of a song or composition. This process not only sparks new ideas but also creates a shared emotional and symbolic language, deepening the collaboration. The cards become a bridge between individual experiences, allowing each musician to contribute their unique perspective while remaining attuned to the collective vision.

Tarot's connection to archetypes makes it particularly powerful for musicians seeking to explore universal themes. Music has a unique ability to transcend cultural and linguistic boundaries, reaching into the shared human experience. Similarly, the archetypes of the tarot, love, loss, transformation, and triumph resonate across time and space. By engaging with these archetypes, musicians can create work that feels timeless and universally relevant, music that speaks to the deepest parts of the human soul. A song inspired by the Death card, for example, might explore themes of endings and rebirth, touching on emotions that are both deeply personal and universally understood.

The relationship between tarot and music is not limited to inspiration and emotion; a live performance is often a transformative experience, a ritual of connection between the artist and the audience. Tarot can enhance this ritualistic quality, serving as a thematic or symbolic anchor for a performance. A musician might design a setlist based on the journey of the Major Arcana, taking the audience through the Fool's journey from innocence to wisdom. The cards can also be integrated visually into the performance, with their imagery adding an additional layer of meaning and atmosphere.

On a personal level, tarot can help musicians navigate the emotional highs and lows that often accompany a creative life. The pursuit of music is filled with moments of doubt, fear, and elation, and the cards offer a way to process these experiences. A musician facing rejection or criticism might turn to the cards for reassurance, drawing the Star as a reminder of hope and inspiration. Similarly, in moments of success, the cards can help the artist remain grounded and connected to their deeper purpose. Tarot becomes a companion on the creative journey, offering wisdom, comfort, and perspective.

In essence, tarot complements the creative and emotional life of musicians by serving as a source of inspiration, a tool for introspection, and a medium for storytelling. It bridges the gap between the inner and outer worlds, transforming personal experiences into universal expressions of art. Through tarot, musicians can access new realms of creativity, explore the depths of their emotions, and connect more deeply with themselves and their audiences. It is a relationship that enriches not only the artist but also the art, infusing music with a sense of magic, meaning, and timeless resonance.

Tarot As A Tool For Musicians

Tarot, long celebrated for its ability to provide insight and guidance, has found an increasingly meaningful place in the lives of musicians seeking to navigate the complexities of their creative and professional worlds. As both a deeply introspective practice and a source of creative inspiration, tarot offers musicians a unique way to explore their inner landscapes, unlock their artistic potential, and make thoughtful decisions in their careers. The cards, with their rich symbolism and archetypal narratives, serve as mirrors of the human experience, allowing musicians to reflect on their emotions, creative journeys, and professional challenges.

At its core, tarot is a tool for introspection, a way to pause, reflect, and connect with one's inner self. Musicians, often immersed in the demands of creation, performance, and industry pressures, can benefit immensely from this kind of reflection. Tarot creates a sacred space where one can confront doubts, insecurities, and creative blocks with honesty and clarity. A musician struggling with self-doubt before a performance might draw the Strength card, a gentle reminder of their inner resilience and courage. Similarly, someone grappling with feelings of stagnation in their creative work may encounter the Hanged Man, encouraging them to see their situation from a new perspective and embrace the value of stillness and surrender. These moments of introspection can lead to profound personal growth, helping musicians better understand their motivations, fears, and aspirations.

Tarot also functions as a wellspring of inspiration, especially for musicians who feel stuck in their creative process. The imagery on the cards is deeply evocative, often sparking new ideas for melodies, lyrics, or themes. A musician might draw the Star and feel inspired to write a song about hope and renewal, or see the Tower and channel its themes of chaos and transformation into a bold, experimental composition. The suits of the Minor Arcana, with their elemental associations, can guide musicians toward exploring different emotional tones in their work: the fiery passion of the Wands, the introspective depth of the Cups, the intellectual clarity of the Swords, and the grounded rhythm of the Pentacles.

By engaging with these symbols, musicians can tap into their subconscious, uncovering creative insights that might otherwise remain hidden.

Beyond its role in fostering introspection and inspiration, tarot can also serve as a practical tool for professional decision-making. Musicians often face challenging choices, from deciding whether to collaborate with a particular producer to determining the best time to release an album. Tarot can provide a structured way to explore these decisions, offering clarity and perspective without dictating specific actions. For instance, a musician considering signing with a new record label might use a tarot reading to explore the potential dynamics of the partnership. Drawing the Lovers might indicate harmony and alignment, while the Devil might prompt a closer examination of the terms and potential pitfalls of the agreement. Importantly, tarot does not predict outcomes or provide definitive answers but rather encourages musicians to engage with their intuition and think critically about their options.

The practice of tarot for professional guidance also extends to understanding one's audience and the broader music industry landscape. A reading focused on the reception of an upcoming project might reveal patterns or themes that resonate with listeners, offering valuable insights into how to connect with them more authentically. Similarly, tarot can help musicians navigate the ebb and flow of the industry, offering reassurance during periods of uncertainty and encouraging bold action when opportunities arise. The Wheel of Fortune, for example, might remind a musician of the cyclical nature of their career, inspiring them to embrace both the highs and lows with equal grace.

Tarot's relevance to musicians lies not only in its ability to provide answers but also in its power to spark meaningful questions. By engaging with the cards, musicians are invited to think deeply about their artistic identities, creative processes, and professional aspirations. This reflective practice can lead to a greater sense of alignment and purpose, enabling musicians to move forward with confidence and clarity. Tarot's imagery and symbolism resonate deeply with the artistic mind, offering a language through which musicians can explore their own narratives and transform their experiences into art.

Moreover, tarot encourages musicians to trust their intuition, a skill that is as vital in music as it is in life. Whether improvising on stage, composing a new piece, or making strategic career decisions, musicians rely heavily on their instincts. Tarot readings provide a space to hone this intuition, helping musicians recognize and trust their inner voice. This can be especially empowering in an industry that often demands conformity and external validation. Through tarot, musicians can reconnect with their unique artistic visions and make choices that honor their authenticity.

Finally, tarot fosters a sense of connection and community, which is invaluable for musicians who may often feel isolated in their creative pursuits. Group readings or collaborative tarot practices can bring musicians together, fostering deeper understanding and alignment among bandmates or collaborators. Sharing insights from the cards can lead to richer creative exchanges and a stronger sense of unity, both on and off the stage. Tarot's universal language of symbols and archetypes creates a shared space where musicians can explore their journeys together, celebrating their collective experiences while honoring their individual paths.

In essence, tarot offers musicians a multidimensional tool that supports their personal, creative, and professional growth. By engaging with the cards, musicians can gain deeper insights into their own emotions and motivations, unlock new sources of inspiration, and navigate the complexities of their careers with greater clarity and confidence. Tarot's rich tapestry of symbols and archetypes speaks directly to the artistic spirit, making it an invaluable companion for musicians seeking to harmonize their inner and outer worlds. Whether used for introspection, inspiration, or decision-making, tarot invites musicians to embark on a journey of self-discovery, creativity, and empowerment, illuminating the path toward their fullest potential.

Trusting Instincts

Instinct is the quiet, guiding voice that exists within every person, a voice that whispers truths often obscured by logic or external noise. In both music and tarot readings, trusting instincts is not just a helpful tool, it is an essential part of the creative and interpretive process. Both disciplines require a balance between knowledge and intuition, and the moments of greatest insight and beauty often come when one surrenders to the instinctual flow that exists beneath conscious thought.

For musicians, instinct manifests as an almost ineffable connection to their instrument, voice, or composition. It is the way a guitarist's fingers seem to move effortlessly across the fretboard or how a singer naturally knows when to linger on a note to heighten its emotional impact. This sense of innate knowing does not come solely from technical skill or years of practice, though these are important foundations. It arises from a deeper place, one that listens not only to the music itself but also to the emotions, atmosphere, and energy surrounding it.

Similarly, tarot readings often rely on the intuitive leaps that occur when interpreting the cards. While the meanings of the cards and their traditional associations form a critical framework, the heart of a reading lies in the reader's ability to trust their instincts. A card like the Three of Cups might traditionally signify celebration and friendship, but in a particular reading, a reader's instincts might guide them to see it as a call to reflect on relationships that have grown stagnant or unbalanced. This intuitive interpretation emerges not from logic but from an inner sense that draws upon both the cards and the reader's connection to the querent's energy.

The relationship between instinct and preparation is key in both music and tarot. A musician learns scales, chord progressions, and techniques to provide a foundation, but true artistry comes when they transcend these structures and allow instinct to guide their expression. Similarly, a tarot reader studies the cards and their meanings, but the most profound readings occur when they trust their gut feelings to weave these meanings into a story tailored to the querent's unique situation. This dynamic highlights the importance of preparation, not as an endpoint but as a gateway to instinctual fluency.

In both practices, the concept of flow, moments when time seems to disappear and actions feel effortless, is deeply connected to trusting instincts. For musicians, these are the moments when the music seems to play itself, as if the artist is merely a vessel through which the melody emerges. Improvisation is a perfect example of this. When a jazz musician takes a solo, they rely on their instincts to navigate uncharted territory, making split-second decisions that reflect their emotions and the energy of the moment. These decisions are not random, they are deeply informed by both their technical knowledge and their ability to listen to their inner voice.

In tarot, the flow state emerges during readings where the cards seem to unfold a story with clarity and resonance. A skilled reader trusts their instincts to connect seemingly unrelated cards into a coherent narrative, finding meaning in the interplay between them. This process often feels like a dialogue between the reader, the cards, and the querent's energy: a dynamic, instinctual interaction that transcends the intellectual understanding of the cards' meaning.

Trusting instincts also involves embracing vulnerability. Both music and tarot require a willingness to step into the unknown and take risks. A musician who plays purely by the book might produce technically perfect but emotionally sterile performances. Similarly, a tarot reader who rigidly adheres to textbook definitions of the cards might miss the nuances and depth that arise from intuitive interpretation. Trusting instincts means accepting the possibility of mistakes, knowing that these moments of uncertainty are often where true creativity and insight are born.

Fear of judgement can be a significant obstacle to trusting instincts in both fields. Musicians may worry about how their improvisations or compositions will be received, while tarot readers may fear giving an interpretation that deviates from traditional meanings. Overcoming this fear requires cultivating confidence in one's unique voice and perspective. A musician must believe in their ability to create something meaningful, even if it defies convention. A tarot reader must trust that their instincts are a valid and valuable part of the reading process. Both must learn to quiet the inner critic that questions their instincts and instead embrace the authenticity that comes from trusting themselves.

The act of listening is central to trusting instincts. For musicians, this means not only listening to the notes they play but also to the silence between them, the subtle dynamics of their fellow performers, and the emotional tone of the audience. For tarot readers, listening involves paying attention to the querent's energy, the symbolic language of the cards, and the intuitive nudges that arise during the reading. In both practices, listening is not passive, it is an active engagement with the moment, an openness to what is emerging without judgment or preconception.

Trusting instincts also involves a deep connection to the present moment. In music, this might mean being fully immersed in a performance, responding instinctively to the shifting dynamics of the band or the emotional energy of the room. In tarot, it means being fully present with the cards and the querent, allowing the reading to unfold naturally rather than trying to force a particular interpretation. This presence creates a space where instincts can flourish, free from the constraints of other thinking or second-guessing.

Both music and tarot offer practices that can help individuals strengthen their trust in their instincts. Meditation, for example, can help musicians and readers alike develop the mindfulness necessary to tune into their inner voice. Journaling about musical improvisations or tarot readings can provide insights into patterns and moments of instinctual clarity, fostering a deeper understanding of how instincts manifest in each practice. Over time, these practices build a sense of trust and confidence in one's ability to rely on instinct, even in high-pressure situations.

Ultimately, trusting instincts in music and tarot is about embracing the mystery of creation and interpretation. It is about surrendering to the process, allowing the music or the reading to emerge organically rather than trying to control or predict the outcome. In this surrender, there is freedom, a freedom that allows for the full expression of one's unique voice and perspective. Whether playing a haunting melody or uncovering the hidden truths of a tarot spread, trusting instincts opens the door to moments of profound connection, insight, and beauty.

A Not So Brief History of Tarot

The history of Tarot is as complex and intriguing as the cards themselves, a tale shaped by art, culture, mysticism, and human curiosity. It spans centuries, bridging the medieval courts of Europe, the mystical traditions of the Enlightenment, and the modern resurgence of spirituality in the digital age. To fully understand the tarot's rich and layered history, it is necessary to explore its origins, evolution, and the cultural forces that transformed it from a card game to a profound tool for self-discovery and divination.

The story of tarot begins in the late medieval period, with the emergence of playing cards in Europe. These early playing cards were likely introduced through trade routes from the Islamic world, where card games had already gained popularity. The Mamluk card decks of the 14th century, which featured ornate designs and suits of cups, swords, coins, and polo sticks, are thought to be the direct predecessors of European playing cards. These suits were eventually adapted into the familiar Latin suits of wands, cups, swords and pentacles, which remain a cornerstone of traditional tarot decks.

In the early 15th century, a new type of card deck began to appear in northern Italy: the tarot, or tarocchi as it was called in Italian. The tarot decks of this period were elaborate and often hand-painted, created for the noble families of cities like Milan and Ferrara. Unlike standard playing card decks, which typically had four suits and a set of face cards, tarot decks featured an additional set of twenty two trump cards, known as the Major Arcana, as well as a card called the Fool. These additional cards depicted allegorical figures and scenes, drawing on themes from classical mythology, Christian iconography, and Renaissance philosophy.

Visconti-Sforza

One of the most famous early tarot decks is the Visconti-Sforza, created in the mid-15th century for the Visconti and Sforza families, who were powerful patrons of the arts in Milan. This deck, which is only partially preserved, is celebrated for its exquisite craftsmanship and artistic detail. The cards feature gilded backgrounds and finely painted figures, reflecting the opulence and sophistication of the Italian Renaissance. However, these early tarot decks were not used for divination or mystical purposes; rather, they were primarily used for a game known as tarocchi, a trick-taking card game similar to modern bridge.

The Visconti-Sforza tarot deck holds a unique and significant place in the history of tarot, representing one of the earliest and most elaborate examples of the cards as both an artistic achievement and a cultural artifact. Created in the mid-15th century during the Italian Renaissance, this deck reflects the opulence, intellectual sophistication, and complex symbolism of its time. It is not merely a deck of cards; it is a masterpiece of craftsmanship, a window into the lives of the Italian nobility, and a foundational piece in the development of what we now know as tarot. Its legacy has shaped both historical understanding and contemporary appreciation of tarot as a tool of art and mysticism.

The Visconti-Sforza deck emerged during a period of great cultural and artistic flourishing in northern Italy, a region dominated by powerful city-states and ruled by influential families. The deck was commissioned by the Visconti and Sforza families, who were prominent rulers of Milan and ardent patrons of the arts. Their wealth and influence allowed them to support some of the finest artists and intellectuals of their time, and the tarot deck was an extension of this cultural patronage. The cards were not merely objects of leisure; they were symbols of status, refinement, and an appreciation for the emerging humanist ideals of the Renaissance.

The creation of the Visconti-Sforza deck is commonly attributed to the renowned painter Bonifacio Bembo, although other artists may have contributed to its design. Bembo was a highly skilled artist known for his delicate use of color, intricate detailing, and ability to capture the grandeur of the noble families he served. The cards he created for the Visconti and Sforza families are breathtakingly beautiful, adorned with gold leaf, rich pigments, and finely detailed imagery. Each card feels like a miniature painting, carefully crafted to convey both elegance and symbolism.

What sets the Visconti-Sforza deck apart from other early decks is its extraordinary size and artistic detail. The deck originally consisted of 78 cards, including the traditional four suits of the Minor Arcana (swords, cups, coins, and batons), each with ten numbered cards and four court cards, as well as twenty-two Major Arcana cards. However, not all the original cards have survived, and the existing examples are incomplete. Despite this, the surviving cards offer a glimpse into the World of Renaissance symbolism and allegory.

The Major Arcana cards in the Visconti-Sforza deck are particularly notable for their rich imagery and depth of meaning. These cards depict a series of allegorical figures and concepts, including the Fool, the Magician, the Empress, and the World. The designs are heavily influenced by the philosophical and cultural ideas of the Renaissance, including classical mythology, Christian theology, and the humanist emphasis on individual potential and moral virtue. Each card is a visual representation of ideas and ideals, designed to inspire contemplation and intellectual engagement.

The Minor Arcana, while less allegorical in nature, are equally stunning in their artistry. The suits of swords, cups, coins, and batons reflect themes of medieval and Renaissance life, with their symbolism tied to chivalry, commerce, and the natural elements. The court cards, knights, pages, queens, and kings, are richly dressed figures, likely modeled after members of the Visconti and Sforza families themselves. These cards serve not only as game pieces but also as representations of power, hierarchy, and social order.

The exact purpose of the Visconti-Sforza deck is a subject of ongoing scholarly debate. One possible occasion for the creation of the deck was the marriage between Francesco Sforza and Bianca Maria Visconti in 1441. This union between two powerful families solidified their control over Milan and marked a new era in the region's political and cultural history. The tarot deck may have been designed to commemorate this alliance, with its images reflecting themes of love, power, and divine order. The inclusion of the Visconti and Sforza family emblems in the deck's design supports this theory, as does the lavish quality of the materials used.

The survival of the Visconti-Sforza deck is itself a remarkable story. Over the centuries, many of the original cards were lost or damaged, and the remaining examples are now scattered across various museums and private collections. The cards that do survive are cherished not only for their historical value but also for their artistic brilliance. They offer a rare glimpse into the world of the Italian Renaissance, where art, philosophy, and symbolism converged in extraordinary ways.

The influence of the Visconti-Sforza deck on later decks cannot be overstated. Its imagery and structure set the standard for future tarot designs, and many of its themes and symbols continue to be used in modern tarot decks. The Rider-Waite-Smith deck, one of the most popular decks of the 20th century, owes much of its symbolic language to the foundation laid by the Visconti-Sforza deck. Even as tarot has evolved into a tool for divination and self-discovery, the legacy of the Visconti-Sforza deck remains a touchstone for its artistic and historical significance.

The Visconti-Sforza deck is more than just a deck of cards; it is a symbol of the interplay between art, culture, and human imagination. Its history is a testament to the power of creativity and the ways in which symbols can transcend time, offering insights and inspiration to generations. Whether viewed as a historical artifact, a work of art, or a tool for contemplation, the Visconti-Sforza deck continues to captivate and inspire, standing as a monument to the enduring allure of tarot.

Antoine Court de Gebelin

For several centuries, tarot remained primarily a game, enjoyed by the European aristocracy and later by the middle classes. It was not until the late 18th century that the tarot began its transformation into a tool for divination and esoteric study. This shift occurred in France, where occultists and mystics began to reinterpret the cards through the lens of ancient wisdom and mystical traditions. One of the key figures in this transformation was Antoine Court de Gebelin, a French clergyman and freemason.

Antoine Court de Gebelin was a pivotal figure in the history of tarot, known for his influential contributions to the perception and interpretation of tarot as a mystical and symbolic system. Born in 1719 in Nimes, France, Court de Gebelin was a Protestant pastor, linguist, and scholar who became deeply involved in the intellectual and cultural movements of the Enlightenment. He was a man of vast curiosity and ambition, driven by a belief in the power of symbols, language, and ancient wisdom to unlock profound truths about the human experience and the universe. His work on tarot, though now understood as largely speculative, marked a turning point in the evolution of tarot from a card game into a tool for esoteric study and divination

Court de Gebelin's interest in tarot emerged during a time when intellectuals across Europe were captivated by the idea of rediscovering ancient knowledge. This is the Age of Enlightenment, a period that saw an explosion of interest in history, philosophy, science, and the arts. Scholars and thinkers sought to uncover the hidden connections between cultures and traditions, often with a focus on ancient civilizations such as Egypt, Greece, and Rome. Within this intellectual climate, Court de Gebelin became convinced that the tarot was more than a mere deck of playing cards. He believed it was a repository of ancient wisdom, encoded in symbols and imagery, waiting to be deciphered.

In 1781, Court de Gebelin published his magnum opus, "Le Monde Primitif, Analyse et Compare avec le Monde Moderne ("The Primitive World, Analyzed and Compared with the Modern World"). This multi-volume work was an ambitious attempt to trace the origins of human civilization and uncover the universal truths that underpinned all cultures and religions. It was in the eighth volume of this work that Court de Gebelin introduced his ideas about the tarot. This section of the text, titled "Recherches sur les Tarots et sur les Divertissements qu'on en tire" ("Research on the Tarot and the Entertainments Derived from It"), presented the tarot as a profound and ancient symbolic system.

Court de Gebelin's thesis was that the tarot had its origins in ancient Egypt, a civilization he regarded as the cradle of wisdom and esoteric knowledge. He asserted that the cards contained hidden messages passed down through the ages, encoded in their imagery and symbols. According to his theory, the tarot had survived the fall of ancient civilizations and had been preserved through the centuries, eventually finding its way to Europe. He believed that the cards were introduced to Europe by Gypsies, whom he mistakenly thought were descendants of the ancient Egyptians. This idea, though later debunked, became one of the enduring myths of tarot history.

In his analysis, Court de Gebelin argued that the Major Arcana, the twenty two trump cards of the tarot, were the most significant part of the deck. He saw these cards as a series of archetypes and allegories that conveyed universal truths about the human condition and the cosmos. For example, he interpreted the Fool as a representation of the human soul on a journey through life, while the Magician symbolized the power of intellect and creativity. Each card, in his view, was a key to understanding the mysteries of existence, a notion that resonated with the Romantic and esoteric currents of his time.

What is remarkable about Court de Gebelin's work is the sheer conviction and creativity with which he presented his ideas, despite the lack of historical evidence to support them. Modern scholars now know that his claims about the Egyptian origins of the tarot were unfounded; the tarot deck as we know it actually originated in 15th-century Italy as a card game. There is no evidence to suggest that the tarot predates this period or that it was connected to ancient Egypt. Nevertheless, Court de Gebelin's theories captivated the imaginations of his contemporaries and laid the groundwork for the esoteric interpretation of tarot that continues to this day.

One of the most significant outcomes of Court de Gebelin's work was its influence on the development of tarot as a tool for divination. While there is little evidence that tarot was widely used for divination before the 18th century, Court de Gebelin's writings helped to establish this practice as a central aspect of tarot's identity. His work inspired other thinkers, such as Jean-Baptiste Alliette (known as Etteilla), who expanded on his ideas and created one of the first tarot decks specifically designed for divination.

Court de Gebelin's emphasis on the symbolic and archetypal nature of the tarot also had a profound impact on later interpretations of the cards. His writings encouraged readers to view the tarot as a mirror of the human psyche, a concept that would later be explored by figures such as Carl Jung in the 20th century. By framing the tarot as a symbolic system with universal significance, Court de Gebelin helped to elevate it from a game to a subject of serious intellectual and spiritual inquiry.

Despite the flaws in his historical claims, Court de Gebelin's work remains a milestone in the history of tarot. His imaginative and speculative approach opened the door to new ways of understanding and using the cards. He demonstrated the power of narrative and interpretation in shaping the meaning of symbols, a concept that continues to resonate in contemporary tarot practice. Court de Gebelin's legacy is a testament to the enduring allure of tarot as a cultural and intellectual phenomenon. His work reminds us that the significance of tarot lies not in its historical accuracy, but in its capacity to inspire reflection, creativity, and exploration. Whether viewed as a tool for divination, a work of art, or a source of personal insight, the tarot owes much of its modern identity to the vision and passion of Antoine Court de Gebelin.

Etteilla

Building on Court de Gebelin's work, Jean-Baptiste Alliette, better known by his pseudonym Etteilla, became one of the first individuals to popularize tarot as a tool for fortune-telling. Etteilla (his surname spelled backward), holds an essential place in the history of tarot as one of the first individuals to formalize and popularize its use for divination. Born in Paris in 1738, Alliette's life coincided with a period of intellectual upheaval and growing interest in mysticism, esotericism, and the rediscovery of ancient traditions. His contributions to tarot extended beyond interpretation; he laid the groundwork for the design of decks specifically intended for divinatory purposes and established a systematic approach to reading the cards. Etteilla's work was instrumental in transforming tarot from a game rooted in Renaissance Europe into a mystical tool for insight, self-discovery, and fortune-telling.

Etteilla's early life is shrouded in mystery, and much of what is known about him comes from his later years as he rose to prominence. He worked as a seedsman and a hairdresser, but he was also drawn to the study of occult sciences, astrology, and alchemy. This curiosity brought him into contact with the growing interest in tarot sparked by Antoine Court de Gebelin's writings. Court de Gebelin's assertion that tarot originated in Egypt, as outlined in his influential work "Le Monde Primitif," inspired Etteilla to delve deeper into the cards and their potential meanings. However, while Court de Gebelin's focus was primarily academic and speculative, Etteilla approached tarot as a practitioner, aiming to make its divinatory applications accessible to the public.

In 1783, Alliette published his first work on tarot, "Etteilla, ou manière de se recréer avec un jeu de cartes" ("Etteilla, or a Way to Entertain Oneself with a Deck of Cards"). This text marked the first comprehensive attempt to explain how tarot could be used for divination, predating the now-familiar Rider-Waite and other modern decks by more than a century. It also signified a departure from earlier perceptions of tarot as purely a game or an intellectual curiosity. For Alliette, tarot was a bridge between the physical and metaphysical worlds, a means to access hidden knowledge and offer guidance about the past, present, and future.

What made Alliette unique was his systematic and organized approach to tarot. He restructured the deck to suit his purposes, creating one of the earliest tarot decks explicitly designed for divination. Known as the Grand Etteilla, this deck reimagined the traditional structure of tarot, incorporating Egyptian-inspired imagery, symbols, and correspondences. Alliette believed that the tarot's origins lay in the wisdom of ancient Egypt, a misconception he inherited from Court de Gebelin, and his deck reflected this belief. The cards were imbued with astrological associations, elements of alchemy, and numerical associations, elements of alchemy, and numerical correspondences, creating a comprehensive symbolic system.

One of the innovations that Etteilla introduced was the inclusion of divinatory keywords on the cards. Each card was inscribed with meanings for upright and reversed positions, offering readers clear guidance on how to interpret them during a reading. This approach differed significantly from the earlier Visconti-Sforza or Marseille tarot decks, which lacked explicit instructions for divination. By providing a framework for interpretation, Etteilla made tarot more accessible to a wider audience and established the foundation for modern tarot practices.

Etteilla's contributions extended beyond the design of his deck. He founded one of the first societies dedicated to the study and practice of tarot, known as the Societe des Interpretes du Livre de Thot (Society of Interpreters of the Book of Thoth). Through this organization, he sought to elevate tarot to a respected and legitimate field of study, framing it as a continuation of ancient wisdom rather than mere superstition. The society's name referenced the Egyptian god Thoth, whom Etteilla and his contemporaries believed to be the originator of tarot's symbolic language. While this claim was historically inaccurate, it captured the imagination of those seeking to connect with a deeper mystical heritage.

Alliette's writings further solidified his influence on the development of tarot. Over the course of his career, he published several works on tarot, astrology, and the occult sciences. These texts outlined his methods for reading the cards, explained the symbolic connections he saw between tarot and other esoteric systems, and offered practical guidance for diviners. His books were widely read and helped to popularize tarot as a tool for spiritual exploration and fortune-telling.

Despite his contributions, Etteilla was not without his critics. Some of his contemporaries dismissed his work as fanciful or overly commercial. His reinterpretation of the tarot deck, with its emphasis on Egyptian symbolism, was seen by some as a departure from the authentic tradition of tarot as it had been practiced in Italy and France. However, Etteilla's vision resonated with many, and his influence persisted long after his death in 1791.

Etteilla's legacy lies in his role as a pioneer of modern tarot. His system introduced several concepts that remain integral to tarot practice today, including the use of reversed meanings, the incorporation of astrological and elemental associations, and the idea of tarot as a structured tool for divination. His emphasis on creating a consistent methodology for interpreting the cards set a standard that would be adopted and adapted by later tarot readers.

In hindsight, Alliette's work can be seen as both a product of its time and a harbinger of the future. His fascination with Egypt and his belief in the ancient origins of tarot reflect the Romantic and esoteric currents of the 18th century, which sought to uncover hidden truths and connect with lost wisdom. At the same time, his practical approach to tarot reading and his efforts to make the practice accessible anticipated the broader popularization of tarot in the 19th and 20th centuries.

Today, Etteilla is remembered as one of the founding figures of tarot as a divinatory practice. His contributions paved the way for the development of later systems, including the Rider-Waite-Smith deck, which drew on many of the principles he established. While the specifics of his theories have been revised or replaced, the framework he created endures as a testament to his vision and creativity.

In the ever-evolving history of tarot, Jean-Baptiste Alliette remains a central figure, a man who transformed an intriguing deck of cards into a profound and versatile tool for insight, reflection, and exploration. His life and work demonstrate the power of imagination and innovation to shape how we understand and engage with symbols, stories, and the mysteries of existence. Whether one views him as a visionary or an opportunist, his impact on tarot is undeniable, and his name continues to resonate in the world of divination and the occult.

Rider-Waite-Smith

The Rider-Waite-Smith tarot deck, one of the most iconic and influential tarot decks in history, stands as a cornerstone of modern tarot practice. First published in 1909 by the London-based publisher William Rider & Son, this deck was the collaborative creation of Arthur Edward Waite, a British mystic and scholar, and Pamela Colman Smith, an artist whose vivid imagery brought Waite's vision to life. While often referred to simply as the Rider-Waite deck, the inclusion of Smith's name in its title is a more recent acknowledgment of her essential contribution to its design and enduring legacy. Together, Waite and Smith created a deck that not only reshaped tarot's visual and symbolic language but also made it accessible to a broader audience, sparking a global fascination that persists to this day.

Arthur Edward Waite, a prominent member of the Hermetic Order of the Golden Dawn, played a pivotal role in conceptualizing the deck. The Golden Dawn was a 19th-century magical order devoted to the study of occultism, mysticism, and esotericism, and it served as the intellectual and spiritual foundation for Waite's exploration of tarot. Waite's scholarly interest in the esoteric traditions of Western mysticism, including Kabbalah, alchemy, and Christian mysticism, heavily informed his approach to tarot. He viewed the cards not merely as tools for divination but as a profound repository of symbolic and spiritual knowledge. Waite sought to create a deck that would encapsulate the deeper, hidden meanings of the cards, drawing upon the Golden Dawn's teachings while also making the tarot more comprehensible to the general public.

Pamela Colman Smith, the artist commissioned to illustrate the deck, was a member of the Golden Dawn herself, though her role in the group was less prominent than Waite's. An accomplished illustrator, Smith had already established a reputation for her work in book illustration and theater design. Her artistic sensibility, characterized by bold colors, flowing lines, and an evocative use of symbolism, made her an ideal collaborator for Waite's project. While Waite provided the conceptual framework for the deck, it was Smith's artistic vision that brought the cards to life, infusing them with a vibrancy and narrative quality that set them apart from earlier decks.

One of the most significant innovations of the Rider-Waite-Smith deck was its treatment of the Minor Arcana, the fifty six cards that accompany the twenty two Major Arcana in a standard tarot deck. In traditional tarot decks, such as the Marseille Tarot, the Minor Arcana were depicted with simple, pip-style designs that lacked detailed imagery. For example, the Five of Cups might show five cups arranged in a straightforward pattern, leaving much of the interpretation to the reader's intuition or knowledge of the card's symbolic meaning. In contrast, Smith's illustrations for the RWS deck featured fully realized scenes for each card, complete with human figures, landscapes, and symbolic elements that suggested a narrative or emotional context. The Five of Cups, for instance, depicts a cloaked figure standing before three spilled cups while two upright cups remain behind them, evoking themes of loss, grief, and hope. This narrative approach made the Minor Arcana far more accessible to readers, allowing for a richer and more intuitive connection to the cards.

The Major Arcana of the RWS deck also underwent significant reinterpretation. Waite and Smith imbued these twenty two cards with a depth of symbolic meaning that reflected Waite's esoteric interests. Each card was carefully designed to convey multiple layers of meaning, drawing on a wide range of influences, including Christian iconography, alchemical symbols, and the Kabbalistic Tree of Life. The High Priestess, for example, represents intuition and mystery, with her imagery evoking the ancient mysteries of the feminine divine. She sits between two pillars marked with the letters "B" and "J," references to the pillars of Boaz and Jachin from Solomon's Temple, signifying duality and balance. The Fool, often considered the most enigmatic card in the deck, represents the soul's journey through life, embodying innocence, spontaneity, and the potential for transformation.

The artistic style of the RWS deck is both distinctive and venturing. Smith's use of vibrant colors, intricate details, and expressive figures created a visual language that has become synonymous with tarot itself. Her illustrations are rich with symbolic elements that invite contemplation and interpretation, from the white roses and lilies that appear in various cards to the sunlit landscapes that suggest optimism and renewal. The deck's imagery strikes a balance between simplicity and complexity, making it accessible to beginners while offering endless layers of meaning for experienced readers. Smith's art is not merely illustrative but evocative, drawing the viewer into the world of the cards and inviting them to engage with their symbolic depths.

Another notable aspect of the Rider-Waite-Smith deck is its accessibility. Prior to its publication, tarot was largely the domain of scholars, occultists, and mystics, and many decks were either handmade or produced in limited quantities. The RWS deck was one of the first to be mass-produced, making it widely available to the general public. Its accompanying guidebook, "The Pictorial Key to the Tarot," written by Waite, provided readers with interpretations and insights into the deck's symbolism, further demystifying the cards and encouraging their use as a tool for personal and spiritual exploration.

The impact of the RWS deck on the world of tarot cannot be overstated. It set a new standard for tarot design and interpretation, influencing countless decks that followed. The deck's narrative approach to the Minor Arcana became a hallmark of modern tarot, and its imagery has been reimagined and reinterpreted in a wide variety of styles and cultural contexts. From the 20th century to the present day, the RWS deck has remained one of the most popular and widely used tarot decks in the world, a testament to its enduring appeal and relevance.

In recent years, there has been a growing recognition of Pamela Colman Smith's role in the creation of the deck. For much of the 20th century, her contributions were overshadowed by Waite's prominence as the deck's conceptual creator. However, contemporary scholars and tarot enthusiasts have sought to restore Smith to her rightful place in the history of tarot, celebrating her artistry and vision. Her work on the Rider-Waite-Smith deck is now widely acknowledged as a groundbreaking achievement, and her name is increasingly included alongside Waite's in references to the deck.

The RWS tarot deck represents a fusion of mysticism, artistry, and accessibility, a deck that transcended its origins to become a universal symbol of tarot itself. Its creation marked a turning point in the history of tarot, bridging the gap between its esoteric roots and its modern-day role as a tool for self-discovery, guidance, and connection. As one of the most enduring and beloved tarot decks, it continues to inspire, inform, and illuminate the paths of those who turn to it, ensuring its place as a timeless artifact of human imagination and spirituality.

The Basics of Tarot

Tarot and music may seem, at first glance, like distinct worlds with little in common. One is a visual, symbolic system that invites introspection and interpretation, while the other is an auditory, expressive art that stirs emotion and connects people. Yet, the basics of tarot align surprisingly well with the inner workings of music, particularly for musicians seeking clarity, inspiration, or a deeper understanding of their craft and journey. Tarot provides a framework through which musicians can reflect on their creative processes, navigate the challenges of their profession, and connect more authentically with their personal artistic vision. The basics of tarot, when applied to the realm of music, become a unique tool for both introspection and outward creative action, offering a fresh perspective on the symbiotic relationship between symbolism, intuition, and expression.

At its core, tarot is a system of seventy eight cards divided into two main sections: the Major Arcana and the Minor Arcana. The Major Arcana consists of twenty two cards, each representing significant archetypes or themes that resonate universally, such as transformation, self-discovery, and purpose. For musicians, these archetypes often align with the overarching themes in their own journeys, from the innocence of the Fool embarking on a creative endeavor to the transformative energy of Death, signaling the end of an old musical style or identity to make way for something new. The Major Arcana serves as a symbolic mirror for the pivotal moments in a musician's life, reflecting both their internal evolution and the larger narrative of their artistry.

The Minor Arcana, on the other hand, is composed of fifty six cards divided into four suits: Cups, Wands, Swords and Pentacles. Each suit corresponds to an element and focuses on different aspects of life. For musicians, these suits can be seen as representing different facets of their professional and personal worlds. Cups align with emotional connection and inspiration, essential for crafting music that resonates with audiences. Wands speak to creativity, ambition, and the fire that drives musicians to compose, perform, and innovate. Swords, often representing mental clarity and challenges, reflect the intellectual and logistical aspects of music-making, including overcoming writer's block or navigating difficult collaborations. Finally, Pentacles embody the material and practical side of a musician's career, including financial stability, industry negotiations, and the grounding work of managing a career in the arts.

One of the most powerful aspects of tarot lies in its ability to provide guidance without dictating specific answers. Musicians often grapple with ambiguity, be it creative decisions, career crossroads, or the unpredictable nature of inspiration. Tarot embraces this ambiguity, offering a symbolic language that invites reflection rather than imposing a definitive outcome. For example, pulling the Hermit during a reading might suggest a period of introspection, a time for retreating from the public sphere to focus on developing one's craft or reconnecting with the deeper reasons for making music. Similarly, the Ten of Wands could point to the burdens of overcommitment or creative burnout, prompting the musician to reconsider their priorities. These cards don't prescribe a single path forward but instead open the door for a nuanced exploration of possibilities.

The process of engaging with tarot parallels the creative process itself. Just as a musician draws upon intuition, emotion, and technical skill to compose or perform, reading tarot involves interpreting symbols, trusting one's instincts, and weaving a narrative from the interplay of the cards. This shared reliance on intuition makes tarot a natural fit for musicians, who are often accustomed to listening for what feels right rather than relying solely on logic. When applied thoughtfully, tarot can amplify this intuitive practice, helping musicians tune into their inner voices and uncover creative solutions or insights that might otherwise remain hidden.

Tarot also speaks to the storytelling aspect of music. Every song, composition, or performance tells a story, whether explicit or abstract. Similarly, a tarot spread lays out a story through its arrangement of cards, each one contributing to a larger narrative. For a musician, this can be an invaluable tool for exploring the stories they want to tell through their art. If a musician is struggling with writer's block or feeling stuck in their creative process, drawing a spread of cards can inspire new ideas or perspectives. For example, a spread that includes the Star, the Tower, and the Chariot might suggest a narrative arc of hope, upheaval, and eventual triumph. These are elements that could inform the emotional journey of a new song or album. In this way, tarot becomes a collaborative partner in the creative process, sparking inspiration and guiding artistic choices.

The relationship between tarot and music extends beyond personal reflection to encompass the larger dynamics of collaboration and audience connection. Musicians often work with others, whether as bandmates, producers, or collaborators on a single project. Tarot can provide insight into these relationships, shedding light on potential conflicts, shared goals, or unspoken dynamics. For instance, if a musician is navigating tensions within a band,a tarot reading might reveal underlying issues through the interplay of the cards. The Three of Cups, symbolizing harmony and shared celebration, might highlight the importance of fostering mutual respect and camaraderie, while the Five of Swords could point to unresolved conflicts or competition that need to be addressed.

Similarly, tarot can help musicians connect more deeply with their audience. Every performance is an exchange of energy between the artist and the listener, and tarot's focus on intuition and emotional resonance can enhance this connection. By using tarot as a tool for introspection before a performance, a musician might gain clarity on the emotions or themes they want to convey, allowing them to approach their performance with greater intention. Tarot can also inspire innovative ways to engage with an audience, whether by incorporating its symbolism into album art, music videos, or stage design, or by using its archetypes to inform the themes of a live set or concept album.

The ethical and spiritual dimensions of tarot further enrich its relevance to music. Tarot encourages a deep engagement with one's values, aspirations, and challenges, providing a framework for musicians to align their work with their higher purpose. This can be especially meaningful in an industry that often emphasizes external success over internal fulfillment. By grounding their practice in tarot's principles of self-awareness and authenticity, musicians can navigate their careers with greater integrity and resilience, staying true to their artistic vision even in the face of external pressures.

The Structure of Tarot

The structure of tarot is a carefully constructed system that reflects the rhythms, dynamics, and narrative arcs found in music. Both disciplines are built on foundational frameworks, tarot with its 78 cards divided into the Major and Minor Arcana, and music with its scales, chords, and harmonic progressions. Within these frameworks lies an infinite potential for creativity and interpretation, with each card or note serving as a building block in the larger composition of meaning. By examining the parallels between the structure of tarot and the principles of musical composition, one can uncover a rich interplay of form and function that enhances both practices.

The Major Arcana, composed of 22 cards, forms the backbone of its symbolic universe, much like the tonal centers and key signatures in music provide the foundation for harmonic organization. The Major Arcana follows a distinct narrative arc often referred to as the Fool's Journey, a cycle that begins with pure potential (The Fool) and culminates in fulfillment and integration (The World). This arc mirrors the structure of many musical compositions, particularly those that follow a sonata form or symphonic structure, where an initial theme is introduced, developed, and resolved. Each Major Arcana card can be seen as a distinct movement within this overarching symphony, contributing its unique energy and symbolic resonance.

In music, the concept of tension and resolution is central to creating emotional impact, and this principle finds a direct parallel in the Major Arcana. Cards like the Tower and Death represent moments of dissonance and upheaval, akin to the heightened tension of a diminished chord or an unexpected key change. These moments are balanced by the harmony and resolution found in cards like the Star or the Sun, which bring a sense of clarity and hope. Just as a composer carefully balances moments of tension and release to guide the listener through an emotional journey, the Major Arcana's structure ensures a dynamic interplay between challenge and growth.

The Minor Arcana, divided into four suits (Wands, Cups, Swords and Pentacles), serves as the rhythmic and melodic counterpoint to the Major Arcana's grand themes. Each suit corresponds to an element (water, air, fire, and earth) that reflects a specific aspect of the human experience. This division is akin to the way musical modes or tonalities convey distinct emotional landscapes. The Cups, with their focus on emotion and intuition, might align with the lyrical, flowing qualities of a minor key melody, while the fiery Wands evoke the driving energy of an upbeat tempo or a syncopated rhythm. Swords, associated with intellect and clarity, might resonate with intricate counterpoint or sharp, staccato phrasing, while the grounded Pentacles find their counterpart in steady, harmonic bass lines or repetitive motifs that evoke stability.

The numbered cards of the Minor Arcana, ranging from Ace to Ten, provide a developmental arc within each suit, similar to the progression of a musical phrase. The Ace introduces the theme, serving as a tonal center or initial motif that sets the stage for what follows. The subsequent cards build upon this foundation, adding layers of complexity and variation. By the time the progression reaches the Ten, the theme has reached its full expression, completing a cycle that mirrors the resolution of a musical cadence. This progression allows for a nuanced exploration of a single theme, much like a composer might take a simple melody and develop it into a rich, multi-layered composition.

The court cards (Page, Knight, Queen, and King) add another layer of complexity to the tarot's structure, representing archetypal roles or states of being within each suit. In music, these cards might be likened to different instruments within an ensemble or voices within a choir, each contributing its unique timbre and perspective to the overall composition. The Page, with its youthful curiosity, could correspond to the exploratory improvisation of a soloist testing the waters. The Knight, with its dynamic and action-oriented energy, might reflect the driving rhythm of a percussion section. The Queen, embodying emotional depth and nurturing wisdom, could be likened to the rich, resonant tones of a cello or alto voice. The King, symbolizing mastery and authority, might parallel the grounding presence of a bass line or the commanding clarity of a trumpet fanfare.

The interplay between the Major and Minor Arcana can be understood as a dialogue between melody and harmony in music. The Major Arcana provides the overarching themes and motifs, the central narrative that gives the piece its shape and purpose. The Minor Arcana, with its focus on everyday experiences and details, provides the harmonic richness and textural depth that support and enhance the melody. This relationship emphasizes the importance of both the universal and the personal, the grand and the intimate, in creating a complete and resonant work of art.

In both music and tarot, structure serves as a framework for creative expression rather than a constraint. A jazz musician might begin with a standard chord progression but use it as a springboard for improvisation, creating something entirely unique within the bounds of the original structure. Similarly, a tarot reader begins with the established meanings of the cards and the layout of the spread but allows their intuition and connection to the querent to shape the reading in a way that transcends the rigidity of the system. This interplay between structure and spontaneity is where the true magic of both practices lies.

The Major Arcana

The Major Arcana, a collection of twenty two archetypal cards within the tarot deck, represents profound themes, experiences, and turning points in life. When considered in relation to music, these cards offer a rich symbolic language through which musicians can explore their creative journeys, challenges, and triumphs. The Major Arcana can serve as a guide for understanding the deeper aspects of musical artistry, from the emotional and spiritual to the practical and professional. Each card reflects universal truths that resonate deeply with the process of creating, performing, and experiencing music, making them invaluable tools for introspection and inspiration.

The Major Arcana also addresses the darker, more challenging aspects of the musical journey. The Tower, for instance, reflects upheaval and sudden change, which can manifest in a musician's life as unexpected setbacks, creative crises, or shifts in direction. While this card may seem ominous, it also carries the potential for renewal and growth, as the destruction of old structures makes way for new possibilities. Similarly, the Devil highlights the temptations and attachments that can hinder a musician's progress, from self-doubt and perfectionism to external pressures and unhealthy habits. These cards invite musicians to confront and release what no longer serves them, paving the way for greater authenticity and freedom.

The Fool

The Fool is the beginning, the boundless leap into the unknown, and the embodiment of pure potential. In music, the Fool is the first note played on an instrument you've never touched before, the song written without thought of structure, the performance given with fearless abandon. It is the essence of creativity untethered, a reminder that music is not just a craft to be mastered but an adventure to be lived.

When the Fool appears, it calls the musician to embrace curiosity and spontaneity. It speaks to the joy of exploration, of finding melodies and rhythms not through calculation but by surrendering to the moment. The Fool doesn't ask whether the notes make sense or if the lyrics are perfect, it simply invites the artist to play, to experiment, to allow the music to flow freely without judgment. This is the energy of new beginnings, untainted by fear or expectation.

In music, the Fool can signify the start of a creative journey. It is the first attempt at writing a song, the decision to join a band, or the courage to perform in front of others for the first time. These moments are often accompanied by a mix of excitement and uncertainty, but the Fool encourages musicians to step forward regardless. It is a card that celebrates the act of trying, of trusting in one's ability to learn and grow through the experience itself.

The Fool also represents freedom, a quality that is essential to true artistic expression. It reminds musicians that music is not bound by rules, that it thrives in the spaces where convention is challenged and boundaries are blurred. Under the influence of the Fool, a musician might abandon traditional forms in favor of improvisation or embrace an entirely new genre without concern for how it will be received. This card urges the artist to follow their instincts and passions, to create not for approval but for the sheer joy of the process.

There is a sense of innocence in the Fool, a childlike wonder that is deeply connected to the essence of music. For a musician, this might mean rediscovering the pure pleasure of playing an instrument, the thrill of hearing a new melody for the first time, or the simple act of singing without restraint. The Fool invites the artist to return to this state of wonder, to strip away the pressures of perfection and reconnect with the heart of why they make music in the first place.

The Fool's journey is not without its risks. In music, this could manifest as stepping into unfamiliar territory or taking creative leaps that feel uncertain. Perhaps it's playing an instrument in front of an audience before mastering it, or releasing a song that feels deeply personal. These risks, however, are where the greatest growth occurs. The Fool teaches that vulnerability is a strength, that the willingness to risk failure is what allows for true innovation and authenticity.

For those who feel stuck or uninspired, the Fool can be a powerful reminder to let go of expectations and simply begin. It doesn't matter if the first note is perfect or if the composition makes sense, what matters is the act of creating. The Fool encourages musicians to break free from the weight of doubt and to trust in the process. In this way, it can be a spark that reignites a passion for music and opens the door to new possibilities.

The Fool's energy is infectious, and it often inspires others to join in. A jam session that starts with one person experimenting can quickly grow into a collaborative explosion of sound, with each participant feeding off the uninhibited energy of the moment. The Fool is a reminder that music is a shared experience, one that connects people across boundaries and brings them together in the spirit of play.

Ultimately, the Fool is a celebration of the journey itself. In music, it is the reminder that the act of creating is its own reward, that the missteps and experiments are just as important as the polished performance. It urges musicians to embrace the unknown, to let go of the need for control, and to trust that the path will reveal itself as they move forward. With the Fool, there are no limits, only possibilities.

To embody the Fool in music is to embrace the freedom to be yourself, to play with abandon, and to trust in the power of your own creativity. It is a card that asks musicians to step into the unknown with open hearts and fearless minds, knowing that each note they play, each song they write, is a step into a boundless and infinite world. The Fool does not promise certainty, but it does promise adventure and in music, as in life, that is often more than enough.

The Magician
The Magician is a card of manifestation, mastery, and creative power. It symbolizes the artist as an alchemist, transforming raw inspiration into tangible sound, blending skill and passion to create something that resonates. It is the moment when ideas move from the abstract into reality, when the tools of the craft, whether instruments, voice, or technology, become extensions of the musician's will. The Magician represents the connection between intention and action, the ability to shape the intangible into something that can be heard, felt, and shared.

At its core, the Magician is about potential realized. It reflects the musician who has not only discovered their creative spark but also learned how to channel it effectively. There is an understanding here of the balance between inspiration and discipline, the knowledge that while music can be spontaneous and instinctual, it also requires focus and dedication to bring it fully to life. The Magician's table is full of tools, each representing a different aspect of the musician's craft: the strings of a guitar, the keys of a piano, the timbre of a voice, or the infinite possibilities of a digital soundboard. The card celebrates the mastery of these tools and the way they come together to serve the artist's vision.

The Magician often appears at moments of innovation or breakthrough. It speaks to a time when the artist is fully in their element, weaving together technique and emotion to create something unique. This could be the songwriter who finds the perfect lyric to express an elusive feeling, or the producer who layers sounds in a way that transforms a simple melody into a symphonic experience. The Magician is the architect of sound, the one who sees beyond the notes and rhythms to the deeper story they can tell.

This card also carries a sense of confidence and authority. It reflects the moment when a musician steps into their own power, trusting their instincts and their abilities. It is the guitarist who improvises a solo with effortless grace, or the vocalist who holds a note with unwavering conviction. The Magician knows their strengths and uses them with purpose, unafraid to take risks because they understand their craft. This confidence doesn't come from arrogance but from a deep connection to their art, a sense of alignment between their inner vision and the external world.

The Magician's connection to the element of air, which governs intellect and communication, also speaks to music's ability to convey meaning. Under this card's influence, a musician might find themselves not only creating sound but also crafting messages such as lyrics that tell a story, melodies that evoke a mood, or compositions that reflect personal truths. The Magician reminds the artist that music is not just entertainment but a language, a way to bridge the gap between minds and hearts, to connect on levels that words alone cannot reach.

One of the Magician's greatest powers is its ability to transform limitations into opportunities. For a musician, this might mean working with a restricted budget or limited equipment but still managing to create something extraordinary. It could also signify finding inspiration in adversity, using personal struggles or experiences as fuel for artistic expression. The Magician sees possibilities where others see obstacles, reminding musicians that creativity is not about having everything but about making the most of what is at hand.

The Magician also embodies the idea of being a channel. In music, this speaks to the mysterious way ideas often seem to come from somewhere beyond the self. A melody might arrive unbidden, or a lyric might flow as if whispered by an unseen muse. The Magician encourages musicians to honor this process, to trust the flow of inspiration and allow themselves to be vessels for creativity. Yet it also reminds them that they are not passive in this exchange; they must actively shape and refine what comes through, bringing it into form with intention and care.

In a performance setting, the Magician's energy can be electric. A musician embodying this card has a magnetic presence, captivating their audience not just with technical skill but with an undeniable charisma. They command the stage, drawing listeners into their world and making them feel as if the music is speaking directly to them. This is the magic of the Magician in action: the ability to create a moment that feels both intimate and transcendent, to weave an invisible thread between themselves and their audience.

The Magician is a card of empowerment. It reminds musicians that they hold the tools they need to create, that their ability to manifest their vision lies within them. It is an invitation to step into the fullness of their creative power, to trust their skills, and to embrace the infinite potential of their art. Music, under the Magician's influence, becomes not just a craft but a form of magic, a way to transform the ordinary into the extraordinary, to turn emotions into sound, and to make the invisible visible.

For musicians, the Magician is a call to action. It asks them to take their ideas and bring them to life, to use their talents boldly and unapologetically. It is a reminder that the creative process is both a gift and a responsibility, a chance to shape the world through sound and expression. With the Magician, music becomes not just something heard but something felt, an alchemy of the heart, the mind, and the spirit. It is the art of making magic real.

The High Priestess
The High Priestess is a card of intuition, mystery, and the deep currents of the subconscious. In music, she represents the unseen forces that guide creativity, the whispers of inspiration that emerge from silence, and the profound connection between sound and emotion. She is the keeper of secrets, the guardian of the intangible realms where music begins before it becomes a note, a lyric, or a rhythm. To encounter the High Priestess in music is to step into a

space of reflection and discovery, where answers are not given but revealed through the act of listening.

When the High Priestess appears, she invites the musician to turn inward, to explore the depths of their own intuition and emotional landscape. She speaks to the moments when music is not driven by technique or external goals but by an inner knowing, a feeling that guides the hands, the voice, or the pen without explanation. Under her influence, the creative process becomes less about control and more about surrendering to the flow, trusting that the music will find its way if the artist allows it to.

This card is closely tied to the mysteries of sound itself, the way a single note can evoke memories, the way a melody can reach into the soul and touch something unspoken. The High Priestess reminds musicians that music is more than patterns and frequencies; it is a way to bridge the gap between the conscious and unconscious mind. When creating under her energy, a musician might find themselves drawn to subtlety and nuance, crafting pieces that resonate not just with the ears but with the heart and spirit.

The High Priestess is also a symbol of patience and stillness. This might manifest as the quiet moments between notes, the spaces that allow sound to breathe and meaning to emerge. She teaches musicians to honor these silences, to recognize that what is not played is as important as what is. This can be a powerful lesson for artists who feel the pressure to fill every moment, to always produce or perform. The High Priestess encourages them to trust the process, to let the music unfold naturally, and to understand that inspiration often comes in the pauses.

In the act of composing or performing, the High Priestess speaks to the intuitive choices that defy logic but feel right. A songwriter under her influence might pair unexpected chords or find themselves drawn to a lyric that seems to come from nowhere but carries profound meaning. A performer might instinctively slow a tempo or linger on a note, creating a moment that feels timeless. These are not decisions made with the mind but with the soul, guided by a deeper understanding that cannot be easily articulated.

The High Priestess also reminds musicians of the transformative power of music as a personal practice. Playing an instrument, singing, or even listening to music can become a form of meditation, a way to connect with one's inner self and the larger mysteries of existence. Under her guidance, music becomes a mirror, reflecting back truths that the conscious mind might struggle to see. This is the kind of music that heals, not because it provides answers but because it creates space for questions, for emotions, and for the unknown.

Her connection to the moon ties her energy to cycles and rhythms, reminding musicians of the natural ebb and flow of creativity. There will be times of inspiration and times of stillness, and both are essential to the process. The High Priestess teaches the importance of honoring these cycles, of not forcing the music but allowing it to arise in its own time. This can be a challenge in a world that often demands constant output, but she offers reassurance that creativity cannot be rushed or confined; it is a deep well that must be tended with care.

In performance, the High Priestess brings an almost otherworldly quality. A musician embodying her energy creates an atmosphere of mystery and depth, drawing the audience into an experience that feels both intimate and expansive. This is the kind of performance that lingers, leaving listeners with a sense of having touched something beyond themselves. It is not about spectacle but about presence, about the quiet power of being fully in the moment and allowing the music to speak for itself.

Ultimately, the High Priestess in music is a reminder of the sacred nature of art. She calls musicians to approach their craft with reverence, to see it not just as an act of creation but as a journey into the unknown. She asks them to trust their instincts, to listen deeply, not only to music but to themselves, and to honor the mysteries that guide their work.

Under the influence of the High Priestess, music becomes a portal. It is no longer just sound but a journey inward, a way to connect with the hidden parts of the self and the vast, unknowable universe. It is a reminder that music, like the High Priestess herself, holds secrets that can only be discovered through patience, intuition, and the willingness to explore the depths. To create music in her presence is to step into the sacred, to trust in the unseen, and to let the mysteries of sound and silence lead the way.

The Empress

.The Empress is a card of creation, abundance, and the nurturing power of life itself. She represents the act of bringing something beautiful into the world through a process that is as organic as it is inspired. She embodies the essence of creativity in its most fertile form, where ideas take root, grow, and flourish in harmony with the natural rhythms of life. With the Empress, music is not only an act of expression but also an act of love, a way of tending to both the self and others through sound.

When the Empress appears in the context of music, she invites the artist to embrace the fullness of their creative energy. She encourages musicians to see their work not as a product of effort alone but as a natural extension of who they are. Under her influence, the act of making music feels less like labor and more like giving life to something that already exists within, waiting to be born. It is the kind of creativity that flows effortlessly, guided by intuition and a deep connection to the world around us.

The Empress's connection to nature is profound, and in music, she speaks to the organic quality of sound. A musician working under her influence might find inspiration in the patterns of the natural world such as the rustling of leaves, the rhythm of waves, and the song of birds. These elements remind us that music is not separate from life but deeply intertwined with it. The Empress encourages musicians to listen not only to their instruments but to the world itself, finding harmony in the interplay of natural and human-made sounds.

There is a sensuality to the Empress that is reflected in the richness of her energy. In music, this translates to an embrace of beauty and emotion, a willingness to indulge in the lush textures of sound. Her presence encourages musicians to explore the depth and breadth of their craft, layering harmonies, experimenting with dynamics, and creating compositions that evoke a sense of fullness and warmth. She teaches that music, like life, is meant to be savored, experienced fully with all the senses.

The nurturing aspect of the Empress is also central to her role in music. She reminds musicians of the importance of care and patience in the creative process. Just as a gardener tends to their plants, a musician must nurture their ideas, giving them the time and attention they need to grow. The Empress teaches that creativity cannot be rushed or forced; it must be allowed to unfold naturally. This approach fosters a deep sense of connection between the artist and their work, a relationship built on trust and devotion.

The Empress also reflects the communal power of music. She understands that creativity is not just about the individual but about the connections it fosters. In this way, the Empress represents music as a unifying force, bringing people together in celebration, healing, and joy. A concert, a song shared between friends, or even a simple lullaby sung to a child; all of these moments carry the energy of the Empress, where music becomes a bridge between hearts.

The Empress's energy manifests as a presence that is both commanding and inviting. A musician embodying her essence creates an atmosphere of warmth and inclusivity, drawing the audience into an experience that feels deeply personal yet universally resonant. This is the kind of performance that leaves people feeling enriched, as though they've been nourished by the music itself. The Empress reminds musicians that their art has the power to heal and uplift, to provide comfort and inspiration in equal measure.

Her connection to abundance also speaks to the idea that creativity is limitless. For musicians, this means that inspiration is always available, even in times of doubt or struggle. The Empress encourages artists to trust in the cycles of creativity, knowing that even periods of quiet or stagnation are part of the process. She teaches that there is always more to discover, more to create, and that the well of inspiration is never truly empty.

The Empress is a celebration of life and the ways in which music can reflect its beauty. She reminds musicians that their craft is not just a skill but a gift, one that allows them to bring joy and meaning into the world. Under her influence, music becomes a living thing, a creation that grows, evolves, and touches the lives of others in ways that cannot always be measured but are deeply felt.

To create music in the spirit of the Empress is to embrace the fullness of one's creativity, to trust in the process of growth, and to share the results with an open heart. It is to see music not as something separate from life but as a part of its great, interconnected web. With the Empress, music becomes a celebration of existence itself; a testament to the beauty of creation and the boundless potential of the human spirit.

The Emperor

The Emperor stands as a figure of structure, authority, and stability. In music, his energy manifests in the discipline and organization that turns raw inspiration into mastery. Where the Empress represents the organic flow of creativity, the Emperor brings the framework to give it form and endurance. He embodies the principle that art, no matter how inspired, needs a foundation to thrive, reminding musicians that structure does not stifle creativity, it elevates it, providing the boundaries within which it can grow and flourish.

When the Emperor appears in the realm of music, he calls attention to the importance of craftsmanship. This is the time for the artist to focus on honing their skills, practicing their scales, refining their technique, and mastering the tools of their trade. While passion and intuition are vital, the Emperor emphasizes that dedication and discipline are what transform potential into excellence. The musician under his influence learns to respect the rigor of their craft, understanding that mastery is built over time, through effort and persistence.

The Emperor also represents the architecture of music itself, the structures that underpin its beauty. He governs rhythm, form, and harmony, the elements that give music its shape and coherence. His energy can be seen in the symmetry of a classical sonata, the tight arrangement of a jazz ensemble, or the steady pulse of a drumbeat that holds a band together. For a musician, working with the Emperor means engaging with these elements intentionally, recognizing that even the most freeform improvisation benefits from a solid foundation.

In composition, the Emperor encourages clarity and order. He is the voice that asks the songwriter to consider the structure of a piece: how verses and choruses interact, how tension builds and resolves, how themes develop over time. This is not about rigidity but about purpose, about creating music that feels cohesive and complete. The Emperor's influence helps the musician to organize their ideas, to take scattered fragments of melody or lyric and weave them into a unified whole.

Yet the Emperor's energy extends beyond the technical. He is also the ruler, the leader who commands presence and respect. For a musician, this can translate to the confidence and authority needed to own their stage, their sound, and their vision. The Emperor reminds artists that they have the power to define their identity, to set their boundaries, and to take control of their creative journey. Whether it's managing a band, producing an album, or navigating the music industry, his guidance helps musicians to assert themselves and make decisions with clarity and strength.

The Emperor's connection to stability also speaks to the importance of consistency. In music, this could mean maintaining a regular practice routine, honoring commitments to performances or collaborations, or simply showing up for the work even on days when inspiration feels distant. The Emperor teaches that creativity thrives in an environment of reliability, where the artist creates a foundation of habits and practices that support their long-term growth.

For musicians who struggle with chaos or uncertainty, the Emperor offers a sense of grounding. He encourages them to take stock of their resources and use them wisely. His energy might lead an artist to set goals, create a schedule, or establish systems that help them stay focused and productive. While this structured approach may seem at odds with the fluidity of creativity, the Emperor shows that boundaries and order can create a safe space for inspiration to thrive.

In performance, the Emperor brings a sense of authority and command. A musician embodying his energy does not merely play; they lead. Whether it's the conductor guiding an orchestra or a solo artist commanding the attention of a crowd, the Emperor's presence is undeniable. He reminds performers that their role is not just to share music but to guide an experience, to hold space for the audience and carry them through the journey of sound.

The Emperor represents the balance between vision and execution. He understands that while creativity begins in the realm of dreams and ideas, it must eventually take root in the material world. This means not only imagining what could be but also doing the work to make it real. He teaches musicians to value both inspiration and effort, to respect the process as much as the result.

The Emperor's presence in music is a reminder of the power of discipline, focus, and determination. He calls artists to rise to their potential, to take responsibility for their craft, and to build something enduring from their talents. Under his influence, music becomes not just an expression of creativity but a testament to the strength of the artist's will and the clarity of their vision.

With the Emperor, music takes on a sense of purpose and permanence. It is no longer just sound but a structure, a legacy, something that can stand the test of time. To create under his guidance is to honor both the inspiration that fuels art and the discipline that brings it to life, crafting music that is as solid and enduring as the foundations on which it rests.

The Hierophant

The Hierophant represents tradition, wisdom, and the transmission of knowledge. His energy can be seen in the rituals and teachings that connect musicians to their craft, to their audience, and to one another. He is the bridge between the past and the present, the keeper of traditions who ensures that the wisdom of those who came before is preserved, shared, and honored. To encounter the Hierophant in music is to step into a space where learning and respect for the foundations of the art form take precedence, where the act of creating and performing becomes part of a larger, timeless narrative.

The Hierophant's influence is felt most strongly in the formal study of music. He is the teacher, the mentor, the conductor who imparts knowledge and instills discipline in their students. Under his guidance, musicians learn the theory and techniques that provide a framework for their creativity. Scales, chord progressions, rhythm patterns, these are the tools he provides, the building blocks that allow musicians to express themselves with clarity and precision. The Hierophant reminds artists that while inspiration may strike like lightning, it is the foundation of knowledge and practice that allows them to channel that energy effectively.

In the broader sense, the Hierophant speaks to the traditions and institutions that shape music as a cultural and communal experience. He represents the lineage of composers, performers, and innovators whose work has built the vast, intricate tapestry of musical history. Whether it's the centuries-old traditions of classical music, the oral histories of folk songs, or the cultural movements that birthed genres like jazz or hip-hop, the Hierophant reminds musicians that they are part of something larger than themselves. By engaging with these traditions, they gain not only technical skills but also a deeper understanding of their place within the continuum of musical expression.

Yet the Hierophant is not merely a figure of rigid adherence to the past. His presence calls for balance between honoring tradition and finding one's voice within it. He encourages musicians to learn from the masters, to study the rules and structures that have stood the test of time, but also to recognize when those rules can be bent, reshaped, or transcended. The Hierophant teaches that innovation is most powerful when it is grounded in understanding, when it grows out of respect for what has come before.

The communal aspect of the Hierophant is another essential part of his energy. In music, this is the connection between teacher and student, performer and audience, composer and interpreter. The Hierophant reminds musicians that their work is not reacted in isolation; it is shared, received, and transformed through the act of listening. This dynamic is most evident in traditions where music is passed down through generations, where each performer adds their own nuance and personality while remaining faithful to the essence of the piece. Under the Hierophant's influence, music becomes a dialogue, a living exchange of ideas and emotions.

There is also a spiritual dimension to the Hierophant's connection to music. He represents the sacred nature of sound, the way music can transcend the material world and connect us to something greater. In this sense, the Hierophant might appear in the form of a church choir, a devotional chant, or the deep resonance of a drum circle. He reminds musicians that music is not just entertainment but a way to access the divine, to bridge the gap between the earthly and the eternal. When creating or performing under his guidance, the artist taps into this sacred energy, using their craft as a means of exploration and connection.

In performance, the Hierophant's energy can be seen in moments of reverence and tradition. This could be the careful interpretation of a classical symphony, the respectful cover of a beloved song, or the continuation of cultural practices through music. The musician embodies the role of the Hierophant when they take on the responsibility of preserving and sharing something meaningful, offering their audience a chance to engage with the depth and richness of the music's history and significance.

The Hierophant also challenges musicians to reflect on their relationship with authority and tradition. While he celebrates the value of knowledge and structure, he also asks the artist to consider where these elements may limit their growth or expression. Musicians under his influence might wrestle with questions about their identity and authenticity, wondering how to stay true to themselves while honoring the traditions they hold dear. This is part of the Hierophant's lesson: to find freedom within the framework, to make the teachings one's own.

The Hierophant in music is a symbol of connection; connection to the past, to the community, and to the transcendent power of sound. He reminds musicians that their craft is both personal and collective, that every note they play carries echoes of the traditions, teachings, and influences that have shaped them. Under his guidance, music becomes not just an act of creation but an act of communion, a way to honor the threads that bind us to one another and to the deeper mysteries of life.

To create or perform in the spirit of the Hierophant is to embrace the wisdom of the ages while remaining open to the possibilities of the present. It is to recognize that music is a gift passed down through time, a sacred inheritance that carries with it the responsibility to learn, to teach, and to share. With the Hierophant, music becomes more than sound; it becomes a bridge between worlds, a testament to the enduring power of tradition, and a reminder that every musician is part of a greater story.

The Lovers

The Lovers is a celebration of union, harmony, and the choices that shape the core of who we are. It speaks to the profound connections that are formed through sound whether it be between a musician and their instrument, between collaborators creating together , or between the performer and their audience. The Lovers embody the magic of synergy, the way music can bring elements together in perfect balance, creating something greater than the sum of its parts.

At its essence, the Lovers represents the bond between passion and purpose. In music, this is the meeting of inspiration and intention, the alignment of the heart and the craft. When a musician taps into the energy of the Lovers, they find themselves in a state of flow, where creativity feels effortless and deeply fulfilling. This is not simply about making music for the sake of making it; it is about creating something that resonates with one's truest self, something that feels like an extension of the soul.

The Lovers also symbolizes duality and the dance between opposing forces. In music, this can be heard in the interplay of melody and harmony, tension and release, sound and silence. The card reminds musicians that these contrasts are what give music its depth and emotion. It is the push and pull, the moments of discord resolving into beauty, that create the narrative of a piece. To work with the Lovers is to embrace this balance, to find harmony in the contrasts and to trust the interplay of elements as they come together.

Collaboration is another key theme of the Lovers in music. This card highlights the power of working with others, of combining talents and perspectives to create something extraordinary. Whether it's a band, a songwriting partnership, or an orchestra, the Lovers speaks to the connection and mutual respect that make collaboration thrive. When musicians truly listen to one another, when they allow their individual voices to blend and complement each other, they create a unity that transcends their separate contributions. The Lovers reminds us that music is often at its most powerful when it is shared, when it becomes a dialogue rather than a monologue.

This card also reflects the vulnerability and intimacy inherent in music. To create or perform is to open oneself up, to share something deeply personal with others. The Lovers encourage musicians to lean into this vulnerability, to trust that authenticity will resonate more powerfully than perfection. Music born from genuine feeling has a way of touching hearts, of creating connections that are as profound as they are intangible. The Lovers teaches that it is through this openness, this willingness to be seen and heard, that the most meaningful connections are formed.

In the act of performance, the Lovers represents the electric bond between artist and audience. This is the moment when the music becomes a shared experience, a meeting place where emotions and energy flow freely between the two. Under the influence of the Lovers, a performance feels like an intimate conversation, where the artist and the audience are not separate but united in the moment. It is this connection that makes music feel alive, that transforms it from notes and rhythms into something that can move and inspire.

Choice is another vital aspect of the Lovers. In music, this could manifest as the decisions that shape an artist's path such as what genre to pursue, which collaborators to work with, what stories to tell through their songs. The Lovers reminds musicians that these choices should come from a place of alignment with their values and passions. It is not about following trends or external expectations but about choosing the path that feels most true to their creative spirit. The Lovers encourages musicians to trust their instincts, to honor their desires, and to create from a place of authenticity.

The Lovers also reflects the relationship between a musician and their craft. This is not just about skill or technique but about the love and dedication that fuel the act of creation. To play an instrument, to sing, to compose, it is an act of devotion, a commitment to something that feels larger than oneself. The Lovers reminds musicians to nurture this relationship, to find joy in the process as much as in the outcome. Music is not just something they do; it is a part of who they are, a reflection of their connection to the world and to themselves.

The Lovers in music is a card of connection, harmony, and purpose. It is a reminder that music is a bridge, a way to unite the inner and outer worlds, to bring people together, and to express the deepest truths of the heart. Under the influence of the Lovers, music becomes more than an art form; it becomes a language of love, a way to communicate what words cannot.

To create music in the spirit of the Lovers is to embrace both the joy and the vulnerability of connection. It is to honor the relationships that shape the music, the bond with one's instrument, the partnership with collaborators, the dialogue with the audience. With the Lovers, music is not just heard; it is felt, experienced as a union of energy, emotion, and soul. It is through this unity that music reaches its fullest expression, reminding us of the beauty of connection and the infinite possibilities that arise when harmony is found.

The Chariot

The Chariot is a card of determination, control, and triumph through focused effort. In music, it represents the drive to push forward, to conquer challenges, and to channel one's willpower into creating something extraordinary. It is the force that compels a musician to persevere through difficulty, to refine their craft, and to bring their vision to life with unwavering confidence. The Chariot carries the energy of momentum, the unstoppable rhythm of progress that moves the artist closer to their goals.

This card is about mastery, not just of the external world but of the self. In music, this mastery can be seen in the discipline required to hone technique, the focus needed to perfect a performance, or the resilience demanded in the face of setbacks. A musician guided by the Chariot is someone who refuses to be deterred by obstacles, who meets challenges head-on with determination and resolve. They understand that success in music, as in life, requires a balance of passion and control, a willingness to harness both the creative and the practical.

The Chariot's energy is forward-moving, propelling the musician to take action. This is not the card of passive inspiration or waiting for the right moment. Instead, it is a call to seize the reins and make things happen. In music, this might mean pursuing opportunities with vigor, pushing through the discomfort of growth, or stepping onto a stage with the confidence that comes from preparation and self-belief. The Chariot reminds the artist that progress is achieved not by luck or chance but by intentional effort and direction.

In the realm of music performance, the Chariot represents the power of presence. When a musician embodies this card, they command attention, projecting confidence and control through every note they play or sing. Their focus is palpable, their energy magnetic. This is the performer who captivates an audience not just with their skill but with their sheer force of will, their ability to hold the space and drive the emotional journey of the music. The Chariot teaches that true mastery in performance comes not only from technical precision but from the conviction and intensity that bring music to life.

The Chariot also speaks to the idea of balance in motion. In the imagery of the card, the charioteer often holds the reins of opposing forces, symbolizing the need to harmonize conflicting energies. In music, this might manifest as the balance between creativity and discipline, improvisation and structure, or individual expression and collaboration. The Chariot shows that success comes not from suppressing these tensions but from learning to guide them, to use their dynamic interplay as a source of power. A musician aligned with the Chariot learns to navigate the complexities of their craft with precision, steering their efforts toward a clear and purposeful goal.

Another aspect of the Chariot's energy is its connection to confidence and identity. In music, this is the moment when an artist steps fully into their own, embracing their unique voice and perspective. The Chariot encourages musicians to assert themselves, to claim their space in the world of sound without hesitation or doubt. This is the card of owning one's power, of recognizing that the journey forward requires not just skill but belief in one's ability to succeed. It asks the musician to trust in their path, even when the road ahead is uncertain or fraught with difficulty.

The Chariot is not a card of ease; it acknowledges that progress often comes with struggle. For musicians, this might mean overcoming self-doubt, navigating the competitive nature of the industry, or finding the strength to push through creative blocks. The Chariot offers reassurance that these challenges can be overcome, that the same force that drives the struggle also holds the power to resolve it. It teaches that perseverance is not just a virtue but a necessity, the key to breaking through barriers and achieving greatness.

In composition and creativity, the Chariot symbolizes clarity of vision. It urges the musician to focus on their goals, to move past distractions and commit fully to the act of creation. Whether it's writing a symphony, producing an album, or crafting a single melody, the Chariot reminds the artist to stay true to their purpose, to pour their energy into the work with unrelenting dedication. It is this clarity and focus that turn ideas into reality, that transform inspiration into tangible, impactful music.

Ultimately, the Chariot in music is a symbol of triumph through determination and willpower. It reminds musicians that the path to mastery is not always smooth but that every challenge faced and overcome is a step closer to fulfillment. Under the Chariot's influence, music becomes a vehicle for growth and achievement, a testament to the power of perseverance and self-belief.

To create or perform with the energy of the Chariot is to embrace the journey, to harness the opposing forces within and use them to propel forward. It is to stand in one's power, to trust in the direction chosen, and to commit fully to the pursuit of excellence. With the Chariot, music becomes not just an art form but a statement of triumph, a reflection of the strength and resolve that fuel the artist's journey.

Strength

The Strength card represents inner power, resilience, and the harmony between force and gentleness. In music, its energy resonates deeply with the journey of mastering both the technical and emotional aspects of the craft. Strength is not merely about the outward display of talent but about the quiet, unwavering force that allows a musician to persist, to create with authenticity, and to connect with the deepest layers of their being through sound.

Strength speaks to the courage required in music. It is the courage to be vulnerable, to share a piece of oneself through song, and to face the fears and insecurities that often accompany the creative process. Music can feel like a raw and exposed form of expression, and the Strength card reminds the musician that this vulnerability is not a weakness but a testament to their bravery. It takes fortitude to bare one's soul, to channel emotions into melodies and lyrics, and to trust that the audience will not only hear but also feel the truth embedded in the music.

Strength teaches the importance of balance in music. It embodies the fusion of technical skill and emotional depth, of precision and flow. A musician guided by this card understands that true mastery comes not from domination or rigid control but from a relationship of mutual respect with their instrument, their voice, or their craft. Strength whispers that the finest music emerges when the artist allows themselves to be both disciplined and free, commanding yet yielding, powerful yet tender.

The lion often depicted on the Strength card symbolizes raw energy and instinct. In music, this can be likened to the wild, untamed power of inspiration, the flashes of creativity that feel almost feral in their intensity. The figure on the card, gently taming the lion, represents the ability to channel that energy into something meaningful. For a musician, this means finding ways to transform raw emotion into structured artistry. Strength is the force that bridges these two worlds, reminding the artist that their greatest power lies in their ability to shape their inspiration without stifling its essence.

In performance, the energy of Strength shines through in moments of vulnerability met with composure. It is the singer who allows their voice to crack with emotion but continues singing, or the pianist who loses themselves in a piece, surrendering to the flow without losing their technical grounding. Strength shows in the ability to convey the full spectrum of human experience through music while maintaining a sense of control and presence. It is not about perfection but about authenticity, about finding beauty in the interplay of fragility and resilience.

Strength also represents the patience required in the pursuit of musical excellence. Learning an instrument, developing one's voice, or composing a piece often requires months, even years, of dedication. Strength encourages musicians to trust in this process, to approach their practice with perseverance and kindness toward themselves. It reminds them that growth is not always immediate or linear, that setbacks and plateaus are a natural part of the journey. Strength teaches that the true power lies in showing up, in continuing to play, sing, or write even when progress feels elusive.

The card's connection to compassion extends to collaboration. In music, this might manifest as the ability to listen deeply to fellow musicians, to adapt and respond in the moment, and to create an environment of trust and mutual respect. Strength in a musical ensemble is not about overpowering others but contributing one's voice in a way that supports and enhances the whole. It is the bassist who locks in with the drummer to create a solid foundation, the guitarist who steps back to let the vocalist shine, the conductor who leads with sensitivity and care.

Strength also holds a spiritual dimension in music. It is the recognition that music has the power to heal, to comfort, and to uplift. A musician working with the energy of Strength understands the profound impact their art can have, not just on themselves but on others. They play not only for recognition or achievement but as an act of service, offering their music as a balm for the soul. Strength reminds musicians that their work is meaningful, that the sounds they create can touch hearts and transform lives.

The Strength card in music is a reminder of the power of perseverance, compassion, and authenticity. It teaches that true strength is not about force or domination but about understanding, balance, and the courage to be vulnerable. Under its influence, music becomes a reflection of the artist's inner journey, a testament to their resilience and their capacity to find harmony within themselves and with the world around them.

To create with the energy of Strength is to embrace the dualities of music: the raw and the refined, the controlled and the free, the powerful and the tender. It is to approach the craft with humility and courage, to trust in the process, and to allow music to be both a source of strength and an expression of it. Strength reminds us that through music, we can find our truest selves, and through that discovery, we can share something timeless and profound with the world.

The Hermit

The Hermit is a beacon of introspection, solitude, and the search for deeper meaning. Its energy invites a journey inward, a retreat from the noise of the external world to uncover the truths and inspiration that lie within. The Hermit represents the quiet, sacred space where creativity is born, nurtured, and refined in a space where the musician is free to explore the depths of their soul and allow the music to become a reflection of their inner world.

To embrace the Hermit's energy in music is to seek clarity through silence and stillness. It is the act of stepping away from distractions, from the demands of performance or recognition, and instead focusing on the purity of creation. This is the moment when a musician sits alone with their instrument, not to practice or perform but to commune with it, to allow the sound to guide them toward something that feels true. The Hermit's lantern symbolizes the light of wisdom that emerges from such solitary exploration. This is a light that illuminates not only the path forward but also the deeper purpose behind the music itself.

The Hermit teaches that music is not always about being heard by others. Sometimes, it is about listening to oneself, to the quiet whispers of inspiration, to the emotions and experiences that linger beneath the surface. In this way, the

Hermit invites musicians to approach their craft as a form of meditation, a way to connect with their innermost thoughts and feelings. The music created in this space may never be shared with an audience, but its value lies in the connection it fosters between the artist and their own essence.

Solitude is not loneliness but a deliberate choice to step away from the world in order to recharge and reflect. For musicians, this solitude can be a powerful tool for growth and discovery. It is in these quiet moments that they can experiment without fear of judgment, explore new ideas, and take creative risks. The Hermit reminds them that some of the most profound musical breakthroughs happen not in the spotlight but in the privacy of a room where they are free to make mistakes, to wander, and to find their way.

The Hermit's connection to wisdom also speaks to the idea of seeking guidance in music. This guidance might come from studying the works of great composers, reflecting on the teachings of mentors, or drawing inspiration from the natural world. Yet, the Hermit also teaches that true wisdom is not about imitation or external validation, it is about integrating these influences into one's unique voice. In this sense, the Hermit encourages musicians to trust their instincts, to follow their own path even when it diverges from convention or expectation.

The Hermit's energy manifests as a deeply introspective and intimate connection to the music. A musician aligned with this card plays not for the applause but for the act itself, for the way it allows them to express and explore their inner landscape. Their performance feels like a moment of communion, as though they are sharing a private conversation with the music that others are fortunate enough to witness. This quality of presence, of being fully immersed in the act of creation, is what makes their artistry resonate on a profound level.

The Hermit also reminds musicians of the importance of rest and retreat. In a world that often demands constant output and visibility, the Hermit offers permission to step back, to honor the cycles of creativity that include both activity and stillness. A musician who heeds the Hermit's wisdom understands that the quiet periods, the times of reflection and pause, are as essential to the creative process as the moments of inspiration and action. It is in these spaces of stillness that the seeds of future music are sown.

The spiritual aspect of the Hermit cannot be overlooked. This card speaks to the transcendent power of sound, the way music can serve as a bridge to something greater than oneself. For a musician, the Hermit represents the sacredness of this connection, the way a single note or melody can evoke a sense of awe and wonder. When working under the Hermit's influence, music becomes not just an art form but a spiritual practice, a way to seek and share truth.

The Hermit is a reminder of the value of introspection, solitude, and authenticity. It teaches that the journey inward is just as important as the journey outward, that the act of creating music is as much about self-discovery as it is about expression. The Hermit encourages musicians to trust in their path, to honor the quiet moments, and to seek meaning not in the applause of others but in the resonance of their own heart.

To create with the Hermit's energy is to embrace the silence, to allow the music to emerge from a place of stillness and authenticity. It is to trust in the wisdom of solitude, to use the quiet as a canvas for exploration and growth. With the Hermit, music becomes a reflection of the inner world, a lantern that lights the way for both the artist and those who hear their song.

Wheel of Fortune

The Wheel of Fortune is a card of cycles, change, and the unseen forces that shape the trajectory of life. It speaks to the ebb and flow of creativity, the unpredictable rhythms of inspiration, and the opportunities that arise when one learns to move in harmony with the tides of fate. This card captures the essence of transformation, the way music itself constantly evolves, reflecting the shifting landscapes of the artist's inner and outer worlds.

The Wheel of Fortune represents the interplay of chance and choice. It acknowledges the role of serendipity in their journey, the unexpected encounters, the sudden sparks of inspiration, the doors that open when least expected. A song may be born from a random chord progression stumbled upon in a moment of playfulness or from an unplanned collaboration that reveals something entirely new. The Wheel reminds musicians that much of what shapes their artistry lies beyond their control, in the spontaneous magic of the moment.

At the same time, the Wheel of Fortune does not suggest passivity. It challenges musicians to remain alert and adaptable, ready to seize opportunities as they arise. In music, this might mean saying yes to a chance to perform at the last minute, exploring a genre or style outside of one's comfort zone, or following a creative impulse without questioning where it might lead. The Wheel encourages trust in the process, a willingness to ride its cycles with faith that each twist and turn is part of a larger, meaningful design.

Music itself embodies the energy of the Wheel of Fortune in its cyclical nature. Melodies loop and evolve, rhythms rise and fall, and themes are introduced, varied, and revisited. This card calls attention to the way music mirrors the natural cycles of life, from the steady repetition of a beat to the dynamic shifts of tempo and tone that keep a piece alive. A musician working with the Wheel understands that no moment in music, or life, is static. The beauty lies in its movement, its constant reinvention.

The Wheel also speaks to the unpredictable nature of success in music. A single song can unexpectedly capture the world's attention, or a career may rise and fall with the ever-changing tastes of the audience. The card reminds musicians that the highs and lows are part of the same cycle and that both triumph and challenge offer opportunities for growth. The Wheel's turning is impartial, offering lessons in humility during periods of success and resilience during times of struggle. It urges musicians to embrace each phase with grace, knowing that change is inevitable and often necessary for evolution.

Creatively, the Wheel of Fortune invites musicians to embrace the unknown. It asks them to step into the flow of inspiration, even when the destination is unclear. This might involve experimenting with new sounds, letting go of preconceived ideas about what a song "should" be, or allowing the music to take shape organically rather than forcing it into a fixed structure. The Wheel teaches that some of the most profound musical moments arise from surrendering to the process, trusting that the music knows where it wants to go.

The Wheel's connection to cycles also reflects the broader arc of a musician's journey. There are periods of intense productivity and times of rest, moments of clarity and times of uncertainty. The card reminds artists that all these phases are essential and interconnected. A creative block, for instance, may feel like a low point, but it often sets the stage for a breakthrough, a turning of the wheel that brings new insight and energy. The Wheel encourages musicians to honor each stage of the journey, trusting that the path unfolds as it should.

In performance, the Wheel of Fortune represents the unpredictable energy of live music, the way each performance is unique, shaped by the mood of the audience, the environment, and the spontaneity of the moment. A musician attuned to the Wheel embraces this unpredictability, finding joy in the surprises that arise and adapting to the shifts with grace. They understand that no two performances are the same and that this variability is part of what makes live music so electric and alive.

On a spiritual level, the Wheel of Fortune speaks to music's role as a universal force, something that transcends individual experience and connects us to the greater cycles of existence. A musician working with this card may feel a sense of alignment with something larger than themselves, as though they are a channel through which the music flows. The Wheel reminds artists that their work is part of a greater whole, a contribution to the ever-turning, ever-evolving symphony of life.

The Wheel of Fortune is a symbol of transformation, movement, and trust in the unfolding journey. It teaches that music, like life, is full of surprises, opportunities, and challenges, and that the key to navigating its cycles lies in adaptability, openness, and faith. The Wheel reminds musicians to celebrate the highs, endure the lows, and embrace the in-betweens, knowing that each moment is part of a larger rhythm, a greater song.

To create with the energy of the Wheel of Fortune is to dance with the unpredictable, to find harmony in change, and to trust the process of creation and evolution. It is to honor the cycles of music, the way it mirrors the constant turning of the world, and to recognize that through this movement, something timeless and beautiful is always being born, With the Wheel, music becomes not just an expression of self but a reflection of the infinite and ever-changing rhythms of life itself.

Justice

The Justice card embodies balance, fairness, truth, and accountability, concepts that resonate deeply within the world of music. In its essence, music seeks harmony, between notes, rhythms, and emotions, and Justice reminds us that this harmony must also extend to the intentions and actions of the artist. To align with the energy of Justice is to approach music with integrity, to honor the craft with authenticity, and to create work that reflects an honest connection to oneself and the world.

Justice calls for clarity and purpose. It is the moment when an artist pauses to consider why they create, what they wish to communicate, and how their work contributes to the larger narrative of humanity. Music, at its most profound, holds the power to reveal truths, to challenge perspectives, and to bring people together in shared understanding. Justice reminds the musician that this power comes with responsibility to wield their voice with care and to remain true to their vision.

Justice also speaks to the importance of balance. In the technical realm, this balance manifests in the interplay between melody and harmony, rhythm and space, light and shade. A composition or performance that feels "just" is one that respects these dynamics, where every element has its rightful place and contributes to the whole. Justice invites musicians to refine their craft, to edit and adjust until the work feels honest and complete, not through perfectionism but through a commitment to honoring the essence of the piece.

On a deeper level, Justice reflects the equilibrium within the artist. It asks musicians to confront their own truths, to face the inner questions that shape their art. What motivates the music they create? Is it a genuine expression of their soul, or does it cater to external pressures or expectations? Justice does not judge but encourages self-examination, urging the musician to align their work with their values and beliefs. Music created under the influence of Justice carries this authenticity; it resonates not because it conforms but because it is undeniably true.

In collaboration, Justice demands fairness and respect. The act of making music with others is a delicate balance of giving and receiving, of finding harmony between diverse voices and perspectives. Justice reminds musicians to listen as much as they play, to honor the contributions of their collaborators, and to work toward a shared vision. This is not about compromise for the sake of peace but about creating something richer and more meaningful through mutual understanding and effort.

Justice also holds a mirror to the societal role of music. Throughout history, music has been a vehicle for justice, a way to amplify voices, challenge injustices, and inspire change. Whether through protest songs, anthems of unity, or compositions that confront difficult truths, the Justice card reminds musicians of the profound impact their art can have on the collective. It calls them to use their platform with intention, to consider how their work reflects and influences the world around them.

The connection between Justice and accountability is especially significant for musicians. To work with this card is to take responsibility for one's actions, to honor commitments, and to uphold the integrity of the art form. This might mean putting in the effort to learn and practice, respecting the intellectual property of others, or acknowledging the cultural roots of the music they draw from. Justice asks musicians to approach their craft with humility and respect, understanding that every choice they make contributes to the larger fabric of music.

Justice also serves as a reminder that music is not just about the individual but about the relationships it fosters between the artist and their audience, between collaborators, and within the community. When a musician creates or performs, they enter into an unspoken contract with those who listen, offering a part of themselves in exchange for the listener's time and attention. Justice calls for sincerity in this exchange, urging musicians to give their best and to trust that the audience will meet them with the same openness.

In performance, the energy of Justice can be felt in the way a musician commands presence, not through force but through authenticity. A performance aligned with Justice feels balanced and grounded, as though the artist is completely attuned to the music and to the space they are sharing with the audience. There is an honesty in their expression, a sense that every note or word is delivered with intention and care. This kind of performance doesn't just entertain; it resonates, leaving a lasting impression because it speaks to something real.

The Justice card is a reminder of the profound interplay between truth, intention, and action. It challenges musicians to create with awareness, to honor the craft and its impact, and to strive for balance in every aspect of their work. Under its influence, music becomes more than just sound; it becomes a reflection of the artist's integrity, a testament to the power of authenticity, and a force for connection and understanding.

To embrace the energy of Justice is to approach music with a clear mind and an open heart, to seek balance in the creative process, and to trust in the transformative power of honesty. Justice teaches that when music is created and shared with sincerity, it has the potential to reveal truths, heal wounds, and inspire change. In this way, it becomes not just an art form but a form of justice in itself, offering harmony to a world that often longs for it.

The Hanged Man

The Hanged Man is a card of surrender, suspension, and the profound transformation that comes from seeing the world from a different perspective. In the context of music, it calls for a willingness to let go of preconceived notions, to embrace stillness, and to trust in the process of creation, even when it feels uncertain or uncomfortable. The Hanged Man invites musicians to pause, to release the need for control, and to allow the music to emerge in its own time and way.

At its heart, the Hanged Man represents a shift in perspective. For musicians, this might mean stepping back from the technical aspects of their craft to reconnect with the emotional or spiritual core of their work. It could involve exploring a new genre, instrument, or approach, allowing themselves to be a beginner again and seeing the world of music through fresh eyes. The Hanged Man teaches that growth often comes not from pushing forward but from stepping back, observing, and allowing oneself to be transformed by the experience.

The Hanged Man also speaks to the value of patience and the importance of the creative pause. There are times when inspiration seems distant, when the effort to create feels like a struggle. The Hanged Man reminds musicians that these moments of suspension are not failures but opportunities. In the stillness, the subconscious continues to work, weaving together ideas and emotions that will eventually find their way into the music. Trusting in this process requires faith and humility, qualities the Hanged Man embodies.

Surrender is a central theme of the Hanged Man, and in music, this can mean releasing the ego and allowing the music itself to take the lead. Musicians often speak of moments when the song seems to write itself, as though they are merely a channel for something greater. The Hanged Man teaches that these moments of surrender are where the deepest magic of music lies. By letting go of the need to control every detail, musicians open themselves to the flow of inspiration, to the melodies and rhythms that come from a place beyond conscious thought.

The Hanged Man's energy can also be felt in the way it challenges conventional expectations. Music, like any art form, is full of rules like scales, time signatures, and genres, but the Hanged Man asks musicians to question these boundaries, to experiment, and to embrace the unconventional. It suggests that the most transformative and innovative music often comes from a willingness to break the rules, to turn the familiar on its head, and to explore the unfamiliar with curiosity and openness.

In performance, the Hanged Man's influence might manifest as a moment of stillness, an unexpected pause that creates tension and anticipation. It could be a choice to strip a song down to its essence, allowing silence and space to speak as powerfully as sound. A musician guided by the Hanged Man understands that music is not only about what is played but also about what is left unplayed, the spaces between the notes that give the music its depth and meaning.

The spiritual aspect of the Hanged Man cannot be overlooked. This card speaks to the transcendent power of surrender, the way music can serve as a bridge between the earthly and the divine. For a musician, working with the Hanged Man's energy might mean approaching their craft as a form of meditation or prayer, a way to connect with something greater than themselves. It suggests that the act of creating music is as much about listening as it is about playing or composing.

The Hanged Man also teaches the importance of sacrifice in the pursuit of music. This is not sacrifice in the sense of suffering but in the sense of letting go of what no longer serves. A musician may need to release old habits, outdated beliefs, or fears of failure in order to move forward. The Hanged Man reminds them that this letting go is not a loss but a necessary step toward growth and transformation.

The Hanged Man in music is a symbol of trust, patience, and the power of perspective. It challenges musicians to embrace the unknown, to let go of the need for immediate results, and to find beauty and meaning in the process itself. Under its influence, music becomes a journey of discovery, a reflection of the artist's willingness to surrender and be transformed.

To create with the energy of the Hanged Man is to embrace stillness, to trust in the unfolding of the creative process, and to see music not just as an end but as a path of growth and self-discovery. It is to recognize that sometimes, the most profound truths emerge when we let go, step back, and allow ourselves to be guided by the rhythm of life itself. The Hanged Man reminds us that through surrender, we find freedom, and through stillness, we find the deepest music within.

Death

The Death card is a symbol of transformation, endings, and new beginnings. It speaks to the cycles of creation and destruction that are essential to the artistic process. It challenges musicians to let go of what no longer serves them, whether it's a creative block, a limiting belief, or even an attachment to a particular identity as an artist. Death is not an end in the final sense but a gateway to renewal, a reminder that within every conclusion lies the seed of something new.

Death can appear as the moment when a musician realizes that a particular piece or project must be abandoned. It might be a song that refuses to come together, a sound that no longer feels authentic, or an approach to music-making that has grown stagnant. The act of letting go can feel painful or even terrifying, especially when it involves walking away from something familiar. But the Death card reminds musicians that these endings are necessary for growth. By releasing what is no longer alive, space is made for the unexpected and the transformative.

Death is also about the evolution of the artist. A musician's journey is rarely linear; it is marked by phases of exploration, mastery, and reinvention. The Death card encourages musicians to embrace these natural cycles of change, to shed old identities and embrace new possibilities. This might mean leaving behind a successful genre to explore uncharted territory, or allowing a deeply personal experience to reshape their music in ways they never anticipated. Under the influence of Death, transformation becomes an act of courage and renewal.

Inspiration itself is an echo of the Death card's energy. Often the most profound creative breakthroughs arise in the aftermath of endings such as a heartbreak, a loss, or a moment of profound change. Music becomes a way to process these experiences, to give form to emotions that seem too vast for words. The Death card reminds musicians that the creative act is deeply tied to transformation, that it is through confronting and honoring these endings that some of the most powerful music is born.

Death also speaks to the way music itself undergoes cycles of death and rebirth. A song might change form through reinterpretation, a forgotten melody might resurface years later with new meaning, or an artist might rework an old idea, breathing new life into it. These acts of renewal mirror the essence of the Death card, showing that even in music, endings are rarely final, they are simply transitions.

The Death card can represent the courage to take risks, to leave behind what feels safe in favor of something raw and real. It is the moment of vulnerability onstage, when a musician decides to share something deeply personal or to improvise without knowing where the music will lead. In these moments, the old structures fall away, and what remains is pure expression, unfiltered and alive.

The spiritual aspect of the Death card cannot be ignored. Music itself is often seen as a bridge between the physical and the transcendent, a way to connect with something larger than oneself. The Death card amplifies this connection, reminding musicians that their art can serve as a vessel for transformation, not just for themselves but for their listeners. A piece of music inspired by the energy of Death has the power to move people, to help them process their own losses, and to find meaning in the cycles of life.

Death also teaches musicians about resilience. While the act of letting go can be difficult, it is through this process that strength and clarity emerge. A musician who embraces the lessons of the Death card learns to trust in the cycles of creation, knowing that even in the midst of an ending, the seeds of the next beginning are already taking root. This faith in the process allows them to face challenges with grace and to find beauty in the transitions.

The Death card is a reminder that endings are an integral part of the artistic journey. It encourages musicians to embrace change, to trust in the power of transformation, and to find inspiration in the cycles of life and death. Music created under the influence of Death is imbued with authenticity, depth, and the recognition that within every ending lies the potential for rebirth.

To create with the energy of the Death card is to honor the natural flow of life, to release what no longer resonates, and to step fearlessly into the unknown. It is to recognize that every note, every silence, and every pause is part of a larger symphony of transformation. Through Death, music becomes not just an art form but a testament to the enduring cycles of renewal, reminding us that even in the quietest moments of loss, there is always the promise of a new beginning.

Temperance

Temperance is a card of balance, harmony, and integration, qualities that resonate deeply within the world of music. At its core, this card invites musicians to find a sense of flow, where opposing elements blend seamlessly to create something greater than the sum of their parts. It speaks to the delicate art of combining discipline with spontaneity, structure with creativity, and emotion with intellect. In music, Temperance embodies the alchemy of composition, performance, and the transcendent experience of harmony.

The energy of Temperance is present in the process of creation. When a musician sits down to compose or play, they are engaging in a dance of opposites: tension and release, complexity and simplicity, experimentation and tradition. Temperance encourages the musician to embrace these dualities, not as contradictions but as complementary forces. It is the reminder that every dissonance has its resolution and that even in the boldest moments of musical exploration, there is a thread of coherence that ties it all together.

Balance is not about sameness or uniformity but about dynamic interplay. A piece of music might juxtapose a gentle melody with a driving rhythm or shift between quiet introspection and soaring intensity. Temperance celebrates this interplay, urging musicians to trust their intuition as they weave diverse elements into a unified whole. It teaches that true harmony is not static but alive, always adjusting and evolving, much like the process of mixing colors to create a perfect hue.

Temperance also speaks to the inner balance of the musician. Creating music often requires walking a fine line between control and surrender, between the careful crafting of a piece and the openness to let it take on a life of its own. A musician attuned to Temperance learns to navigate this balance, blending technical skill with emotional vulnerability, planning with improvisation, and effort with ease. The card suggests that the most profound music arises when the artist is neither overthinking nor completely detached, but fully present in the moment.

Collaboration is another domain where Temperance shines. When musicians come together, they bring with them their unique voices, styles, and perspectives. Temperance guides the group to find harmony, not by suppressing individuality but by allowing each contribution to enhance the whole. It speaks to the magic that happens when the egos are set aside, and the focus shifts to the shared goal of creating something meaningful. In this way, Temperance reminds musicians that the act of making music together is an alchemical process, one that transforms separate elements into a unified, transcendent experience.

Temperance also resonates with the rhythm of practice and performance. A musician's journey is not one of constant exertion but of cycles such as times of intense focus and times of rest, moments of deep exploration followed by periods of reflection. The card teaches the importance of pacing oneself, of honoring the natural flow of energy and inspiration. It suggests that just as music depends on the spaces between notes, so too does the musician benefit from pauses and balance in their creative life.

Temperance reveals the sacred nature of music as a bridge between the material and the divine. To create music is to channel something that feels greater than oneself, to bring into harmony the tangible world of sound and the intangible realm of emotion and meaning. For many musicians, this process feels like a form of alchemy, where raw ideas are transformed into something that touches the soul. Temperance encourages musicians to honor this sacred connection, to see their work not merely as a craft but as a communion with something greater.

Temperance also speaks to the emotional power of music, its ability to soothe, heal, and uplift. A song that embodies the energy of Temperance feels balanced and restorative, offering the listener a sense of harmony and peace. It may blend genres or cultures, draw on diverse influences, or seamlessly weave together disparate ideas, creating something that feels timeless and universal. This is music that bridges divides, offering a sense of unity in a fragmented world.

For performers, Temperance manifests as the ability to adapt and flow with the energy of the moment. A live performance is never static; it is shaped by the connection between the musician, the music, and the audience. Temperance encourages the performer to stay grounded yet open, to find balance in the dynamic interplay of these forces. It is the reminder that a performance is not just about technical precision but about the deeper resonance that comes from being fully present and attuned to the energy of the room.

Ultimately, Temperance is a reminder of the beauty that arises from integration and balance. It encourages musicians to embrace the complexities of their craft, to find harmony in contrast, and to trust in the transformative power of the creative process. Music created under the influence of Temperance is imbued with a sense of wholeness, a feeling that every element is in its rightful place, contributing to a greater unity.

To create with the energy of Temperance is to embrace the art of blending, to honor the interplay of opposites, and to find harmony both inside and out. It is to recognize that music, like life, is an ongoing process of balancing, adjusting, and refining, and that in this process lies the potential for profound beauty and meaning. Temperance reminds us that through the alchemy of sound, we can find not only harmony in music but also a deeper sense of harmony within ourselves.

The Devil

The Devil is a complex and multifaceted symbol, representing themes of temptation, indulgence, power, and bondage. It explores the shadowy, alluring aspects of creativity and the ways in which musicians confront their desires, fears, and constraints. The Devil does not seek to condemn but to illuminate the darker corners of the soul where unexamined impulses and suppressed emotions reside. In music, this energy becomes both a challenge and an opportunity for profound expression.

The Devil often appears as the allure of excess. It's the pull toward perfectionism, overworking, or chasing fame and validation at the expense of authenticity. Musicians can become ensnared by the seductive promise of success, where the artistry itself takes a back seat to external measures of worth. The Devil invites reflection on these dynamics, asking the musician to question whether their creative choices are driven by genuine passion or by the desire to appease external expectations. The card is not inherently negative; it simply reveals the chains, encouraging the artist to recognize and, if necessary, break free from them.

In the creative process, the Devil embodies both the struggle and the power of confronting one's inner demons. Music is often a vessel for the raw, unfiltered emotions that society teaches us to suppress: anger, desire, fear, or grief. These emotions, when channeled through music, can create works of intense beauty and catharsis. The Devil urges musicians to dive into these darker places, to explore the shadows without fear, and to transform what they find into something meaningful. In this sense, the card serves as a reminder that the parts of ourselves we might prefer to hide often hold the greatest creative potential.

The Devil also speaks to the intoxicating power of music itself. Music has a way of captivating the senses, drawing listeners into its rhythms and melodies in a way that feels almost otherworldly. This power can be both exhilarating and dangerous. A haunting melody, a driving beat, or a lyric that cuts to the bone can evoke visceral responses, stirring emotions that may feel overwhelming or even uncomfortable. The challenge lies in wielding this power responsibly, understanding that music has the ability to both liberate and ensnare.

Temptation, a central theme of the Devil, often plays a role in the life of a musician. This could be the temptation to take shortcuts, to compromise artistic integrity for commercial gain, or to avoid the hard work of genuine self-expression by settling for superficiality. Yet, the Devil's energy is not inherently destructive. It offers a mirror, reflecting back the musician's choices and motivations. By confronting this reflection honestly, the artist can reclaim their power, finding freedom in self-awareness and the courage to create authentically.

The Devil is also tied to the idea of indulgence, particularly the indulgence of pleasure and the sensory experiences music provides. For both creators and listeners, music is a form of escape, a way to lose oneself in a moment of unrestrained emotion. This can be liberating, but it can also become a trap if it leads to avoidance or addiction. A musician might find themselves clinging to the highs of performance or the rush of inspiration, struggling to maintain balance. The Devil reminds them to confront these tendencies, understanding that indulgence without awareness can lead to stagnation.

In performance, the Devil's energy can manifest as a raw, magnetic presence. There's a certain allure in watching a musician who channels their shadow self, who allows the unfiltered intensity of their emotions to bleed into their art. Audiences are drawn to this authenticity, even when it's dark or uncomfortable, because it reflects something primal and universal. The Devil reminds musicians that vulnerability and intensity are not weaknesses but powerful tools for connection if wielded with care and consciousness.

On a deeper level, the Devil speaks to the chains that bind artists to their fears. Fear of failure, fear of judgment, fear of not being good enough. These are shackles that can stifle creativity and prevent growth. The Devil challenges musicians to confront these fears head-on, to see them for what they are: illusions that can be dismantled with self-awareness and courage. In facing their fears, musicians often discover new depths of expression and authenticity, breaking free of constraints they once thought unshakable.

The Devil highlights the transformative power of music to confront and process the shadows of the human experience. Music has long been a space where taboo topics are explored, where unspoken desires are given voice, and where the boundaries of societal norms are tested. The Devil revels in this aspect of music, celebrating its ability to challenge, provoke, and disrupt. It reminds musicians that their work has the potential to bring hidden truths to light, to offer catharsis, and to create space for collective healing.

The Devil, when understood in its fullness, is not a force to be feared but a force to be reckoned with. In music, it serves as a guide to the depths, offering both temptation and insight. It asks musicians to confront their shadow selves with honesty, to explore the raw and messy parts of life, and to transform what they find into art that resonates with truth and intensity. Through this process, the musician not only liberates themselves but also creates a space for others to confront their own shadows, finding freedom in the shared experience of music.

The Tower

The Tower is a card of upheaval, destruction, and sudden transformation. It represents the moments when everything seems to collapse, when the structures that once supported an artist's work are shattered. Yet within this chaos lies a powerful opportunity for growth and renewal. The Tower reminds musicians that destruction is often the first step toward reinvention, that the collapse of the familiar can clear space for something entirely new to emerge.

In the creative process, the Tower often manifests as a moment of reckoning. It might be a sudden realization that a piece of music is not working, that a long-held belief about one's artistry no longer holds true, or that external circumstances have disrupted the path forward. These moments can feel devastating, shaking the musician's confidence and leaving them unsure of where to turn. Yet the Tower urges them to embrace this destruction as a necessary part of the journey, to see the rubble not as an end but as the foundation for something greater.

The energy of the Tower is raw and intense, reflecting the unpredictable nature of inspiration and the ways in which it can disrupt a musician's plans. A melody might arrive unexpectedly, demanding attention and reshaping the course of a project. A sudden shift in life circumstances such as a heartbreak, a loss, or even a moment of unexpected joy can throw everything into disarray, forcing the musician to adapt and respond. The Tower teaches that creativity is not a linear process; it is often chaotic, marked by breakthroughs that arise only after the old ways of thinking have been torn down.

For performers, the Tower might appear as a disastrous rehearsal, a failed performance, or a moment of public vulnerability. These experiences, though painful, are often transformative. They strip away pretenses, forcing the musician to confront their fears, their limitations, and their resilience. The Tower reveals what is essential, encouraging the artist to rebuild with greater authenticity and strength. It is a card of humility, reminding musicians that failure is not the opposite of success but an integral part of growth.

In music itself, the Tower can be heard in moments of dissonance, disruption, and catharsis. It is the crescendo that breaks into silence, the unexpected shift in tempo or key, the rawness of an unpolished recording that captures something real and unfiltered. The Tower's energy challenges traditional notions of harmony and beauty, pushing musicians to explore the edges of their craft and to embrace the imperfections that make their work unique. It is a reminder that music, like life, is often most powerful when it breaks the rules.

The Tower also speaks to the way external forces shape a musician's journey. A sudden change in the industry, a cultural shift, or the impact of a global event can upend everything, forcing artists to adapt or risk being left behind. These moments of upheaval are challenging, but they also spark innovation. The Tower encourages musicians to see disruption as an opportunity to rethink their approach, to break free from outdated systems, and to create work that responds to the present moment with urgency and relevance.

On a deeper level, the Tower represents the breaking down of internal barriers. Many musicians carry fears, doubts, and limiting beliefs that hold them back from fully expressing themselves. The Tower's energy can feel like an internal earthquake, shaking loose those blocks and exposing the truth beneath. While this process can be uncomfortable, it is ultimately liberating. By confronting what no longer serves them, musicians can access new depths of creativity and vulnerability, creating music that resonates with raw honesty.

The spiritual aspect of the Tower is one of awakening. In music, this might mean a sudden realization of one's purpose, a moment of clarity that shifts the direction of a career, or a performance that feels like a direct channel to something greater. The Tower reminds musicians that these moments of awakening often come through challenge and struggle. It is through the breaking down of old structures that new pathways are revealed, leading to a deeper connection with the self, the audience, and the music.

Ultimately, the Tower is a force of transformation. It strips away what is false or outdated, leaving behind only what is real and necessary. It challenges musicians to face their fears, to embrace the chaos, and to trust in the process of rebuilding. Music created under the influence of the Tower carries the weight of this transformation. It is raw, powerful, and uncompromising, a testament to the resilience of the artist and the power of creation to rise from the ashes.

To work with the energy of the Tower is to surrender to the unpredictable, to allow destruction to make way for renewal. It is to recognize that in both life and music, the greatest breakthroughs often come after the greatest disruptions. Through the chaos of the Tower, musicians find not only their strength but also the freedom to create without limitations, transforming destruction into a symphony of rebirth.

The Star

The Star is a card of inspiration, hope, and renewal. It is a beacon of light guiding us through the darkness. In music, it represents the transcendent moments when creativity flows effortlessly, when the artist feels connected to something larger than themselves. The Star speaks to the purity of artistic expression, to the healing power of music, and to the unshakable faith that even in times of struggle, the act of creation can bring clarity and peace.

To musicians, the Star is a source of inspiration. It whispers of the infinite potential that lies within, encouraging the artist to dream boldly and to trust in their vision. Music created under the influence of the Star often feels otherworldly, as though it is reaching toward something divine. It carries an essence of timelessness, an ability to touch the soul in a way that words alone cannot. The Star reminds musicians that their work has the power to uplift and transform, not only for themselves but for those who listen.

The energy of the Star is expansive, encouraging musicians to look beyond limitations and embrace the boundless possibilities of their craft. It is the moment when a melody arrives as if from nowhere, shimmering with clarity and beauty. It is the quiet confidence that builds during a creative breakthrough, when everything seems to align, and the music flows with ease. The Star invites musicians to trust these moments, to recognize them as gifts, and to honor them by bringing their visions into the world.

In the process of creating, the Star is a reminder of the importance of authenticity. Music that resonates with the energy of the Star is honest and unguarded, stripped of ego and pretense. It is music that comes from the heart, unafraid to be vulnerable. The Star encourages musicians to express their truth, knowing that their authenticity will shine through in their work and connect with others on a profound level. It teaches that the act of sharing one's inner light through music is an act of courage and generosity.

The Star is also deeply tied to the healing power of music. For both creators and listeners, music has the ability to soothe, to mend broken spirits, and to offer a sense of solace. A song that captures the energy of the Star feels like a balm, providing a sense of hope and renewal. It speaks to the universal human experience, reminding us that we are not alone in our struggles. Creating this kind of music can be a deeply healing process, a way to process their own emotions while offering something meaningful to the world.

In performance, the Star shines as a quiet yet powerful presence. It is the sense of connection that fills the space between the musician and the audience, a shared moment of transcendence. Performers guided by the Star's energy radiate an openness and sincerity that draws people in, creating an atmosphere of trust and intimacy. The Star teaches musicians to let go of the need to impress and instead focus on the act of sharing their light, trusting that it will touch those who are ready to receive it.

The Star also represents the renewal that comes after a period of difficulty. For musicians, this might mean rediscovering their passion after a creative block, finding joy in their craft after a time of disillusionment, or reconnecting with their purpose after a setback. The Star reminds them that no matter how dark things may seem, the light of inspiration is always within reach. It speaks of resilience and the ability to keep going, knowing that each step forward brings them closer to the fulfillment of their dreams.

The Star represents the sense of unity that music can create. Music has the power to transcend barriers, to bring people together in a shared experience of beauty and emotion. The Star celebrates this unifying quality, reminding musicians that their work is part of something much larger. It invites them to see their music as a gift, a way of contributing to the greater harmony of the world.

The Star also encourages musicians to embrace the role of inspiration in their work. Just as they are inspired by others, they too have the power to inspire. A piece of music born under the Star's influence can spark creativity in another artist, offer hope to someone in need, or simply provide a moment of beauty in a chaotic world. The Star reminds musicians that their light, no matter how small it may seem, has the power to illuminate the lives of others.

In the end, the Star is a symbol of faith in oneself, in the creative process, and in the transformative power of music. It teaches musicians to trust in their journey, to honor their inner light, and to share it freely with the world. Through the energy of the Star, music becomes more than just sound; it becomes a beacon, a source of hope and inspiration that resonates far beyond the moment of its creation. For musicians, the Star is both a guide and a reminder that their work has the power to touch hearts, heal souls, and shine brightly even in the darkest of times.

The Moon

The Moon is a card of mystery, intuition, and the unknown, casting its silver light over the hidden corners of the psyche. The energy of the Moon is both enchanting and elusive, guiding the artist into the depths of their imagination where clarity is scarce but inspiration is boundless. It is the space between waking and dreaming, where music becomes a vessel for expressing the intangible. To create under the influence of the Moon is to embrace uncertainty and to trust in the process of discovery.

The Moon represents the subconscious, the realm of intuition and emotion that drives much of artistic creation. Musicians who follow the Moon's call may find themselves drawn to melodies or lyrics that feel as though they've emerged from nowhere, as if whispered by unseen forces. The creative process under the Moon is often nonlinear, marked by unexpected shifts and surprising revelations.

It invites musicians to surrender to the flow of their intuition, to let the music guide them rather than forcing it into a predefined shape.

Music shaped by the Moon often carries an air of mystery, a sense of ambiguity that leaves room for interpretation. It evokes emotion without spelling out its meaning, allowing listeners to project their own experiences onto the sound. This type of music can feel dreamlike or otherworldly, with harmonies and rhythms that seem to mirror the ebb and flow of the subconscious. The Moon reminds musicians that not everything must be understood to be felt, that the power of music often lies in its ability to evoke what cannot be named.

The shadow side of the Moon is its ability to obscure, to confuse, and to unsettle. For musicians, this can manifest as self-doubt, creative blocks, or the fear of being misunderstood. The Moon teaches that these experiences are part of the journey, that the moments of uncertainty are often the prelude to profound insight. It encourages musicians to embrace the discomfort of not knowing, to explore the shadows without fear, and to trust that clarity will come in its own time.

The Moon also speaks to the emotional depth of music, the way it can tap into the hidden layers of the self. A song born under the Moon's influence might be one that confronts unspoken fears, explores unacknowledged desires, or expresses a vulnerability that feels too raw for the light of day. These are the songs that resonate deeply, that create an intimate connection between the artist and the listener. The Moon reminds musicians that the emotions they dare to share through their music can serve as a mirror, reflecting the shared humanity of those who hear it.

Performance under the Moon's energy can be an ethereal experience, both for the musician and the audience. It is the magic of a live performance that feels unrepeatable, where the boundary between the artist and the listener dissolves, and everyone present is swept into a shared moment of transcendence. The Moon encourages musicians to lean into these moments, to trust their instincts, and to allow their emotions to flow freely. It is in these unguarded moments that music becomes something greater than the sum of its parts, a channel for something mysterious and profound.

The Moon's influence also extends to the themes musicians explore in their work. Songs inspired by the Moon often delve into the realms of dreams, secrets, and the unconscious. They may explore the complexity of emotions, the duality of light and shadow, or the tension between illusion and reality. The Moon challenges musicians to push beyond the surface, to seek the truths that lie hidden beneath layers of fear, doubt, and illusion. In doing so, they create music that feels deeply authentic and resonant.

The Moon's influence also extends to the themes musicians explore in their work. Songs inspired by the Moon often delve into the realms of dreams, secrets, and the unconscious. They may explore the complexity of emotions, the duality of light and shadow, or the tension between illusion and reality. The Moon challenges musicians to push beyond the surface, to seek the truths that lie hidden beneath layers of fear, doubt, and illusion. In doing so, they create music that feels deeply authentic and resonant.

At its heart, the Moon is a card of trust; trust in the self, trust in the process, and trust in the unknown. Musicians working with the Moon's energy must learn to navigate their own inner landscapes, to listen to the quiet whispers of intuition even when they are hard to decipher. The Moon teaches that not every path is illuminated, that sometimes the only way forward is to take a step into the darkness and see where it leads. It is in these moments of surrender that the most profound creative breakthroughs often occur.

The Moon reminds musicians that art is not about having all the answers. It is about exploring the questions, embracing the ambiguity, and finding beauty in the unknown. Music created under the Moon's influence is a reflection of the human experience in all its complexity. Through the energy of the Moon, musicians are called to dive deep into their inner worlds, to bring the shadows into the light, and to trust in the transformative power of their art.

The Sun

The Sun is a card of vitality, clarity, and joy. It has a radiant energy that illuminates everything it touches. In music, the Sun represents those moments of pure creative bliss when inspiration shines brightly, and everything feels aligned. It is the heartbeat of celebration and the warmth of self-expression, reminding musicians of the life-affirming power of their art. Under the Sun's influence, music becomes a channel for light and positivity, a reflection of the boundless potential within and around us.

When the Sun appears, it calls attention to the joy that music can bring, both to the creator and the listener. It is the song that makes people dance, the melody that brings a smile, the rhythm that pulses with the energy of life itself. The Sun reminds musicians of the simple, profound pleasure of creating for the sake of joy, free from doubt or overthinking. It speaks of the magic that happens when the artist allows themselves to revel in the act of making music, unburdened by expectations or fear.

The Sun's energy also brings clarity, cutting through confusion and illuminating the path forward. For a musician, this might mean gaining insight into their creative process, finding confidence in their voice, or recognizing the direction they wish to take. The Sun encourages artists to step fully into their power, to embrace their unique gifts, and to share them boldly with the world. It is a card of self-assurance, celebrating the ability to shine without hesitation or apology.

In the realm of performance, the Sun is the bright spotlight, the applause that fills a room, the connection that electrifies a shared space. It speaks to the joy of being seen and appreciated, of knowing that the music created has the power to uplift and inspire others. Performers under the Sun's influence radiate warmth and confidence, creating an atmosphere where musicians that their work is a gift, one that can bring people together and create moments of collective happiness.

The Sun also reflects the universal quality of music, its ability to transcend barriers and connect people on a deep, emotional level. Music created in the spirit of the Sun carries an openness, a universality that invites everyone to partake in its light. Whether through a triumphant anthem, a carefree melody, or a song that captures the beauty of everyday life, the Sun's energy infuses music with a sense of unity and shared humanity.

The Sun can be a reminder of the importance of balance, of taking time to recharge and enjoy the fruits of their labor. The creative journey is often demanding, but the Sun encourages moments of pause and celebration, a chance to bask in the joy of what has been accomplished. It is a card of gratitude, urging artists to recognize the beauty in their work and the impact it has on themselves and others. In doing so, they find the energy to continue creating from a place of abundance and love.

The Sun's influence on music is also deeply tied to authenticity. It invites musicians to express themselves fully, to let their true selves shine through their art. Music under the Sun is fearless and open-hearted. It carries the unique fingerprint of the artist, resonating with an honesty that draws people in. The Sun teaches that when musicians embrace their truth, their work becomes a beacon of light for others, a source of inspiration and joy.

The Sun's energy is expansive, reminding musicians of the infinite possibilities within their craft. It encourages exploration, playfulness, and the willingness to take risks. Under the Sun, creativity feels boundless, a joyful exploration of sound and expression. It is the burst of energy that comes with a new idea, the satisfaction of finishing a piece of music that feels true to one's vision. The Sun reminds artists to trust in their abilities and to approach their work with a sense of wonder and excitement.

At its core, the Sun is about connection to oneself, to others, and to the greater world. Music created under the Sun's influence is a bridge, linking the personal to the universal, the individual to the collective. It carries the artist's unique light while inviting others to see themselves reflected in its warmth. The Sun speaks of the power of music to heal, to unite, and to celebrate life in all its richness and beauty.

The Sun is a reminder of the transformative power of music. It is the soundtrack to life's happiest moments, the spark that reignites passion and hope. For musicians, the Sun is both a guide and a source of inspiration, urging them to embrace their light and share it freely. Through the energy of the Sun, music becomes more than sound; it becomes a radiant expression of life itself, a celebration of the boundless creativity and joy that lies at the heart of the human spirit.

Judgment

Judgment is a card of awakening, transformation, and reckoning, a powerful moment when the past is confronted, and a new path is chosen. In music, the energy of Judgment is profound and deeply personal. It calls musicians to reflect on their journey, to evaluate their work and their choices, and to make peace with what has come before. It is not a card of condemnation but of liberation, offering the opportunity to rise above self-imposed limitations and step into a fuller expression of artistic purpose.

Judgment often represents a turning point. It might appear as a moment of clarity, when the pieces of a long-standing creative puzzle suddenly fall into place. It may also emerge as a call to confront doubts, fears, or regrets that have held them back. Judgment asks musicians to look honestly at their past at their successes, their failures, and everything in between, not with shame, but with a willingness to learn and grow. Through this process of self-assessment, they find the freedom to move forward with renewed purpose.

The creative process under the influence of Judgment is transformative. It often involves revisiting old ideas, unfinished compositions, or abandoned projects and seeing them in a new light. What once felt incomplete or flawed may now reveal hidden potential, as if waiting for this precise moment is understood. Judgment encourages musicians to trust that their journey has brought them to this point for a reason, that every experience, no matter how difficult, has shaped their artistic voice.

In music, Judgment is the sound of awakening. It is the triumphant crescendo that resolves years of struggle, the song that captures the essence of an artist's growth. Music created under Judgment's influence often carries a sense of catharsis, a release of emotions that have long been buried. These are the songs that speak to redemption, transformation, and the power of second chances. They resonate deeply, offering listeners not only a window into the artist's journey but also a reflection of their own.

The performance aspect of Judgment is one of authenticity and vulnerability. It is the moment when a musician steps onto the stage, fully present and unapologetically themselves. Under Judgment's energy, performances become opportunities for connection and healing, for sharing the truth of one's experiences through music. The card teaches that it is through this honesty, through embracing both strengths and imperfections that artists can truly touch their audiences.

Judgment also speaks to the collective power of music. It reminds musicians that their work does not exist in isolation but is part of a greater story. Music has the ability to inspire change, to call people to action, and to remind them of their shared humanity. Under Judgment's influence, musicians may feel a heightened sense of responsibility to use their platform for something meaningful, to create work that challenges, uplifts, and transforms. It is a call to recognize the impact their music can have on the world and to rise to the occasion with purpose and integrity.

At its heart, Judgment is about liberation. This liberation often comes from letting go of self-doubt, of perfectionism, of the need to please others. It is the freedom to create without fear, to embrace one's unique voice, and to trust in the path that lies ahead. Judgment teaches that the past does not define the future and that every ending holds the seed of a new beginning. Through this lens, music becomes a tool for transformation, a way of breaking free from old patterns and stepping into a brighter, more authentic expression of self.

On a spiritual level, Judgment reminds musicians of the transcendent nature of their craft. Music has the power to reach beyond the material, to touch the soul and evoke a sense of the divine. Under Judgment's influence, musicians may find themselves drawn to themes of renewal, forgiveness, and higher purpose. They are called to create music that not only entertains but also elevates, music that speaks to the eternal and their universal.

The journey of Judgment is not without challenge. It requires courage to face the truth, to confront the shadows of the past, and to take responsibility for one's path. Yet it is through this process of reckoning that true transformation occurs. Judgment offers the opportunity to shed what no longer serves them, to rise above the constraints of fear and doubt, and to step into the fullness of their potential. It is an invitation to create not from a place of striving but from a place of alignment, where music becomes an authentic expression of their innermost being.

Judgment is ultimately a card of renewal. It marks the moment when the artist hears the call to rise, to let go of the old, and to embrace the new with open arms. Music born under Judgment's influence carries the weight of this transformation. It is bold, honest, and deeply resonant. Through the energy of

Judgment, musicians find not only their voice but also their purpose, creating work that reflects their journey and inspires others to embark on their own.

The World

The World is a card of completion, unity, and wholeness. It represents the culmination of a journey, the fulfillment of purpose, and the realization of interconnectedness. The World speaks to the moments when everything comes together, when the hours of practice, the sparks of inspiration, and the struggles along the way converge to create something that feels complete and transcendent. It is the symphony that resolves in a perfect harmony, the album that tells a story from beginning to end, the song that leaves nothing unsaid. The World reminds musicians that their craft is part of something larger, a thread in the infinite tapestry of creation.

For a musician, encountering the World is an experience of profound satisfaction. It is the sense of accomplishment that comes with finishing a long-awaited project, the joy of hearing one's work resonate deeply with others, and the realization that the journey itself has been as meaningful as the destination. The World is not just about achieving a goal; it is about recognizing the beauty of the entire process. Every note played, every struggle overcome, every fleeting moment of inspiration has contributed to this point of fulfillment.

In the act of creating music, the World represents integration. It is the ability to draw from a wide range of influences, experiences, and emotions to craft something cohesive and meaningful. Under the World's influence, music becomes a reflection of the artist's inner and outer worlds, a synthesis of the personal and the universal. A piece created in this energy feels whole, as if it captures the essence of something larger than the sum of its parts. The World invites musicians to see their work not as isolated fragments but as a connected, harmonious expression of life itself.

The World also carries an energy of transcendence. Music influenced by the World often feels expansive, capable of bridging divides and speaking to the shared human experience. It is music that knows no boundaries, resonating across cultures, generations, and perspectives. This is the power of the World, to remind musicians and listeners alike that, despite differences, there is a fundamental unity that binds us all. Through the language of music, the World offers a glimpse of this interconnectedness, weaving together diverse threads into a single, luminous whole.

Performance under the World's energy is an experience of unity. It is the magic of a concert where everyone, musician and audience alike, feels connected by the music. It is the unspoken understanding that passes between performer and listener, a sense of being part of something greater. The World encourages musicians to embrace these moments, to recognize that their work has the power to dissolve barriers and create a sense of oneness. It is a reminder that music is not just an individual expression but a collective experience, a celebration of the shared human spirit.

The World also speaks to the cyclical nature of creativity. For musicians, completing one project often marks the beginning of another. The World reminds them that endings and beginnings are intertwined, that each fulfilled vision opens the door to new possibilities. The completion of a piece of music is not the end of the journey but a milestone along a continuous path of growth and discovery. The World teaches that fulfillment is not static but dynamic, a living process of creation, reflection, and renewal.

At its core, the World is a card of connection. It reminds musicians of their place within a larger world, of the ways their work interacts with and influences the lives of others. Music created under the World's influence is deeply attuned to this connection, carrying a sense of purpose and responsibility. It is music that not only entertains but also uplifts, inspires, and unites. The World invites musicians to see their craft as a contribution to the greater whole, a way of bringing harmony and understanding into a fragmented world.

On a spiritual level, the World represents the transcendence of ego. This can mean letting go of personal doubts and insecurities, allowing the music to flow freely as an expression of something beyond the self. Under the World's guidance, music becomes a bridge between the inner and outer realms, a way of channeling the universal through the individual. It is a reminder that creativity is not just a personal endeavor but a sacred act of connection and communion.

The World is also a celebration of mastery. It speaks to the culmination of years of practice, dedication, and passion. It is the moment when their skills and vision align, allowing them to create with ease and confidence. Yet the World also humbles, reminding artists that mastery is not about perfection but about embracing the wholeness of their journey. It is about honoring the lessons learned along the way and using them to contribute something meaningful to the World.

The World is a card of fulfillment and unity. It reminds musicians that their work is part of a larger story, a thread in the endless weave of life and creativity. Through the energy of the World, music becomes more than sound; it becomes a testament to the interconnectedness of all things, a celebration of the infinite beauty and complexity of existence. The World is both a destination and a starting point. It is a reminder that the journey of creation is one of constant evolution, infinite possibility, and boundless joy.

The Minor Arcana: Wands

The Wands suit embodies the element of fire and represents creativity, ambition, energy, and passion, making it a powerful metaphor for music and the drive that fuels musicians. Wands capture the spark of inspiration that ignites a creative project, the determination to overcome obstacles, and the sheer vitality required to bring artistic visions to life. Each card in the suit reflects a different aspect of this creative journey, from the initial idea to the completion of a musical endeavor, resonating deeply with the experiences of musicians at every stage of their craft.

Wands speak to the raw energy that propels musicians to pick up an instrument, write a song, or step onto a stage. This energy is often unrefined and full of potential, reflecting the spontaneous bursts of creativity that often drive musical expression. At its best, the suit reflects the joy and fulfillment that come from channeling this energy into a tangible form, whether it's a song, a performance, or a collaborative project. At the same time, Wands also highlight the challenges musicians face, such as burnout, self-doubt, or the pressure to meet external expectations. This duality mirrors the highs and lows of a creative life, emphasizing the importance of maintaining balance and staying connected to the passion that first sparked the journey.

In addition, the Wands suit reflects the communal aspects of music. Music is often a collaborative process, requiring musicians to work together to bring ideas to fruition. Wands capture the dynamic exchange of ideas and the collective energy that can arise when musicians join forces, whether in a band, an orchestra, or a songwriting partnership. This collaboration often brings about growth and transformation, as musicians inspire and challenge one another, pushing the boundaries of their creativity.

Wands also explore the themes of ambition and the pursuit of goals, which are deeply relevant to musicians navigating the competitive world of music. The cards in this suit speak to the drive to succeed, the courage to take risks, and the resilience to face setbacks. For musicians, this may manifest as the determination to perfect a piece, secure a performance opportunity, or establish a unique voice in the industry. Wands remind musicians to stay focused on their vision, even in the face of obstacles, and to harness their passion as a source of strength and motivation.

The Wands suit is about the power of transformation. Music has the ability to transform emotions, perspectives, and even lives, and the Wands reflect this transformative potential. For musicians, the act of creating and performing music is often a deeply personal and transformative experience, one that allows them to explore their inner world and connect with others on a profound level. Wands celebrate this process, encouraging musicians to embrace the journey and the growth it brings.

Finally, Wands remind musicians of the importance of inspiration. Music often begins with a single spark that sets the creative process in motion. Wands celebrate this spark, urging musicians to nurture it and follow where it leads. They emphasize the importance of staying open to new ideas, taking risks, and allowing the creative process to unfold naturally. In this way, the Wands suit serves as both a mirror and a guide for musicians, reflecting their experiences and encouraging them to embrace the passion and energy that drive their art.

Ace of Wands

The Ace of Wands is a card of initiation, a spark of pure creative energy that surges through the mind and soul like an untamed flame. It represents the raw, unfiltered moment when inspiration strikes, like when a melody bursts forth from silence, a rhythm forms out of chaos, or an idea demands to be transformed into sound. It is the essence of beginnings, a symbol of potential yet to be realized, urging the musician to take the first step toward creation without hesitation or doubt.

When a musician draws the Ace of Wands, it is as if the universe is handing them a torch; its fire not only illuminates their path but also invites them to set the world alight with their unique voice. It is the start of something powerful and new: a song, a symphony, a collaboration, or even a complete reimagining of one's artistic identity. This card holds the energy of ignition, the moment when dormant creativity awakens and demands to be expressed. It is not a passive force but an active call to embrace the spark and turn it into something tangible.

Music inspired by the Ace of Wands carries a certain intensity, an urgency that reflects the card's fiery nature. It is the sound of raw emotion, unfiltered and unapologetic. Think of the opening chords of a song that immediately draws you in, or the primal beat of a drum that speaks directly to your heart. This is the energy of the Ace of Wands, a force that bypasses the intellect and goes straight to the soul. It demands expression, not perfection, reminding musicians that the act of creation itself is what matters most.

This card often appears during times of transformation or change, signaling the beginning of a new phase in a musician's journey. It may mark the decision to learn a new instrument, explore a different genre, or finally share one's work with the world. The Ace of Wands does not come with a map or a plan; it offers only the spark, trusting that the musician will find their way through the act of doing. This is a card that celebrates experimentation and risk, urging the artist to step outside their comfort zone and let curiosity lead the way.

In the creative process, the Ace of Wands represents the moment when an idea first takes shape. It is the seed of a song, the initial spark that sets the imagination aflame. For a songwriter, it might be a fragment of a lyric that refuses to leave their mind, or a melody that seems to emerge from thin air. For a composer, it could be the beginning of a theme that grows and evolves into a larger work. Whatever form it takes, this spark carries with it the promise of something greater, a glimpse of what could be if the musician has the courage to pursue it.

This card also speaks to the physicality of music; the act of playing an instrument, feeling its vibrations, and letting its sound flow through the body. The Ace of Wands reminds musicians that creativity is not just an abstract concept but a visceral experience, one that engages the senses and connects them to the primal energy of life itself. It encourages them to lose themselves in the rhythm, to feel the music in their bones, and to let their passion drive the process.

The Ace of Wands is a deeply personal card, yet it also hints at the potential for collaboration. Its fiery energy can spark connections between musicians, creating a shared momentum that pushes each participant to new heights. A jam session that unexpectedly evolves into a masterpiece, or a chance meeting with another artist that leads to a groundbreaking project, are manifestations of this card's influence. It reminds musicians that inspiration is often amplified when shared, and that the collective fire of creative energy can be unstoppable.

For those who feel creatively blocked, the Ace of Wands offers hope and encouragement. It suggests that the spark of inspiration is never truly gone, it is simply waiting to be reignited. The card urges the musician to return to the basics, to rediscover the simple joy of making sound, whether through strumming a single chord, humming a tune, or tapping out a rhythm. By reconnecting with the essence of music, they can fan the spark back into a flame and reignite their passion.

Above all, the Ace of Wands is a card of action. It does not dwell in the realm of ideas or possibilities but pushes the musician to take the first step, no matter how small. It challenges them to move beyond fear and doubt, to trust their instincts, and to follow the energy wherever it leads. In music, as in life, the journey begins with a single note, and the Ace of Wands is the force that compels them to play it.

This card reminds musicians that the power of creation lies within them, waiting to be unleashed. The flame it offers is not something to be observed from a distance; it must be held, nurtured, and allowed to grow. The Ace of Wands is the beginning of a song, a story, a legacy. It asks only one question: What will you create? The answer, like the music itself, is limited only by the imagination and the courage to let the spark burn brightly.

Two of Wands

The Two of Wands is a card of vision and anticipation, a moment when possibilities stretch out before you like an uncharted horizon. It represents the crossroads of inspiration and planning, the space between an idea's birth and its manifestation. It is the pause where the musician looks out, considers their options, and begins to lay the groundwork for what comes next. If the Ace of Wands is the spark, the Two of Wands is the first step toward shaping that fire into something deliberate, intentional, and expansive.

When this card appears, it suggests that the musician has moved beyond the initial rush of inspiration and is now grappling with the question of direction. It's a time of strategy, of looking at the tools and resources at hand and deciding how best to use them. Perhaps there's a melody that demands to become a full composition, or an opportunity to collaborate with others that could open new doors. The Two of Wands doesn't provide answers, but it encourages the musician to step back, reflect, and weigh their choices with care.

This card carries an energy of exploration and expansion. It may signal a desire to push beyond familiar boundaries. A guitarist might feel drawn to experiment with alternate tunings, or a songwriter may find themselves compelled to write in a genre they've never attempted before. The Two of Wands invites musicians to look at the broader landscape of their craft, to see beyond what they already know, and to imagine what could be. It is a call to embrace curiosity and let it guide the next stage of creation.

At its core, the Two of Wands is about potential. It holds the promise of growth, but it also reminds the musician that action must follow vision. There is a tension in this card, a sense of standing on the edge of something vast and uncertain. The musician may feel a pull between staying in the comfort of their current practices and stepping into the unknown. This tension is not meant to paralyze but to motivate. The card encourages taking calculated risks, trusting that the fire of passion will light the way forward.

Collaboration can also be a key theme of the Two of Wands. It often speaks to the possibility of partnerships or the influence of others in shaping one's creative path. This could manifest as joining forces with another artist, producer, or band, or seeking out mentorship to refine one's craft. These relationships, fueled by shared vision and mutual support, can help bring ideas to life in ways that might not have been possible alone. The card reminds musicians that while the initial spark may be solitary, the journey of creation often flourishes through connection.

The Two of Wands also reflects a growing awareness of the audience. For many musicians, the creative process begins as an intensely personal experience, but this card suggests a shift toward sharing that work with the world. It asks the artist to consider how their music might resonate with others, and how it might bridge the gap between inner expression and external impact. This awareness doesn't dilute the authenticity of the work; it enriches it, adding layers of intention and meaning. Yet the card also comes with a quiet caution. The Two of Wands warns against becoming lost in endless planning or second-guessing. While reflection and strategy are important, they must not overshadow the act of creation itself. Music thrives in motion, in the doing, and this card serves as a gentle reminder not to linger too long on the edge of decision. The horizon will always hold infinite possibilities, but only by taking a step can the musician begin to move toward them.

In its more introspective aspect, the Two of Wands invites the musician to reconnect with their purpose. Why do they make music? What drives them to create? This is a moment to align the outer journey with the inner fire, ensuring that the choices made reflect both ambition and authenticity. It's not just about what lies ahead but about how the artist chooses to navigate it.

The Two of Wands is a card of empowerment. It reminds musicians that they hold the power to shape their creative destiny. The vision is theirs, the choices are theirs, and the path forward, while uncertain, is theirs to walk. This card doesn't promise that the road will be easy, but it assures the musician that they are capable of forging it. The Two of Wands stands as a testament to the balance of inspiration and intention, urging the artist to dream boldly and act with purpose.

Music born under the influence of this card often carries a sense of journey, of reaching outward while staying rooted in something deeply personal. It is the sound of exploration, of stepping into the unknown with a mixture of excitement and resolve. The Two of Wands challenges musicians to embrace this energy, to trust in their vision, and to let their music become a map for others who might one day hear it and find their own horizons.

Three of Wands

The Three of Wands is a card of expansion and momentum, a moment when vision becomes action and the horizon begins to shift. It represents the forward movement of creativity, the point at which ideas that were once tentative now begin to take shape in the real world. It is the song being written, the project underway, and the collaboration gaining strength. The Three of Wands is not about dreaming or planning; it is about doing and watching the results of that action begin to unfold.

When this card appears, it speaks of a musician who has stepped into their role as a creator with intention and purpose. Perhaps they've committed to a project, taken the leap to share their work publicly, or found their rhythm in the flow of composition and performance. The Three of Wands reflects a growing confidence, a sense of understanding the terrain and being willing to push further. It is not the arrival at a destination, but the exhilarating realization that the journey is well underway.

This card holds the energy of progress but also carries the weight of responsibility. In music, the creative process is no longer confined to moments of inspiration; it is becoming a practice, something that demands dedication and follow-through. A musician under the influence of the Three of Wands is building something larger than themselves such as a song that will live beyond the moment it is played, an album that captures a chapter of life, or a performance that leaves an imprint on those who experience it. There is an understanding that what they are creating is not fleeting but part of a larger arc.

Collaboration is often a key theme of the Three of Wands, as it is a card that celebrates connections and shared endeavors. A band finding its sound, a producer working to shape an artist's vision, or a songwriter teaming up with a lyricist, these partnerships thrive under the influence of this card. It reminds musicians that while the initial spark of creation may be solitary, the act of bringing music to life often involves others. The synergy between individuals can elevate the work, creating something that transcends what any one person could achieve alone.

The Three of Wands also speaks to the outward expansion of music. Where the Two of Wands is focused on internal planning, the Three turns its gaze outward, toward the audience, the industry, and the wider world. For a musician, this might be the moment when they decide to release a song, book a performance, or pitch their work to potential collaborators. It is a time of risk and reward, of sending one's creative efforts out into the world and trusting that they will find their place. There is a vulnerability in this, but also great power; the acknowledgment that music is not just an inward expression but a bridge to others.

Momentum is central to this card. In the creative process, the Three of Wands signals a time when things are moving, often faster than expected. A song might come together quickly after weeks of struggle, or a project that once felt distant suddenly begins to take form. The energy of this card is dynamic, and it encourages musicians to lean into that motion, to trust the process even when the outcome is unclear. It's a reminder that creation is as much about the journey as the final product and that every step forward is valuable.

The Three of Wands is not without its challenges. Its expansive energy can sometimes feel overwhelming, as the possibilities become real and the scope of what lies ahead grows larger. For musicians, this might manifest as the pressure to meet expectations, the weight of deadlines, or the uncertainty of how their work will be received. The card encourages balance, reminding the artist to stay grounded in their passion and purpose even as they navigate the complexities of bringing their music to life.

The Three of Wands is a card of vision realized. It reflects the musician who has moved beyond the safety of inspiration and planning into the raw, unpredictable world of action. It celebrates the courage it takes to pursue a creative path, to make something from nothing, and to share it with others. Music under the influence of this card often carries a sense of movement and possibility, the feeling of a story unfolding with each note or lyric.

This card teaches that music, like any creative endeavor, is not a solitary act but a dialogue between the artist and their craft, between collaborators, and between the musician and their audience. It reminds us that the act of creation is both deeply personal and profoundly communal, a ripple that starts with the individual but extends far beyond them. The Three of Wands encourages musicians to embrace this connection, to trust in their work, and to let it reach out across the horizon, where its impact will grow in ways they may not yet see.

Ultimately, the Three of Wands is a celebration of forward motion, of the courage to step into the unknown and the joy of seeing that leap begin to bear fruit. For musicians, it is a powerful reminder that the journey is as meaningful as the destination and that every chord struck, every lyric sung, and every note played is a step toward something greater. The horizon stretches endlessly ahead, and the Three of Wands asks: How far will your music take you?

Four of Wands

The Four of Wands is a card of celebration, harmony, and the joyful culmination of creative efforts. It speaks to the moments when the work comes together, the performance resonates, and the shared energy of creation brings people closer. It is a card that celebrates not just individual success but the communal joy that music can inspire, reminding musicians that their art is as much about connection as it is about expression.

When the Four of Wands appears, it often marks a time when a musician's efforts reach a point of recognition or fulfillment. It might represent a concert or recital where all the hard work finds its purpose in the act of sharing. It could signify the completion of an album, the debut of a song, or a rehearsal that feels like everything finally clicks into place. The energy of this card is vibrant and uplifting, reflecting the sense of satisfaction that comes when passion, practice, and intention align.

At its heart, the Four of Wands emphasizes the communal aspect of music. Unlike the solitary spark of the Ace or the introspective planning of the Two, this card thrives on shared experiences. Music is rarely created or enjoyed in isolation, and the Four of Wands reminds musicians of the power of connection, whether it be between bandmates, collaborators, audiences, or even the unseen lineage of artists who have come before. It is about stepping into a space where music becomes a bridge, linking hearts and minds through rhythm, melody, and emotion.

This card often carries the energy of homecoming. In music, it might represent a return to familiar roots such as playing in a hometown venue, reuniting with an old band, or rediscovering the joy of a style or instrument that once felt like home. It's about grounding oneself in a sense of belonging, finding comfort and strength in the spaces where creativity feels most natural. The Four of Wands suggests that music can serve as an anchor, a way to reconnect with one's identity and share it with others in a spirit of celebration.

The sense of stability associated with this card is also important. While creativity often thrives on chaos and risk, the Four of Wands offers a reprieve, a moment to breathe, reflect, and take pride in what has been accomplished. For musicians, this might be a pause in a busy tour to enjoy the camaraderie of fellow artists, or the quiet satisfaction of hearing a finished track for the first time. It's a reminder that moments of rest and appreciation are as vital to the creative process as the work itself.

Performances under the influence of the Four of Wands are often marked by a palpable sense of joy. Whether it's a small, intimate gathering or a large festival, This card suggests that the music will resonate on a deeper level, creating a space where everyone feels a part of something larger. The energy is celebratory but also grounding, a recognition of the beauty of the present moment and the connections it fosters. For musicians, these are the moments when the reasons for creating music feel most clear and most rewarding.

There is also a sense of ceremony in the Four of Wands. Music has long been tied to rituals and celebrations, from weddings to festivals to gatherings around a fire. This card reminds musicians of the sacred role that music plays in marking life's milestones and bringing people together. It invites them to embrace the honor of being a part of such moments, to recognize the weight and beauty of their role in creating the soundtrack to life's most meaningful experiences.

Yet the Four of Wands is not merely a card of completion; it also carries the seeds of what comes next. The foundation it represents is strong, but it is not the end of the journey. For a musician, this might mean that the successful completion of one project provides the stability and confidence needed to embark on the next. The card encourages looking ahead with excitement and gratitude, knowing that each milestone is part of a larger creative path.

The Four of Wands is a card of gratitude and joy. It invites musicians to celebrate their achievements and the community that surrounds them, to honor the work that has brought them to this moment while recognizing the endless potential that still lies ahead. It is a reminder that music is not just about the notes played or the songs written; it is about the connections forged, the lives touched, and the sense of belonging that it creates.

The Four of Wands is a moment of harmony, both within oneself and with others. For musicians, it is a call to savor the magic of music as both a personal expression and a communal gift. It asks them to stand still, even if just for a moment, in the joy of what has been created and shared. And in that stillness, the music becomes not just a sound but a celebration of life itself.

Five of Wands

The Five of Wands is a card of conflict, competition, and the chaotic energy of creative tension. It embodies the struggles and clashes that arise in the pursuit of artistry, both within the musician's inner world and in their interactions with others. The Five of Wands is not a card of destruction but of dynamic growth; it reflects the challenges that push musicians to develop their craft, refine their voice, and navigate the often tumultuous landscape of creativity. It speaks to the passion and energy that emerge when differing ideas, egos, and ambitions collide, creating a spark of potential that can lead to something extraordinary.

In the creative process, the Five of Wands often manifests as a sense of friction or struggle. It could be the battle to find the right melody, the frustration of writer's block, or the challenge of reconciling clashing ideas within a composition. This tension, though uncomfortable, is also a vital part of creation. It forces the musician to confront limitations, question assumptions, and push beyond the familiar. The Five of Wands teaches that the path to artistic growth is rarely smooth and that struggle is not a sign of failure but of engagement with something meaningful and transformative.

For a musician working within a group, the Five of Wands may reflect the dynamics of collaboration. Bands, orchestras, and ensembles often face moments of disagreement, where competing visions and strong personalities create friction. These conflicts can feel overwhelming, but they are also opportunities for growth and innovation. The card suggests that through negotiation, compromise, and mutual respect, a group can harness this chaotic energy to produce something far greater than any individual could achieve alone. The Five of Wands reminds musicians that the creative process is inherently messy and that beauty often arises from the resolution of discord.

On a personal level, the Five of Wands can represent the internal battles a musician faces. Doubts, insecurities, and the pressure to succeed can create an inner mental clatter that feels impossible to quiet. The card acknowledges this struggle while also pointing to its transformative potential. The musician who faces their fears, who grapples with the voices of criticism and self-doubt, ultimately emerges stronger and more self-assured. The Five of Wands reminds artists that growth often requires stepping into the discomfort of the unknown, trusting that the process will yield clarity and strength.

The competitive aspect of the Five of Wands is also relevant in the world of music. Whether it's auditions, competitions, or the race for recognition in a crowded industry, musicians often find themselves pitted against one another. The card reflects the intensity of this environment, where ambition and rivalry can either inspire or discourage. The Five of Wands encourages musicians to view competition not as a threat but as a motivator, a way to refine their skills and clarify their goals. It reminds them that their true measure of success lies not in comparison to others but in their commitment to their craft.

Performance under the influence of the Five of Wands can carry an electrifying energy. The tensions and challenges leading up to a performance often culminate in a moment of heightened intensity on stage. This energy, though chaotic, can also be exhilarating, driving the performer to new heights. The Five of Wands suggests that embracing this tension, rather than resisting it, can lead to a powerful and unforgettable expression of music.

The Five of Wands speaks to the competitive and often volatile nature of the field. It reflects the challenges of navigating an environment where opportunities can feel scarce and success elusive. Yet the card also highlights the vibrant energy that comes from being part of a dynamic, ever-evolving community. Musicians under the influence of the Five of Wands are reminded to stay true to their vision while remaining open to collaboration and learning. The card teaches that perseverance and resilience are key to thriving in a world of constant change and challenge.

On a creative level, the Five of Wands represents the raw, untamed energy of inspiration. It is the spark that ignites when different ideas and influences collide, creating a fertile ground for innovation. The card reminds musicians that the creative process is rarely linear or predictable and that moments of chaos often lead to breakthroughs. By embracing the turbulence and trusting in their ability to navigate it, musicians can transform discord into harmony, crafting music that is dynamic, original, and deeply resonant.

The Five of Wands also speaks to the importance of perspective. In the midst of struggle, it can be difficult to see the bigger picture, to recognize the growth and opportunity that lie within the conflict. The card encourages musicians to step back, to view challenges not as obstacles but as stepping stones on their creative journey. It teaches that every clash, every setback, and every frustration is an integral part of the process, shaping the artist and their work in ways that are both profound and unexpected.

The Five of Wands is a card of transformation through tension. It reminds musicians that the path of creation is rarely easy but is always rewarding. The struggles they face are not roadblocks but catalysts for growth, pushing them to explore new possibilities and to deepen their connection to their craft. Through the energy of the Five of Wands, music becomes not just a product of inspiration but a testament to the power of perseverance, passion, and the willingness to embrace the chaos of creation.

Six of Wands

The Six of Wands is a card of triumph, recognition, and the celebration of accomplishment. It represents the moments when the effort and dedication poured into the craft are met with applause, acknowledgment, and success. It is the song that garners standing ovations, the album that tops the charts, or the performance that lingers in the minds of the audience long after the final note. The Six of Wands signifies a peak in the musician's journey, a moment of victory that validates the struggles and sacrifices along the way. Yet beneath its surface of glory, the card holds deeper lessons about leadership, humility, and the true essence of achievement.

For a musician, encountering the energy of the Six of Wands feels like stepping into the spotlight. It is the culmination of hard work, the realization of long-held dreams, and the joy of knowing that their art has resonated with others. This card celebrates not just the external success but also the inner victory of having stayed committed to one's vision and craft. The Six of Wands reminds musicians that success is not a sudden stroke of luck but the result of perseverance, passion, and an unwavering belief in their creative voice.

On the stage, the Six of Wands is the embodiment of confidence and charisma. It is the energy of a performer who has found their rhythm, who commands the attention of the audience not through arrogance but through authenticity and connection. When musicians are in alignment with the Six of Wands, their performances carry an undeniable energy that captivates and inspires. It is as though every note, every movement, and every expression is imbued with the joy of being fully present and fully themselves. This card teaches musicians to embrace their moment of glory with gratitude and grace, knowing that their success is a reflection of their dedication and the support of those who have journeyed with them.

Collaboration and community also play a significant role in the energy of the Six of Wands. While it often highlights individual achievement, the card acknowledges the collective effort behind any success. This might mean recognizing the contributions of bandmates, producers, mentors, and even the audience who has supported them along the way. The Six of Wands serves as a reminder that triumph is rarely a solo endeavor and that true leadership involves uplifting and honoring those who have played a part in the journey. Musicians who embody this card's energy understand that their success is intertwined with the people around them, and they use their platform to inspire and empower others.

The Six of Wands is about the relationship between the artist and their audience. It reflects the magic that occurs when music transcends the individual, becoming a shared experience that unites and uplifts. When a musician performs under the influence of this card, their work carries a sense of celebration, not just of their personal victory but of the universal power of music to connect, heal, and transform. It is the concert where the crowd sings along as one, the song that becomes an anthem for countless lives, or the piece that brings tears of recognition to a listener's eyes. The Six of Wands reminds musicians of the profound impact their work can have, both on an individual and collective level.

While the Six of Wands is undoubtedly a card of success, it also carries a cautionary note. It invites musicians to reflect on the nature of recognition and to remain grounded in the face of praise. The adulation of an audience, while intoxicating, is fleeting, and the card urges artists to stay connected to the deeper purpose behind their music. Success is a milestone, not an endpoint, and the Six of Wands encourages musicians to celebrate their achievements while continuing to grow, evolve, and explore new creative horizons. It teaches that true triumph lies not in external validation but in the fulfillment of expressing one's authentic self.

The creative energy of the Six of Wands is one of momentum. It reflects the surge of inspiration and motivation that often follows a significant accomplishment. This might mean the excitement of planning the next project, building on the success to reach even greater heights. The card suggests that the energy of triumph can be a powerful driving force, propelling artists toward new challenges and opportunities. Yet it also reminds them to take time to savor their achievements, to acknowledge how far they've come, and to express gratitude for the journey.

The Six of Wands also speaks to the responsibility that comes with recognition. For musicians who find themselves in the public eye, the card highlights the importance of using their platform wisely. It encourages them to remain true to their values, to create work that reflects their integrity, and to use their influence to inspire positive change. The Six of Wands teaches that success is not just a personal victory but an opportunity to contribute something meaningful to the world.

On a deeper level, the Six of Wands is about self-belief. It reflects the inner victory of overcoming doubt, fear, and the obstacles that once seemed insurmountable. For musicians, this might mean finding the courage to share their work, to stand by their creative vision, or to step into the spotlight despite uncertainty. The card celebrates the triumph of authenticity, reminding artists that their unique voice is their greatest strength. It teaches that true success comes not from conforming to expectations but from embracing the fullness of who they are.

The Six of Wands is a card of celebration, connection, and inspiration. It honors the triumphs that come from dedication and passion, while reminding musicians to stay grounded in their purpose. Through the energy of this card, music becomes not just a means of personal expression but a shared experience that unites and uplifts. The Six of Wands teaches that success is not an endpoint but a moment of recognition along the journey, a reminder of the beauty and power of creation. For musicians, it is a call to embrace their victories with gratitude, to honor the support of their community, and to continue sharing their light with the world.

Seven of Wands

The Seven of Wands is a card of perseverance, determination, and standing one's ground in the face of opposition. It carries the energy of defending one's creative voice and maintaining integrity amidst challenges. The Seven of Wands reflects the struggles artists face as they assert their individuality and resist pressures to conform. It is the battle to remain true to oneself while navigating a world that may not always understand or support the path chosen. This card speaks to the courage required to rise above criticism, competition, and doubt, channeling that energy into a steadfast commitment to one's art.

For musicians, the Seven of Wands often appears in moments when their vision is tested. Perhaps they are faced with external criticism such as a song that challenges conventional norms, a performance that doesn't align with audience expectations, or a style that defies industry trends. These moments of resistance, though daunting, are also opportunities for growth. The Seven of Wands reminds musicians that their unique voice is worth defending, even when it feels like the world is pushing back. It teaches that staying true to one's creative identity is an act of strength and that authenticity often requires standing apart from the crowd.

The energy of the Seven of Wands is inherently confrontational, but it is not about aggression or hostility. Instead, it is about holding firm in one's convictions while remaining open to dialogue and growth. This might mean navigating disagreements within a band, handling harsh feedback with grace, or resisting the temptation to dilute one's art for the sake of appeasement. The Seven of Wands encourages musicians to engage with challenges constructively, using them as catalysts to refine their craft and deepen their connection to their creative purpose.

Internally, the Seven of Wands speaks to the struggles musicians face within themselves. Doubts, insecurities, and the constant comparisons that arise in a competitive field can create an inner battle that feels relentless. This card acknowledges the weight of these challenges while encouraging artists to rise above them. It reminds musicians that the fight for self-belief is not an easy one but is essential for their growth and fulfillment. By standing firm in their vision, even when the path feels uncertain, musicians can discover a resilience that fuels their creativity and propels them forward.

The Seven of Wands also reflects the competitive nature of the music world. Whether it's auditions, live performances, or vying for recognition, musicians often find themselves in environments where they must prove their worth. This card doesn't shy away from the intensity of these situations; instead, it empowers artists to meet them with confidence and strength. It suggests that the ability to thrive in competitive settings comes not from defeating others but from remaining grounded in one's own abilities and values. The Seven of Wands teaches that true success lies in authenticity, not in conforming to external pressures or expectations.

In a broader sense, the Seven of Wands speaks to the challenges of innovation in music. Artists who push boundaries, experiment with new sounds, or challenge traditional structures often face resistance before their work is fully appreciated. This card honors the courage of those who dare to be different, who risk rejection in pursuit of something groundbreaking. It reminds musicians that innovation often comes at a cost but that the rewards of staying true to their vision far outweigh the temporary discomfort of opposition. The Seven of Wands encourages artists to see their struggles as part of the larger creative process, a necessary step in bringing something new and meaningful into the world.

The performance aspect of the Seven of Wands is charged with an undeniable intensity. It is the energy of an artist who steps onto the stage with the knowledge that not everyone in the audience may understand or embrace their work and yet performs with unwavering conviction. This card represents the moments when musicians must draw on their inner strength, channeling their passion and determination into every note and gesture. It teaches that the power of performance lies not in universal approval but in the authenticity and courage of the artist.

The Seven of Wands also holds a deeply personal message for musicians: the importance of boundaries. In a field where demands and expectations can be overwhelming, this card urges artists to protect their creative energy and prioritize their well-being. It reminds them that saying no, setting limits, and standing firm in their needs are not acts of weakness but of strength. By honoring their boundaries, musicians create the space necessary for their art to thrive, ensuring that their creative journey remains sustainable and fulfilling.

On a spiritual level, the Seven of Wands, represents the alignment of passion and purpose. It reflects the drive to create music that is not just entertaining but deeply meaningful. This card honors the artist's role as a messenger, a conduit for expression that resonates beyond the self. It teaches that the struggles faced along the way are part of a greater calling, a reminder that the pursuit of art is both a personal and universal act of courage.

The Seven of Wands is a card of resilience and empowerment. It reminds musicians that the path of creativity is rarely easy but is always worth the effort. The challenges and opposition they face are not signs of failure but of growth, opportunities to deepen their connection to their art and to themselves. Through the energy of the Seven of Wands, music becomes a testament to the strength of the human spirit, a powerful expression of authenticity, perseverance, and the courage to stand firm in one's truth. This card is both a call to action and a source of inspiration, a reminder that their voice matters and that their art has the power to rise above all resistance.

Eight of Wands
The Eight of Wands is a card of momentum, swift action, and the unimpeded flow of energy. It signifies the moments when creativity surges forward with unstoppable force, when projects that have been in the works suddenly accelerate toward completion, and when inspiration feels as though it strikes like lightning. The Eight of Wands is the energy of movement, of crossing thresholds

with purpose and clarity, and of embracing the excitement that comes with rapid progress. It embodies the exhilarating rush of ideas, the unfolding of opportunities, and the joy of being in perfect alignment with their creative flow.

When the Eight of Wands appears, it often signals a time when obstacles seem to melt away, allowing the music to take shape with ease and speed. Perhaps a melody that had eluded the musician for weeks suddenly comes together, or a collaboration that seemed distant unexpectedly materializes. The card is a reminder that, in certain moments, the universe conspires to support momentum, and the musician's role is to ride the wave, fully present and responsive to the opportunities that arise. It speaks to the beauty of timing, the synchronicity that can occur when effort, inspiration, and external circumstances align.

In the creative process, the Eight of Wands reflects a period of prolific output. It is the kind of energy that fuels late-night writing sessions, spontaneous jam sessions, or bursts of songwriting where lyrics and harmonies seem to emerge effortlessly. Musicians under the influence of this card often find themselves in a state of flow, where their connection to their craft feels unshakable, and their ideas pour forth faster than they can record them. It is a time of abundance, where the barriers between thought and expression dissolve, allowing the music to emerge in its purest form.

The Eight of Wands also carries an element of communication. This can manifest as the ability to convey complex emotions and ideas with clarity and impact. It is the song that reaches across boundaries, touching hearts and connecting people in ways that words alone cannot. For musicians, the card suggests that their work carries an immediacy and relevance, resonating deeply with their audience and creating a shared sense of understanding. It reminds them of the power of music to transmit energy and emotion directly, bypassing barriers and uniting people in a shared experience.

Momentum, a key aspect of the Eight of Wands, often extends beyond the creative process to the practical aspects of a musician's life. It could signify the rapid progression of a project, such as an album reaching its final stages of production, a tour coming together in record time, or unexpected opportunities for performances or collaborations. The card suggests that the musician's efforts are being met with receptivity and support, creating a dynamic flow that propels them forward. It is a time when things seem to fall into place effortlessly, and the pace of progress can feel both thrilling and overwhelming.

The Eight of Wands is also a card of travel and movement, themes that resonate deeply in the life of a musician. It might symbolize the excitement of hitting the road for a tour, the opportunity to share music with new audiences, or the journey of exploring new musical landscapes. This energy of motion reflects the adventurous spirit of music, the way it invites both the artist and the listener to journey into unknown territories. This card encourages a willingness to embrace the unexpected, to follow where the music leads, and to trust in the transformative power of movement and change.

The card's energy is not without its challenges. The rapid pace of the Eight of Wands can be exhilarating, but it can also feel overwhelming. Musicians may find themselves juggling multiple projects, responding to a flood of opportunities, or trying to keep up with the surge of creative ideas. The card advises balance and focus, reminding artists to channel their energy intentionally and avoid spreading themselves too thin. While the momentum of the Eight of Wands is a gift, it requires clarity and direction to ensure that the progress it brings is sustainable and meaningful.

In performance, the Eight of Wands brings an electric energy that captivates and energizes both the musician and the audience. It is the kind of performance where every note feels charged with purpose, where the connection between the artist and the crowd is palpable, and where the energy of the moment carries everyone to new heights. This card reflects the power of music to create a sense of immediacy and urgency, drawing everyone present into a shared, transformative experience. For musicians, it is a reminder of the magic that occurs when they are fully immersed in their craft, allowing the music to flow freely and unhindered.

On a deeper level, the Eight of Wands speaks to the transformative power of alignment. It represents the moments when a musician feels entirely in tune with their purpose, when their work flows not from effort but from a place of natural harmony. This alignment allows them to move through challenges with grace, to seize opportunities without hesitation, and to create music that feels effortless and authentic. The card teaches that when musicians are connected to their true voice, the universe responds by opening doors, clearing paths, and accelerating their progress.

The Eight of Wands also reflects the way music itself moves. It mirrors the way a melody can travel across distances, the way a song can spread through word of mouth or social media, reaching people in ways that feel almost magical. It speaks to the power of music to transcend boundaries, to carry messages of hope, love, or resilience with speed and precision. For musicians, it is a reminder of the far-reaching impact their work can have and the importance of staying open to the possibilities that arise when they release their music into the world.

The Eight of Wands is a card of excitement, opportunity, and the joy of movement. It celebrates the moments when everything comes together, when creativity flows unhindered, and when the path ahead feels clear and full of potential. For musicians, it is a call to embrace the momentum, to trust in the power of their craft, and to allow the music to lead them toward new horizons. The Eight of Wands teaches that progress is not always linear, that inspiration often comes in waves, and that the beauty of the creative journey lies in its ability to surprise and inspire at every turn.

Nine of Wands

The Nine of Wands is a card of resilience, perseverance, and the determination to endure despite fatigue or obstacles. This card reflects the struggles and triumphs of the artistic journey, the moments when exhaustion threatens to overtake creativity, when doubt lingers like a shadow, and yet the musician refuses to give up. It represents the grit required to see a project through to completion, the courage to stand firm in one's vision, and the understanding that every effort brings the artist closer to their goal. The Nine of Wands is a testament to their strength and a reminder of the transformative power of persistence.

The Nine of Wands often arises during times of weariness. Perhaps it comes after long hours in the studio, rehearsing the same passages over and over in pursuit of perfection. Or maybe it appears during a grueling tour, when the road feels endless, and the spark of joy in performance has dimmed under the weight of exhaustion. These moments of fatigue test not only the musician's physical endurance but their emotional and spiritual commitment to their craft. The Nine of Wands acknowledges this struggle and encourages artists to dig deep, to tap into reserves of strength they may not realize they possess, and to keep moving forward.

At its core, this card is about the balance between vulnerability and resilience. The musician depicted in the energy of the Nine of Wands carries the scars of their journey, the evidence of past battles fought and won. These scars are not marks of failure but of experience, a reminder of the challenges overcome and the lessons learned along the way. For musicians, the Nine of Wands teaches that their struggles are not signs of weakness but proof of their dedication. It urges them to embrace the vulnerability inherent in creation, recognizing that the act of making music is itself an act of courage.

The Nine of Wands often signifies the final push before completion. It is the stage when a song or composition is nearly finished, but the last details demand more effort than anticipated. The card reflects the tension of being so close to the goal yet feeling overwhelmed by the remaining work. This can be a time of frustration, where self-doubt creeps in and questions arise: Is this good enough? Will anyone appreciate it? The Nine of Wands offers reassurance, reminding artists that they have already come so far and that their perseverance will be rewarded. It encourages them to trust in their abilities and to see their vision through to the end.

The Nine of Wands also speaks to the emotional resilience required in the music world. Criticism, rejection, and the constant comparison to others can take a toll on even the most confident artist. This card acknowledges the pain of these experiences while emphasizing the importance of staying true to one's creative voice. For musicians, it is a reminder that their worth is not determined by external opinions but by their commitment to their craft. The Nine of Wands teaches that every setback is an opportunity for growth and that the ability to persevere through adversity is a mark of true strength.

On stage, the energy of the Nine of Wands manifests as a performer who gives their all, even when they feel they have nothing left to give. It is the artist who, despite illness, fatigue, or personal struggles, steps into the spotlight and delivers a performance that is raw, real, and unforgettable. This card reflects the deep well of resilience that musicians draw upon in these moments, the ability to channel their pain and exhaustion into something powerful and moving. It teaches that vulnerability and strength are not opposites but two sides of the same coin, each enhancing the other.

The Nine of Wands also highlights the importance of boundaries in the life of a musician. The drive to succeed, to create, and to share one's art can lead to burnout if not balanced with rest and self-care. This card serves as a warning against pushing too hard and a reminder that resilience does not mean ignoring one's limits. For musicians, it is an invitation to honor their well-being, to recognize when to pause and replenish their energy, and to trust that taking care of themselves will ultimately strengthen their art. The Nine of Wands encourages artists to protect their creative energy, knowing that it is a precious and finite resource.

On a deeper level, the Nine of Wands is about the relationship between struggle and transformation. It reflects the idea that every challenge faced on the artistic path contributes to the musician's growth, shaping their identity and deepening their connection to their craft. For musicians, this card is a reminder that the struggles they endure are not in vain. Each setback, each moment of doubt, and each obstacle overcome becomes a part of their story, enriching their music with authenticity and depth. The Nine of Wands teaches that resilience is not just about enduring but about evolving, using each challenge as fuel for creativity and self-discovery.

In its broader sense, the Nine of Wands speaks to the perseverance required to be true to one's artistic vision in a world that often demands conformity. It is the musician who resists trends to create something original, who refuses to compromise their values for the sake of commercial success, and who continues to make music even when it feels like no one is listening. This card honors the courage it takes to walk such a path, to hold firm in the face of external pressures, and to believe in the power of one's unique voice.

The Nine of Wands is a card of endurance, courage, and the triumph of the human spirit. For musicians, it is both a challenge and an inspiration, a reminder of the strength they possess and the importance of their journey. It acknowledges the pain and exhaustion that come with the creative process while celebrating the resilience that allows artists to rise above these challenges. Through the lens of the Nine of Wands, music becomes a testament to perseverance, a reminder that even in the face of adversity, the artist's voice can endure, creating something that resonates with both struggle and triumph. This card is a call to honor their journey, to embrace their scars, and to continue creating with unwavering determination and hope.

Ten of Wands

The Ten of Wands is a card of burdens, responsibility, and the weight of ambition. It reflects the moments when the love for the craft becomes entangled with the pressures of expectation, obligation, or overcommitment. For musicians, this card resonates with the reality of taking on too much, whether it's the demands of a career, the weight of perfectionism, or the sheer scope of a creative project. While it acknowledges the immense effort required to carry such a load, it also challenges musicians to reflect on what they are carrying and why, encouraging them to assess whether the burden is worth the toll it takes on their spirit.

The image of the Ten of Wands often depicts a figure struggling under the weight of a heavy load, walking toward a distant goal. This can symbolize the journey of pursuing a dream while managing the countless challenges that come with it. It might reflect the long hours spent perfecting a piece of music, the exhaustion of juggling performances, or the relentless demands of maintaining a presence in the ever-changing music industry. The Ten of Wands speaks to the sacrifices made in the pursuit of art, reminding musicians that while hard work is often necessary, it can also become overwhelming if not balanced with rest and reflection.

One of the key messages of the Ten of Wands in music is the danger of losing sight of joy amidst the weight of responsibility. What begins as passion can become a source of stress when burdened by deadlines, expectations, or the pressure to succeed. A musician might find themselves consumed by the technicalities of their craft, striving for perfection at the expense of the emotional connection that first inspired them. The Ten of Wands serves as a warning against this imbalance, urging musicians to reconnect with the heart of their music and remember why they began creating in the first place.

The card also speaks to the emotional burdens musicians often carry. Music is an intensely personal form of expression, and the vulnerability it requires can weigh heavily on the artist. Sharing one's work with the world invites judgment, criticism, and comparison. Over time, these external pressures can accumulate, leaving the musician feeling drained or disconnected. The Ten of Wands acknowledges the courage it takes to bear these burdens while encouraging artists to find ways to lighten their emotional load, whether through collaboration, support systems, or self-compassion.

In the context of collaboration, the Ten of Wands reflects the dynamics of shared responsibility. Working with others, whether in a band, an orchestra, or a production team, can be both rewarding and challenging. The card might appear when a musician feels they are carrying more than their fair share of the work, whether it's organizing rehearsals, managing logistics, or holding the group together creatively. It highlights the importance of communication and balance within collaborative relationships, reminding musicians that the weight of a shared goal should not fail disproportionately on one person's shoulders.

On the creative level, the Ten of Wands can symbolize the overwhelming nature of a large-scale project. Writing an album, scoring a film, or even preparing for a major performance requires immense focus, energy, and time. The excitement of such endeavors can quickly shift into stress as the sheer volume of work becomes apparent. This card serves as a reminder to break down overwhelming tasks into manageable steps and to seek help when needed. It encourages them to recognize that carrying the weight of a project alone is not a sign of strength but of unnecessary strain.

The Ten of Wands also invites reflection on the role of ambition in a musician's life. Ambition can be a powerful motivator, driving artists to reach new heights and achieve their dreams. However, unchecked ambition can also lead to burnout, as the desire for success pushes musicians to take on more than they can handle. This card challenges musicians to examine their goals and priorities, asking whether the weight they carry is truly aligned with their values and aspirations. It suggests that letting go of unnecessary burdens, whether they are self-imposed or externally driven, can create space for more authentic and fulfilling creativity.

In a live performance setting, the Ten of Wands reflects the physical and emotional effort required to bring music to life on stage. Musicians often pour their entire being into a performance, channeling their energy into every note and movement. While this dedication is admirable, it can also be exhausting, particularly when compounded by the logistics of touring, rehearsing, and managing a public image. This card reminds performers to honor their limits, to find moments of rest amidst the chaos, and to trust that their authenticity is more important than perfection.

The spiritual message of the Ten of Wands is one of release. It invites musicians to consider what they can let go of, whether it's outdated expectations, unnecessary obligations, or limiting beliefs. The card suggests that by releasing these burdens, musicians can rediscover the lightness and freedom that first drew them to their craft. It is a call to simplify, to focus on what truly matters, and to trust that letting go doesn't mean giving up but rather creating space for new possibilities to emerge.

The Ten of Wands also speaks to the communal aspect of music. It reminds musicians that they are not alone in their struggles and that sharing the load can ease the burden. Music has always been a collective experience, a way of connecting with others and finding strength in shared expression. This card encourages musicians to lean into this sense of community, knowing that the weight they carry is lighter when shared with others who understand their journey.

The Ten of Wands is a card of perseverance and transformation. It acknowledges the challenges and sacrifices inherent in the pursuit of music while offering the hope of relief and renewal. For musicians, it is a reminder that the burdens they bear are not permanent and that they have the power to choose which weights to carry and which to set down. The Ten of Wands teaches that strength lies not in enduring every challenge alone but in knowing when to seek support, when to rest, and when to let go. Through its lessons, musicians can find a deeper connection to their craft, rediscovering the joy and freedom that make the journey worthwhile.

Page of Wands

The Page of Wands is a card of youthful enthusiasm, curiosity, and the spark of inspiration. This energy is akin to the moment when an idea first takes form, when the sheer excitement of possibility ignites a sense of wonder and exploration. It represents the beginning stages of a creative journey, where passion outweighs experience, and the desire to create eclipses any fear of failure. The Page of Wands embodies the fearless energy of discovery, the willingness to experiment, and the joy of finding one's voice in the ever-expanding world of sound.

This card often appears in the life of a musician at a time when inspiration is abundant but the path forward remains undefined. It reflects the pure, unbridled energy of creating music for the sake of creation itself, unencumbered by the weight of expectation or perfection. The Page of Wands celebrates this phase of exploration, urging musicians to follow their instincts and embrace the unknown. It is about diving into the act of making music without overthinking, allowing curiosity to lead and trusting that every note played or lyric written is part of a greater unfolding.

The Page of Wands is also a messenger of creative opportunity. This might manifest as a sudden burst of inspiration, the chance to collaborate with someone new, or the impulse to try a different genre or instrument. These opportunities often arise unexpectedly, like a melody that comes to mind seemingly out of nowhere. The Page encourages musicians to seize these moments, to act on their impulses, and to trust in their ability to transform raw inspiration into something meaningful. It is a call to be open to experimentation, knowing that even ideas that seem whimsical or outlandish have the potential to grow into something extraordinary.

In its youthful energy, the Page of Wands often brings a sense of playfulness and spontaneity to music. It reminds musicians that the act of creation is as much about enjoyment as it is about discipline. This card suggests that some of the most profound musical experiences come from moments of unstructured exploration such as picking up an instrument with no agenda, improvising freely, or letting the music take shape organically. The Page of Wands invites musicians to reconnect with this playful spirit, to remember the joy of making music simply because it feels good, and to let go of any pressure to produce something polished or perfect.

The Page of Wands also carries a sense of adventure, encouraging musicians to step outside their comfort zones and embrace the unfamiliar. This might mean trying a new instrument, exploring a different cultural tradition in music, or even experimenting with unconventional sounds and techniques. The card speaks to the courage required to take creative risks, to venture into territory where there are no guarantees but infinite possibilities. This adventurous spirit is a reminder that growth comes from exploration and that every step into the unknown brings new insights and skills.

This card is often associated with the early stages of a musical career or project, where the possibilities feel endless, and the future is wide open. For emerging musicians, the Page of Wands reflects the excitement and challenges of finding one's place in the musical landscape. It symbolizes the first performance, the debut recording, or the initial attempts at songwriting, all filled with the thrill of discovery and the eagerness to share one's voice with the world. At this stage, mistakes are not failures but valuable lessons, and every experience adds to the musician's growing sense of identity and purpose.

For more experienced musicians, the Page of Wands can serve as a reminder to reconnect with the beginner's mindset. It asks artists to set aside their accumulated knowledge and approach music with fresh eyes and ears, as if encountering it for the first time. This perspective can reignite creativity, breaking through blocks and opening the door to new ideas. The Page of Wands suggests that no matter how long a musician has been practicing their craft, there is always room for growth and exploration. It is an invitation to stay curious, to remain open to learning, and to embrace the ever-changing nature of music.

The Page of Wands speaks to the passion and excitement that music can evoke. It reflects the way a new melody or rhythm can spark a sense of wonder, how a single note can open the door to a world of possibilities. This card reminds musicians of the deep emotional connection they have with their craft, the way it stirs something primal and joyful within them. It celebrates the power of music to inspire, uplift, and energize, urging musicians to share this energy with others and to let their enthusiasm become contagious.

The Page of Wands also highlights the importance of storytelling in music. Just as the figure on the card holds a wand that seems to hum with potential, musicians wield their instruments and voices to convey ideas, emotions, and narratives. The card encourages artists to tap into their unique perspective, to tell their story in a way that only they can, and to trust that their authenticity will resonate with others. It reminds musicians that their voice, however new or unrefined it may feel, holds value simply because it is their own.

While the Page of Wands is brimming with potential, it also carries a reminder to ground creative energy with action and intention. The enthusiasm of this card can sometimes lead to scattered focus, as the musician is tempted to chase every idea that comes to mind. The Page encourages musicians to channel their inspiration into tangible efforts, to take the first steps toward bringing their ideas to life. It suggests that even small actions can build momentum and turn inspiration into reality.

The Page of Wands is a celebration of beginnings, of the energy and excitement that come with embarking on a new musical journey. It is a reminder that music is an ever-evolving process, one that thrives on curiosity, courage, and the willingness to take risks. This card is both an encouragement and a challenge to embrace their passion fully, to trust in their ability to create, and to allow themselves the freedom to explore without fear or hesitation. Through the lens of the Page of Wands, music becomes a boundless adventure, a journey filled with endless possibilities waiting to be discovered.

Knight of Wands

The Knight of Wands is a card of passion, drive, and fearless energy. It embodies the spirit of action and determination that propels musicians forward, often with an intensity that is both inspiring and overwhelming. The Knight of Wands represents the artist who moves boldly toward their vision, undeterred by challenges or uncertainties. It's about taking risks, embracing the thrill of creation, and allowing the momentum of one's passion to guide the way. This card reminds musicians that energy, when channeled with intention, can spark transformative breakthroughs.

The Knight of Wands speaks to the fire that fuels a musician's creative process. This energy is raw and untamed, urging artists to act on their instincts and trust their impulses. For some, this might mean diving into a new project with fervor, while for others, it could manifest as the courage to step onto a stage for the first time or share their work with the world. The Knight encourages a fearless approach to music, one that prioritizes action over hesitation and passion over perfection. It's not about having all the answers but about forging ahead regardless, confident that the path will reveal itself along the way.

The card often signifies a moment of rapid progress or significant movement in a musician's journey. It could indicate a burst of inspiration that leads to a prolific period of writing, composing, or performing. It might also reflect the urgency of preparing for a major opportunity, such as a tour, album release, or high-profile collaboration. The Knight of Wands thrives on momentum, reminding musicians that sometimes the best way to overcome doubt or stagnation is to simply act. Even if the steps forward are uncertain, the act of moving creates its own clarity and direction.

The Knight of Wands is deeply connected to the idea of risk-taking in music. It's the energy of experimentation, of stepping outside one's comfort zone and trying something bold and new. This might involve blending genres, adopting unconventional techniques, or expressing an idea that feels raw and vulnerable. The Knight is not concerned with playing it safe or following established rules; instead, this card celebrates the audacity to push boundaries and explore uncharted territory. This can be both liberating and intimidating, but the card's message is clear: great art often comes from daring to take risks.

The Knight of Wands reflects the intensity and urgency that music can evoke. It's the feeling of being so deeply immersed in a song or performance that everything else fades away. This card celebrates the passion that drives musicians to pour their entire selves into their craft, to lose track of time as they create, and to feel alive in the act of expression. The Knight of Wands reminds musicians that this kind of energy is a gift, one that can inspire not only their own work but also those who hear and experience it.

However, the Knight of Wands also carries a warning about the potential pitfalls of unbridled energy. While its passion and drive are powerful, they can also lead to impulsiveness or burnout if not balanced with focus and care. For musicians, this might manifest as diving into too many projects at once, neglecting the need for rest, or letting enthusiasm overshadow the importance of planning and preparation. The Knight of Wands urges musicians to harness their energy wisely, to channel it into meaningful efforts rather than scattering it in every direction. It's about finding the balance between action and intention, between spontaneity and discipline.

In a collaborative setting, the Knight of Wands often represents a dynamic and charismatic presence. This could be the musician who brings a spark of energy to a group, inspiring others with their enthusiasm and bold ideas. At the same time, the card can also reflect the challenges of working with such intense energy, particularly if it becomes overpowering or domineering. The Knight reminds musicians to be mindful of how their passion affects those around them, encouraging them to lead with inspiration rather than force. Collaboration thrives when energy is shared and balanced, creating a space where everyone's contributions are valued.

The Knight of Wands is the essence of charisma and stage presence. It's the artist who commands attention through sheer force of will, whose energy radiates outward and captivates an audience. This card celebrates the fearless spirit required to step into the spotlight, to own one's performance, and to connect with others through music. It's about channeling confidence and passion into every note, trusting that the energy put forth will resonate deeply. At the same time, the Knight reminds performers to stay grounded, to temper their fiery energy with authenticity and connection.

The Knight of Wands also reflects the adventurous spirit of music. It's about the journey of discovery, both outward and inward. For some musicians, this might involve exploring new places or cultures, seeking inspiration in unfamiliar sounds and traditions. For others, it could mean delving deeper into their own emotions and experiences, uncovering truths that fuel their art. The Knight encourages musicians to embrace this sense of adventure, to approach their craft with curiosity and openness, and to trust that every step of the journey brings growth and insight.

Spiritually, the Knight of Wands speaks to the transformative power of music. It acknowledges that music is more than sound, it is energy, emotion, and connection. This card celebrates the musician as a vessel for this energy, someone who channels their passion and creativity into something that transcends the individual. The Knight reminds musicians that their work has the potential to inspire, uplift, and ignite change, not only in themselves but also in those who experience it. It is a call to embrace the sacred nature of music, to honor its ability to move and transform.

The Knight of Wands is a card of action, passion, and fearless creativity. It represents the drive to move forward, to take risks, and to embrace the adventure of making music. It challenges artists to harness their energy with intention, to lead with courage, and to trust in the transformative power of their work. Whether it's the spark of a new idea, the thrill of a performance, or the determination to overcome obstacles, the Knight of Wands reminds musicians that their passion is their greatest strength. Through its energy, music becomes a journey of discovery, a celebration of boldness, and a testament to the power of fearless expression.

Queen of Wands

The Queen of Wands radiates confidence, charisma, and an undeniable presence, making her a powerful force in music. She embodies the kind of artist who not only masters their craft but also captivates an audience through sheer energy and magnetism. Her connection to fire and passion fuels creativity, giving musicians the courage to express themselves boldly and unapologetically. The Queen of Wands is a symbol of artistic self-assurance, urging musicians to trust in their unique voice and to step fully into their power.

At the heart of this card is an unshakable belief in one's creative abilities. The Queen of Wands does not second-guess herself; she knows who she is and what she offers to the world. For a musician, this means owning one's sound, embracing one's style, and refusing to dilute artistic vision to fit expectations. It is about playing, singing, or composing with an intensity that comes from deep within, knowing that authenticity is what truly resonates. The music that stems from the energy of this card is fearless, whether it is raw and emotive, bold and theatrical, or deeply personal, it carries a strength that demands to be heard.

This confidence extends beyond the music itself and into the way a musician carries themselves. The Queen of Wands has an undeniable stage presence, not necessarily because she is the loudest or flashiest but because she is completely at home in her expression. A performer embodying this energy does not shy away from the spotlight; they revel in it. They command attention effortlessly, drawing people in with their sheer passion and presence. Their movements, expressions, and even the silences between notes are filled with intention. Whether they are performing in front of a massive audience or an intimate crowd, they make every moment count, infusing it with warmth, charisma, and an infectious enthusiasm that lingers long after the music fades.

Yet, the Queen of Wands is not just about personal power; she is also an inspiration to others. She represents the kind of musician who uplifts, encourages, and ignites passion in those around her. She is the mentor who pushes a young artist to step outside their comfort zone, the bandleader who fosters a sense of unity among musicians, or the songwriter whose lyrics empower listeners to embrace their own strength. Her energy is magnetic, drawing people in not just because of her talent but because of her ability to make others believe in their own potential. Music created under this influence often carries a message of empowerment, resilience, and courage, urging others to find their own fire.

There is a deep connection between the Queen of Wands and creative independence. She does not wait for permission to create; she moves forward with determination, knowing that her artistry is worthy of being heard. This is the energy of a musician who takes control of their own path, whether that means self-producing their work, forming their own band, or carving out a space in an industry that may not always be welcoming. The Queen does not let obstacles deter her. If one path is blocked, she creates another. Her music is not defined by external validation but by her own passion and vision. This card reminds musicians that their power lies in their ability to shape their own artistic destiny.

Another key aspect of the Queen of Wands is the balance between fire and warmth. While she is intense and driven, she is not consumed by ego. She understands that music is not just about self-expression but also about connection. Her fire does not burn others; it illuminates and inspires. This means that musicians embodying this energy can lead with strength while remaining approachable and generous. They are not afraid to share the stage, to collaborate, and to celebrate the successes of others. Their confidence is rooted in a deep sense of self-worth rather than the need for external validation, allowing them to support others without feeling threatened.

The creative energy of the Queen of Wands is dynamic and constantly in motion. She does not linger in stagnation; she thrives on reinvention and exploration. For musicians, this means continually pushing creative boundaries, evolving with each new project, and refusing to be confined to a single style or identity. The Queen encourages experimentation reminding artists that growth comes from embracing change. She is the musician who reinvents themselves with each album, the songwriter who fearlessly explores new themes, or the performer who constantly finds fresh ways to connect with an audience. Her artistry is alive, never static, always moving forward with purpose.

In the realm of inspiration, the Queen of Wands represents an artist who channels passion into every note and lyric. She is not detached or distant, she is fully engaged, pouring her entire being into the music. Her fire burns through hesitation and self-doubt, allowing for the kind of creation that is both cathartic and exhilarating. Music made under her influence often feels electric, charged with emotion and depth, as though it has been infused with the very essence of the artist's soul. It is this raw authenticity that makes it so powerful, drawing listeners in and leaving a lasting impact.

The Queen of Wands represents the ability to turn personal experiences into powerful art. She does not shy away from her emotions, nor does she let them control her. Instead, she harnesses them, transforming even pain and struggle into something meaningful. This is the energy of an artist who writes from a place of deep feeling, yet does so with a sense of strength rather than vulnerability. Her music may tell stories of heartbreak, resilience, joy, or defiance, but no matter the theme, it carries a sense of empowerment. She reminds musicians that their struggles, triumphs, and personal journeys are all fuel for creation, and that their stories, told through music, have the power to inspire others.

The Queen of Wands is also a reminder that music is meant to be felt, not just heard. She does not create passively; she brings her full presence to every note, every beat, every breath. This is the energy of a musician who plays or sings as if their life depends on it, who loses themselves in the music and invites the audience to do the same. Whether in a fiery rock anthem, a soulful ballad, or an experimental composition, the Queen of Wands brings intensity, conviction, and an unshakable belief in the power of expression.

The Queen of Wands represents the artist who refuses to be anything but themselves. She is bold, fearless, and magnetic, leading with both passion and generosity. She reminds musicians to trust in their own creative vision, to own their presence, and to never dim their light for the sake of fitting in. She challenges them to step forward with confidence, knowing that their voice, their music, and their energy have the power to inspire and transform. Through her, music becomes not just an act of creation, but a force of nature.

King of Wands

The King of Wands is the embodiment of vision, leadership, and creative mastery, making him an extraordinary symbol in the world of music. He represents the culmination of inspiration and action, someone who has honed their craft, embraced their passions, and taken command of their artistic journey. The King of Wands is the archetype of the bold and visionary artist who leads with confidence, purpose, and an undeniable fire. He is the master of his sound, someone who not only creates but also inspires others to rise to their potential.

At the core of the King of Wands is a deep connection to passion and creativity. This is the musician who has moved beyond mere experimentation and exploration; they have found their voice and claimed it with authority. The King is not searching for his place in the world of music, he has created it. This card represents the confidence that comes with mastery, the assurance that what one offers is unique, powerful, and worthy of recognition. For musicians, this energy encourages a fearless embrace of their talents, reminding them that their work has value and that they are capable of shaping their own destiny.

The King of Wands is a natural leader, and in music, this often manifests as someone who inspires and directs others with clarity and purpose. He could be the bandleader who drives the group forward, the producer who brings out the best in every collaborator, or the solo artist who sets trends and redefines genres. His leadership is not about control but about vision. The King knows where he wants to go and how to get there, and his energy has a magnetic quality that draws others along with him. He has the ability to motivate and unite, turning disparate talents into a cohesive and powerful force. Under his guidance, creativity flourishes, and everyone involved rises to new heights.

The King of Wands also embodies a deep sense of responsibility. His success is not accidental; it is the result of hard work, perseverance, and an unwavering commitment to his craft. For musicians, this card serves as a reminder that mastery requires discipline and dedication. The King is not content with fleeting inspiration or half-hearted efforts; he invests himself fully in his work, striving for excellence in all that he does. This energy challenges musicians to take their craft seriously, to set high standards for themselves, and to put in the effort needed to reach their goals. At the same time, the King knows the importance of balance, ensuring that his drive does not lead to burnout or rigidity.

In performance, the King of Wands radiates charisma and authority. He is the artist who commands attention the moment he steps on stage, not through flashy antics but through an undeniable presence. His confidence is rooted in authenticity; he knows who he is and what he stands for, and this certainty shines through in every note and gesture. A performer embodying the energy of the King does not need to demand respect, it is given freely, as audiences are drawn to his strength and conviction. His performances are electric, charged with a sense of purpose and passion that leaves a lasting impression.

The King of Wands is also a visionary, someone who sees possibilities where others see limitations. This translates to an artist who pushes boundaries, innovates, and redefines what is possible. The King is not content with repeating the past; he seeks to create something new and transformative. This might involve blending genres, pioneering new technologies, or expressing ideas that challenge conventions. The King of Wands serves as an invitation to think big, to dream boldly, and to trust in their ability to bring their vision to life. He reminds artists that their creativity has the power to shape not just their own journey but the broader landscape of music.

Despite his focus on leadership and vision, the King of Wands does not operate in isolation. He values collaboration and recognizes the importance of community in the creative process. He is generous with his energy and insights, offering guidance and support to those around him. In this way, the King of Wands represents the mentor, the teacher, or the collaborator who elevates others while pursuing his own goals. This might mean sharing knowledge, encouraging younger artists, or fostering an environment where creativity can thrive. The King understands that his success is intertwined with the success of others, and he leads with both strength and compassion.

Emotionally, the King of Wands represents a mature relationship with passion and creativity. He is not ruled by fleeting whims or unbridled impulses; his fire is steady and controlled, allowing him to channel his energy into meaningful endeavors. This means finding a balance between inspiration and discipline, between spontaneity and intention. The King encourages artists to trust in their instincts while also grounding their work in structure and focus. This balance allows for the creation of music that is both deeply personal and polished, both raw and refined.

The King of Wands also carries a spiritual dimension, particularly in his connection to purpose. He understands that music is not just a means of self-expression but also a way to connect with others and with something greater than oneself. For some musicians, this might involve creating work that speaks to universal themes or that uplifts and inspires others. For others, it might mean using their platform to advocate for change or to amplify marginalized voices. The King of Wands reminds artists that their work has the power to influence and transform, and he challenges them to use this power wisely and intentionally.

Ultimately, the King of Wands is a card of mastery, leadership, and vision. In music, he represents the artist who has claimed their place in the world, who leads with confidence and inspires with passion. He challenges musicians to step into their power, to embrace their unique voice, and to take bold steps toward their goals. At the same time, he reminds them of the importance of community, responsibility, and purpose, encouraging a balanced and holistic approach to creativity. Through the energy of the King of Wands, music becomes not just an act of creation but a force for connection, transformation, and inspiration.

The Minor Arcana: Cups

The Cups suit is intimately connected to emotions, intuition, relationships, and the flow of creativity, making it deeply resonant with the essence of music.

Music, at its core, is a language of emotion, an art form that transcends words and communicates directly with the heart. The Cups suit reflects the emotional depth, representing the fluid, often mysterious nature of artistic inspiration and the way music can touch the soul, evoke memories, and foster connections. Through its watery symbolism, the suit of Cups invites us to explore how music expresses the spectrum of human emotion and our capacity to feel, empathize, and connect.

The energy of Cups in music begins with the act of channeling emotion into sound. Whether joy, sorrow, love, or longing, the music inspired by Cups is raw and authentic, unafraid to explore the depths of feeling. This suit encourages musicians to tap into their inner emotional landscapes, transforming personal experiences into melodies and harmonies that resonate with others. Songs born from this space often carry an undeniable vulnerability, an openness that invites listeners to feel seen, understood, and less alone in their own emotional journeys. It is the kind of music that makes you cry, that makes your heart swell, or that stirs a sense of nostalgia for moments you thought you had forgotten.

The intuitive aspect of the Cups suit also plays a crucial role in music. Creativity is rarely a linear or purely logical process; it often arises from a place beyond words, an inner wellspring that defies explanation. Musicians under the influence of Cups learn to trust this intuitive flow, allowing inspiration to guide them without forcing or overthinking the process. It might be a sudden melody that comes to mind, a chord progression that feels just right, or lyrics that seem to pour out effortlessly. Cups remind artists to surrender to this mysterious process, trusting that their intuition will lead them to create something genuine and meaningful.

Cups also speak to the relational nature of music, the way it fosters connection between people. Music is a bridge, a shared language that transcends cultural and linguistic barriers. It creates spaces where emotions can be exchanged, understood, and celebrated. A song inspired by Cups might be a love ballad that captures the intensity of romantic feelings, a lullaby that comforts and soothes, or a piece that expresses solidarity and unity. In this way, the Cups suit reflects how music can heal rifts, build relationships, and deepen bonds, bringing people together in a shared emotional experience.

One of the most beautiful aspects of Cups in music is its ability to reflect both individual and collective emotions. On an individual level, Cups encourage musicians to be honest about their own feelings and experiences, turning their inner world into art. On a collective level, Cups allow music to speak to universal themes such as love, loss, hope, and longing that resonate across time and space. This duality makes Cups an ideal symbol for the way music can simultaneously be deeply personal and profoundly universal, offering both the artist and the listener a sense of connection and belonging.

The Cups suit also acknowledges the ebb and flow of emotions, much like the tides governed by water. In music, this translates to the dynamic range of expression, from quiet introspection to soaring crescendos. The suit reminds musicians that not every moment needs to be dramatic or intense; there is beauty in stillness, subtlety, and simplicity. A quiet piano interlude, a soft vocal phrase, or a delicate string arrangement can carry just as much emotional weight as a powerful anthem. Cups teach us to honor the full spectrum of expression, allowing music to mirror the complexities and nuances of human emotion.

The Cups suit encourages musicians to use their art as a form of emotional release and healing. For many artists, music is a sanctuary, a space where they can process and transform their feelings. Writing a song about heartbreak, performing a piece that captures joy, or improvising a melody that reflects grief that can be cathartic, offering a way to make sense of emotions that might otherwise feel overwhelming. Similarly, for listeners, music inspired by Cups can serve as a form of therapy, providing solace, understanding, and a sense of being held in moments of vulnerability.

Cups also remind us of the spiritual dimension of music. Just as water reflects the moonlight, music can reflect the unseen, offering glimpses of the transcendent. A piece of music inspired by Cups might evoke a sense of wonder, awe, or connection to something greater than oneself. Whether it is a hymn, a meditative chant, or an instrumental piece that feels like it touches the divine, Cups encourage musicians to explore how their art can serve as a bridge between the earthly and the spiritual, the known and the mysterious.

Cups invite musicians to embrace a sense of flow, letting go of rigidity and allowing their art to evolve organically. Just as water adapts to its container, music influenced by Cups is fluid and responsive, shaped by the emotions, experiences, and inspirations of the moment. This adaptability can lead to unexpected and beautiful outcomes, as artists learn to trust the journey rather than fixating on a specific destination. Cups remind musicians that creativity is not a straight line but a river, winding and meandering toward its ultimate expression.

The Cups suit highlights the joy and celebration that music can bring. Water is not only about depth and reflection; it is also about playfulness and vitality. Music inspired by Cups can be lighthearted and uplifting, capturing the essence of laughter, dancing, and celebration. This energy reminds us that while music often explores deep and profound emotions, it is also a source of joy, delight, and connection to the present moment.

In all its aspects, the Cups suit serves as a powerful symbol for the emotional, intuitive, and relational dimensions of music. It encourages musicians to dive deep into their feelings, to trust their creative instincts, and to create art that speaks to the heart. Whether it is a tender ballad, an evocative symphony, or a soulful improvisation, music inspired by Cups has the power to heal, connect, and transform, offering a glimpse into the beauty and complexity of the human experience. Through the lens of Cups, music becomes not just an art form but a vessel for emotion, a mirror for the soul, and a gift to the world.

Ace of Cups

The Ace of Cups is a card of pure emotional expression, overflowing creativity, and the boundless potential of the heart. It represents the initial spark of inspiration, the first swell of feelings that compels an artist to translate their inner world into sound. This card is the essence of emotional connection, and in the realm of music, it symbolizes the moment when the heart opens wide and allows melodies and harmonies to flow freely, unencumbered by fear or limitation. It is the song that emerges from the depths of the soul, raw and unfiltered, offering a glimpse into the beauty and vulnerability of the human spirit.

The Ace of Cups is often depicted as a chalice overflowing with water, a potent symbol of abundance and emotional depth. This imagery mirrors the way music can act as a vessel for feelings that are too vast or profound to be contained in words. When a musician is under the influence of the Ace of Cups, they become a conduit for the emotions that flow through them. The music they create is not calculated or constrained but is instead a spontaneous and genuine expression of their inner world. This card invites musicians to surrender to this flow, trusting that what emerges will be authentic and deeply resonant.

The Ace of Cups speaks to the power of music to connect with the heart. It reminds us that music is not merely an intellectual or technical pursuit but an emotional one, capable of reaching into the depths of the human experience and bringing it to life. A piece of music inspired by the Ace of Cups might feel like an intimate confession, a love letter, or a cathartic release. It is the song that makes you cry, not because of its complexity or virtuosity, but because it speaks to something unspoken within you. This card celebrates the raw, unpolished beauty of music that is created from the heart, reminding artists that emotional authenticity is far more impactful than perfection.

The Ace of Cups also represents the beginning of an emotional or creative journey. In music, this might manifest as a moment when an idea takes shape such as the first chord progression, the fragment of a melody, or the spark of a lyric that hints at something larger. These initial moments are often fragile and fleeting, yet they hold infinite potential. The Ace of Cups encourages musicians to nurture these sparks, to trust in their instincts, and to allow their creativity to unfold naturally. This card reminds artists that the most profound works often begin with the simplest of ideas, born from a place of sincerity and openness.

This card is often associated with divine inspiration, the sense that creativity is a gift from a higher source. For musicians, this might mean feeling as though the music they create is coming through them rather than from them. It is the experience of being "in the zone," where ideas flow effortlessly and the boundaries between the self and the music dissolve. The Ace of Cups invites artists to honor this connection to the divine, to recognize that their creativity is a sacred gift, and to share it with the world as an offering of love and beauty.

The Ace of Cups also highlights the way music can serve as a bridge between people, fostering connection and understanding. A song inspired by this card might be a love ballad that captures the intensity of a new romance, a lullaby that soothes and comforts, or a celebratory anthem that brings people together in joy. Music influenced by the Ace of Cups has the power to heal emotional wounds, to communicate feelings that cannot be spoken, and to strengthen bonds between individuals. It reminds us that music is a universal language of the heart, capable of expressing what words cannot.

The overflowing nature of the Ace of Cups also speaks to abundance and generosity. When a musician channels the energy of this card, they are not creating from a place of scarcity or fear but from a place of fullness and gratitude. Their music is a gift, offered freely and without expectation, simply because it must be shared. This card encourages artists to release their work into the world with an open heart, trusting that it will find its way to those who need it. It also reminds musicians to remain receptive to the inspiration and support that flows back to them, creating a cycle of giving and receiving that fuels their creative spirit.

The Ace of Cups is a card of healing and renewal, and this energy is mirrored in music's ability to soothe and uplift the soul. For the artist, the art of creating music can be a form of self-care, a way to process and release emotions that might otherwise remain trapped. For the listener, music inspired by the Ace of Cups offers a space of comfort and solace, a reminder that they are not alone in their feelings. This card celebrates the transformative power of music, its ability to turn pain into beauty and to bring light into the darkest of places.

The Ace of Cups also invites musicians to approach their craft with a sense of playfulness and joy. While the card is often associated with deep emotion, it also celebrates the lighthearted and celebratory aspects of creativity. It is the spontaneous jam session, the carefree improvisation, the laughter shared over a shared melody. The Ace of Cups reminds artists that music is not only a means of expression but also a source of delight and wonder, a way to connect with the present moment and to celebrate the simple pleasure of creating something beautiful.

The Ace of Cups is a card of potential, inviting musicians to embrace the limitless possibilities of their creativity and to explore the depths of their emotional landscapes. It challenges artists to be open, vulnerable, and fearless in their expression, to trust in their intuition, and to share their gifts with the world. The Ace of Cups is a reminder that every note, every lyric, and every rhythm has the power to touch the heart, to inspire, and to heal. It celebrates the profound connection between music and emotion, offering a glimpse into the infinite well of creativity that resides within each of us.

Two of Cups

The Two of Cups is a card of harmony, connection, and deep emotional resonance, making it a powerful symbol for the role of music in relationships, collaboration, and shared experience. It represents the merging of two energies, the meeting of hearts, and the unspoken understanding that can exist between people. This card speaks to the way sound and emotion intertwine, how music becomes a bridge between souls, and how it can create profound moments of unity and intimacy. The Two of Cups is the love song, the duet, the harmony between voices, the shared rhythm that brings two beings into sync with one another.

Music, at its essence, is an exchange of energy, and the Two of Cups embodies this perfectly. Whether in a literal sense, such as two musicians coming together to create something beautiful, or in a more abstract sense, where a song becomes a conduit for love and understanding, this card represents the magic that happens when two forces align. There is an effortless flow here, a blending of creative impulses that results in something greater than either could have achieved alone. This could be the serendipity of two artists finding their perfect counterpart, a songwriter and a vocalist whose visions complement each other perfectly, or an instrumentalist and a composer whose work brings out the best in both.

The nature of the Two of Cups in music also extends to the emotional connections that songs create between people. A piece of music inspired by this card is one that evokes love in all its forms: romantic, platonic, or spiritual. It might be a love song that captures the tender exchange of emotions between two people, a song of reconciliation that mends a rift, or a melody that feels like a quiet hug. Music shaped by the Two of Cups does not demand or overpower; it is gentle, inviting, and deeply personal. It allows for vulnerability, creating a space where emotions can be expressed and understood without words.

Some of the most legendary songs and performances are the result of two artists finding a perfect balance between their styles, voices, or instruments. The Two of Cups is present in the kind of musical partnerships that feel effortless, where two energies intertwine seamlessly, creating something that resonates on a deeper level. There is an intuitive understanding in these partnerships, a sense of knowing when to step forward and when to pull back, of allowing space for the other person to shine. The best duets in history embody this energy, where two distinct voices come together not to compete, but to complement one another, forming a union that feels destined.

The Two of Cups also speaks to the intimate bond between musician and audience. Music has the power to forge an unspoken connection between the creator and the listener, a shared experience where emotions are exchanged without the need for direct conversation. A song that carries the energy of the Two of Cups feels personal, as though it was written specifically for the listener, even if thousands of others feel the same way. This is the magic of music. It is deeply personal and yet universally relatable. A love song can remind someone of their own relationship, a ballad can rekindle old emotions, and a piece of music can make a person feel seen, understood, and less alone.

There is an element of healing in the Two of Cups, a reminder that music can be a balm for emotional wounds. Just as the card represents reconciliation and the coming together of energies after conflict, music can serve as a bridge for mending relationships and soothing the soul. A song can be an apology, a plea for understanding, or a means of expressing what words cannot fully capture. Music has the ability to break down barriers, to soften anger, and to open the heart, making it one of the most powerful tools for emotional healing and connection.

The water symbolism in the Two of Cups reflects the fluidity of emotions in music. Just as water flows and adapts, music shaped by this card moves effortlessly, weaving between emotions, shifting in tone, and carrying its listener along with it. This is not the chaotic, crashing waves of conflict, but the gentle current of understanding and unity. There is a natural ease to the music inspired by this card, a feeling of alignment and flow, as if everything has fallen into place exactly as it should.

In a broader sense, the Two of Cups reminds musicians and listeners alike of the importance of connection in creativity. Music does not exist in isolation. It is meant to be shared, experienced, and felt by others. Whether it is the connection between two artists, between a performer and an audience, or between a song and the emotions it evokes, this card speaks to the beauty of shared experience. It encourages musicians to embrace collaboration, to seek out kindred spirits in their artistic journey, and to remember that some of the most powerful music is born from the meeting of two souls.

Ultimately, the Two of Cups in music is about love, balance, and harmony. It is the song that brings two people closer together, the melody that speaks to the heart, the performance that feels like a conversation between equals. It is a reminder that music is not just an individual expression but a shared experience, one that has the power to unite, heal, and strengthen the bonds between us. Whether through collaboration, romantic expression, or the deep emotional connection between a song and its listener, the Two of Cups celebrates the beauty of unity in music, reminding us that some of the most profound moments in life are those we share with others.

Three of Cups

The Three of Cups is a card of celebration, connection, and shared joy. It represents the fusion of individual energies into something greater. In the world of music, this card embodies the essence of collaboration, the magic of harmonies, and the profound way melodies bring people together. It speaks to the kind of musical moments that are best enjoyed with others, whether that's a band playing in perfect sync, a choir lifting their voices in unison, or a group of friends lost in the rhythm of a shared song.

At its core, the Three of Cups is about unity, and music is one of the most powerful ways people bond. It carries the image of three figures raising their cups in a joyous toast, much like musicians lifting their instruments voices, or hands in the air, united in the act of creating something beautiful. The energy of this card in a musical sense is not about the lone virtuoso practicing in solitude, it is about the jam session, the festival, the chorus swelling in perfect synchronization. It is the rhythm section locking in together, the blending of tones and textures, the way music fills a space and makes it feel alive with shared emotion.

Musically, the Three of Cups can manifest in a number of ways, It may symbolize the natural chemistry of a group of musicians who intuitively understand each other, the effortless flow of improvisation where each player listens and responds without ego. There's a sense of playfulness here, an invitation to let go and simply enjoy the experience. It is the open mic night where strangers become friends through song, the communal drum circle where beats weave together like an unspoken conversation, the thrill of a live concert where the audience sings in unison, voices merging into one.

This card also resonates deeply with genres of music that emphasize togetherness and joy. Folk music, with its emphasis on communal storytelling, captures the spirit of the Three of Cups. Gospel music, where call and response create a sense of shared worship and celebration, embodies its uplifting energy. Even in jazz, where improvisation reigns, there is an unspoken agreement among musicians that honors both individuality and cohesion.

Beyond performance, the Three of Cups speaks to the way music is experienced emotionally and socially. Think of the songs that define friendships, the anthems that mark a celebration, the playlists carefully curated for road trips or parties. This card reminds us of the sheer joy of singing along with others, of dancing without inhibition, of letting music dissolve barriers between people. It is the track played at a wedding that brings generations onto the dance floor, the festival anthem that unites strangers in euphoric movement, the spontaneous street musician whose melody draws a crowd and turns passersby into a community, even if just for a moment.

On a deeper level, the Three of Cups highlights the emotional connection music fosters. It suggests that some of the most profound musical moments happen when people experience sound as a collective force. In times of happiness, music amplifies joy; in times of sorrow, it reminds us that we are not alone. When this card appears in a reading, it may be an encouragement to seek out collaborative experiences, to share one's art with others, or to find a sense of belonging through sound.

Yet, the Three of Cups does not speak to music as mere entertainment. It captures the alchemy of sound and connection, the way music transcends the sum of its parts. A single voice may be beautiful, but when it is joined by others in harmony, something almost mystical occurs. The interplay of notes, voices, and instruments mirrors the card's deeper message: that unity creates something richer than what exists alone.

The Three of Cups reminds us that music is not just about the notes played, it is about the space between them, the interaction, the feeling of being part of something greater. It is a celebration of sound, of friendship, of the magic that happens when melodies intertwine and become something more than the sum of their parts. Whether through a shared dance, a heartfelt duet, or the simple act of listening together, this card invites us to revel in the joy that music brings and to embrace the harmony of connection.

Four of Cups

The Four of Cups is a card of introspection, discontent, and missed opportunities. It often represents a moment of emotional withdrawal, where something is being offered, yet the person receiving it remains unmoved, lost in their own thoughts. This card speaks to the times when sound no longer stirs the soul, when inspiration fades, or when the joy of playing and listening becomes dulled by repetition or disillusionment. It is the silence between the notes, not in a way that enhances the melody, but in a way that feels heavy, like an emptiness where music once lived.

Music, but its very nature, is an emotional language. It moves us, shapes us, and often provides a sense of connection both to ourselves and to others. But what happens when that connection is severed? The Four of Cups embodies this detachment; the artist who no longer finds joy in their craft, the listener who grows tired of the same melodies, the songwriter staring at a blank page, unable to summon the spark of creation. It is the lull in inspiration, the feeling of stagnation that comes when music loses its magic, even when it surrounds us.

This card often depicts a figure sitting beneath a tree, arms crossed, gazing at three cups in front of them, while a fourth cup is being offered from an unseen hand. The posture is closed off, the eyes cast downward. There is something within reach, but the figure does not look up. In music, this moment can be deeply personal. It might manifest as creative exhaustion, when every note played feels predictable, when practice feels like a chore rather than an expression. It is the musician who has spent years perfecting their technique, only to feel numb to the very sound that once ignited passion. It is the listener who once found solace in a song, but now finds it empty, unable to stir the same emotions it once did.

The Four of Cups also speaks to a kind of alienation within music. Imagine sitting in a room while a song plays, yet feeling untouched by it. Others might be moved, swaying, singing along, but for the one in the energy of this card, the music passes by like background noise, unable to reach the depths it once did. This is not the joyous communal experience of the Three of Cups, nor the solitary but purposeful focus of the Hermit. It is a state of emotional stagnation, where the heart has closed itself off to what could be beautiful.

Yet within this card, there is an unspoken potential. The unseen hand offering the fourth cup suggests that renewal is possible. In music, this is the subtle invitation to reconnect, to listen with fresh ears, to seek out something unfamiliar, to remember why music once mattered. Often, when a musician or composer reaches a creative block, the instinct is to push harder, to force inspiration. But the Four of Cups suggests that forcing may not be the answer. Instead, it asks for stillness, for reflection, for the willingness to sit in the discomfort of disconnection until something shifts.

Perhaps the remedy lies not in more music, but in silence. Just as a song needs pauses to create rhythm and meaning, the spirit sometimes needs space to regain its appreciation for sound. A musician who has grown tired of their instrument may need to step away for a time, allowing absence to rekindle longing. A listener who feels nothing from music may need to stop chasing old songs, allowing their heart to be surprised by something unexpected. This card does not rush the process. It honors the stillness, even the boredom, trusting that something new will eventually emerge.

There is also a hidden lesson in the Four of Cups about the way we consume music. In a world where sound is constant, where streaming platforms make every song instantly available, where playlists are endless, it is easy to become overwhelmed, to lose the ability to truly listen. When music is always present, it risks becoming noise rather than meaning. This card may appear as a reminder to be intentional with what we hear, to seek music that resonates deeply rather than simply filling space. It asks us to pause and ask: What am I truly listening for?

For an artist, the Four of Cups may signal the need to redefine their relationship with their craft. Perhaps they have been chasing external validation rather than genuine expression. Perhaps they have fallen into routine, playing the same chords, writing the same lyrics, out of habit rather than passion. This card suggests that something new is waiting to be discovered, but it cannot be forced, it must be recognized when the time is right. Inspiration is not absent; it is simply waiting for the right conditions to be received.

The Four of Cups is not about the loss of music, but about the moment before rediscovery. It is the pause in which we question, the quiet space before sound regains its meaning. It is the realization that even when music feels distant, it is never truly gone. The heart may be closed for a time, but when it opens again, the first note played, the first song heard, will carry all the more weight for the silence that preceded it.

Five of Cups

The Five of Cups is a card of sorrow, regret, and emotional loss. It carries the weight of grief, not just in what has been lost, but in the difficulty of turning toward what remains. The figure in the card stands cloaked in darkness, gazing down at three spilled cups while two still stand behind them, unnoticed. It is a card of mourning, of longing for what once was, of struggling to move forward when the echoes of the past still ring too loudly. In the world of music, this energy is deeply felt. It is the mournful melody, the song of heartbreak, the sound that carries the weight of absence and remembrance.

Music has always been a vessel for grief. It holds pain in a way that allows it to be expressed, shaping sorrow into something tangible. The Five of Cups exists in the space of lament, where sound becomes a means of mourning. It is the weeping violin, the blues guitar bending notes into sorrowful wails, the aching voice that trembles with the weight of loss. It is the song played at a funeral, the quiet melody that plays in an empty room long after someone has left. This card speaks to the way music intertwines with memory, how a single song can bring someone back in an instant, making absence feel present again.

There is something deeply personal about the way this card manifests in sound. It is not just about sadness, it is about longing, about holding on to something that can no longer be grasped. A musician embodying the Five of Cups may find themselves drawn to minor keys, to slow tempos, to lyrics that explore heartbreak and nostalgia. There is an almost involuntary pull toward songs that match the heaviness within, as if music itself understands and offers a place to rest in sorrow. This is why people return to sad songs in times of grief, not to deepen the pain, but to feel seen within it. The Five of Cups reminds us that music can be a companion in mourning, a way to sit with loss without needing to explain it.

Yet this card does not only speak to loss in the form of death or heartbreak. It also manifests in the grief of change; the dissolution of a band, the fading of artistic inspiration, the realization that something once cherished no longer holds the same meaning. A musician may look back at old compositions and feel a sense of loss, hearing echoes of a person they no longer are. A listener may return to a song that once meant everything, only to find it hollow, the emotions it once evoked now unreachable. The Five of Cups exists in these moments, in the aching recognition that time moves forward, even when we wish it would not.

But within the sorrow of this card, there is a subtle shift waiting to happen. The two upright cups behind the figure are still full, still present, even if they are unseen. This represents the way grief, once expressed, can transform. The saddest songs are often the ones that bring people together. A ballad of heartbreak, sung in isolation, may be heard by another who feels the same, and in that moment, a connection forms. The musician who pours sorrow into their art creates something that resonates beyond themselves, turning personal loss into something universal. This is the hidden gift of the Five of Cups, it does not take away pain, but it reminds us that we are not alone in it.

There is also the eventual turn that comes after mourning. Just as a song of sorrow eventually resolves, this card suggests that healing is possible, though it may not come immediately. The act of playing, singing, or even just listening to music allows emotions to be processed, step by step, note by note. A composer lost in grief may write through their pain, only to realize, one day, that the music has started to shift. A listener drowning in sorrow may hear a song and, instead of breaking down, feel the first small spark of acceptance. The Five of Cups does not erase loss, but it does offer the possibility of moving forward, not by forgetting, but by carrying the memory in a way that no longer weighs as heavily.

This card reminds us that music holds space for every emotion, even the ones that feel too heavy to carry alone. It is the song that allows us to cry when words fail. It is the melody that reminds us of what was, while gently guiding us toward what still is. It is the sound of mourning, but also the quiet promise that even in sorrow, music continues. And where there is music, there is something left to hold on to.

Six of Cups

The Six of Cups is a card of nostalgia, innocence, and the warmth of the past. It is the melody of childhood, the song that brings forgotten moments rushing back, the music that carries us to a time when the world felt simpler, softer, and full of wonder. This card exists in the space where sound and memory intertwine, where a single note or lyric can resurrect long-lost feelings, bringing them forward with the same vividness they had when first experienced. The Six of Cups is the soundtrack of the past, the songs that linger in our hearts, shaping who we are long after the moment has passed.

Music, more than almost anything else, has the power to transport. A song from childhood can bring back the scent of a summer evening, the feeling of small hands gripping a bicycle's handlebars, the echo of a parent's voice singing softly at bedtime. The Six of Cups is this phenomenon in its purest form; a return to something that once brought comfort, a revisiting of melodies that feel like home. It is the old records in a dusty attic, the lullabies once sung in the dark, the music box that plays a tune too familiar to be forgotten. It is the song that comes on unexpectedly and stops us in our tracks, filling the present moment with the ghosts of the past.

There is something deeply emotional about the way this card interacts with sound. Unlike the sorrow of the Five of Cups, which lingers in grief, the Six of Cups holds memory with tenderness. It does not mourn what has passed, it embraces it, allowing it to exist as a source of comfort. A musician embodying this energy might find themselves drawn to melodies that echo the past, writing songs that feel timeless, that capture the bittersweet beauty of remembering. A listener experiencing this card through music may seek out the songs that once meant everything to them, playing old mixtapes, revisiting childhood favorites, reconnecting with the sounds that shaped their earliest sense of self.

This card also speaks to the way music is passed down through generations. It is the folk song taught by a grandparent, the vinyl collection inherited from a parent, the old home videos where a familiar melody plays faintly in the background. These songs are more than just music, they are vessels of history, carrying the emotions, experiences, and stories of those who came before. In this way, the Six of Cups reminds us that music is a bridge between past and present, a thread that connects us to the people and places we have loved. Even when time moves forward, these sounds remain, allowing us to step back, if only for a moment, into the embrace of what once was.

But nostalgia, while beautiful, can also be intoxicating. The Six of Cups, for all its warmth, carries a subtle warning about lingering too long in the past. Music has the power to heal, but it can also hold us in place, trapping us in a loop of memory that prevents us from fully engaging with the present. A song that once brought joy might, over time, become a place of longing, a reminder of something that can never be relieved in the same way. The musician who only plays the songs of their youth may struggle to create something new, and the listener who clings to old favorites may find that nothing in the present resonates as deeply. This card invites us to embrace nostalgia without being consumed by it, to allow music to be a bridge rather than a cage.

Yet, when balanced, the Six of Cups is a reminder that the past is never truly lost. The songs we once loved remain within us, not as something to mourn, but as something to cherish. The lullaby sung in childhood may one day be sung again to another child. The old records may find new life in the hands of someone who was not yet born when they were first played. Music, like memory, is cyclical; it carries forward, weaving itself into new moments, new lives, new hearts.

Ultimately, the Six of Cups teaches us that music is not just about sound. It's about feeling, about connection, about the way certain melodies become intertwined with who we are. It is a love letter to the songs that made us, to the harmonies that cradled us in our earliest years, to the rhythms that shaped our understanding of joy and sorrow. It is a reminder that, though time moves forward, music has the power to bring us home, again and again, for as long as we are willing to listen.

Seven of Cups

The Seven of Cups is a card of dreams, illusions, and the vast possibilities that exist within imagination. It is the feeling of being overwhelmed by choices, the inability to distinguish between reality and fantasy, the intoxicating pull of ideas that shimmer with potential but lack substance. In the world of music, this card exists in the space between inspiration and confusion, between creativity and illusion. It is the artist lost in endless possibilities, the listener, entranced by soundscapes that blur the line between reality and dream, the song that evokes something just beyond reach: haunting, beautiful, fleeting.

Music has always had a way of pulling people into altered states. A melody can transport the mind to another world, a rhythm can hypnotize, a harmony can open doors to emotions never fully realized. The Seven of Cups is this sensation amplified; the moment when sound ceases to be just sound and becomes something otherworldly, something too vast to fully grasp. It is the shimmering echoes of a synthesizer, the layers of voices that melt into one another, the way a song can feel infinite, as though it stretches beyond the constraints of time. This card represents the boundless nature of music, the way it can conjure entire landscapes within the mind, painting scenes that exist only in the space between sound and silence.

But with such vastness comes uncertainty. The Seven of Cups is not just a card of wonder, it is also a warning against illusion. In music, this can manifest as an artist who becomes lost in their own ideas, unable to bring any one vision to life because the possibilities seem endless. It is the songwriter who starts a hundred songs but never finishes one, trapped in a cycle of dreaming rather than doing. It is the producer who layers sound upon sound, searching for perfection but never knowing when to stop, when to step back and say, "This is complete." The energy of this card can be intoxicating, but it also can be paralyzing. Too many choices can lead to no choice at all, too many visions can leave an artist wandering in circles, chasing something that never fully materializes.

For the listener, the Seven of Cups can represent the way music alters perception. It is the song that makes time feel slower, the soundscape that blurs the boundary between waking and dreaming. It is the sensation of getting lost in music, of feeling as though it carries you somewhere beyond yourself. This can be beautiful, even transcendent, but it can also be deceptive. Sometimes, the songs that seem to promise everything are simply mirages. The music industry itself thrives on the illusions of this card, selling artists as myths, promising that certain sounds will define an era, that one song can change everything. But the Seven of Cups reminds us that not all that glitters is gold, and not every dream manifests in the way we expect.

There is also something deeply personal about the way this card interacts with the creative process. Many musicians experience periods of inspiration that feel boundless, as if melodies and lyrics arrive from another realm, flowing effortlessly. This is the Seven of Cups in its most magical form: the moment when creativity is endless, when anything seems possible. But this state cannot last forever. If an artist lingers too long in this dreamlike space without grounding their ideas, the music may remain unfinished, existing only in fragments, in half-formed visions that never find their way into reality.

Yet, for all its illusions, the Seven of Cups is not a card of despair. It is a card of vision, of potential, of music that expands beyond the ordinary. It suggests that there is power in dreams, that some of the most breathtaking sounds come from places we cannot fully explain. It is the artist who follows inspiration wherever it leads, unafraid to experiment, to chase something unseen. It is the listener who allows themselves to be carried away, to explore new sonic landscapes, to hear music not just with their ears but with their entire being.

The lesson of this card is not to reject imagination, but to learn how to navigate it. The Seven of Cups teaches that music is limitless, but that not every idea can, or should, be followed. It reminds musicians to ground their visions in something real, to bring their dreams into form rather than letting them slip away. And for those who listen, it encourages discernment to recognize the difference between music that truly moves the soul and music that only dazzles for a moment before fading into nothingness.

This card reveals the paradox of music: it is both real and unreal, tangible yet intangible, a force that exists between the world we know and the worlds we can only imagine. The Seven of Cups invites us to explore those spaces, to lose ourselves in sound but also to remember that, at some point, we must return to reality and decide which dreams are worth bringing with us.

Eight of Cups

The Eight of Cups is a card of departure, of leaving behind what no longer serves, of walking away from something that once held meaning but now feels hollow. It is the moment when a musician sets down their instrument, when a song that once resonated no longer stirs the heart, when an artist realizes that the music they have been creating is no longer a reflection of who they are. This card exists in the space between sound and silence, in the decision to step away in search of something deeper, something more fulfilling.

Music is an emotional journey, one that often carries people through different phases of life. There are songs that define entire eras, albums that seem to capture the essence of a particular moment in time. But the Eight of Cups represents the realization that something is missing, that the music which once provided comfort, identity, or inspiration no longer fills the same space. This is not a card of sudden endings, it is not the dramatic crash of a cymbal or the sharp cut of a final note. Rather, it is the slow fade-out, the gradual realization that something is no longer enough.

There comes a time in many artists' lives when they must walk away from what they have known, leaving behind familiar sounds, styles, or even the people they once collaborated with. The Eight of Cups is the moment when a musician realizes they have outgrown their own work, when the music they once loved now feels stagnant, unable to express the depth of who they have become. It is the artist who abandons a successful career to pursue something more meaningful, the songwriter who stops writing love songs because their heart is no longer in them, the band member who steps away because they can no longer hear themselves in the music they play.

This card also speaks to the listener's experience. There are times when a favorite song suddenly feels empty, when an album that once felt like a personal anthem no longer resonates. Sometimes, this shift is subtle, a gradual drift away from old favorites, a slow embrace of new sounds that reflect an inner change. Other times, it is abrupt; a song that once brought joy now only brings discomfort, reminding the listener of a past they no longer wish to dwell in. The Eight of Cups represents this emotional detachment, the quiet moment when we realize we have moved on, even if we cannot see what comes next.

In many ways, this card mirrors the journey of silence in music. Silence is not merely the absence of sound. It is a choice, a space that allows for reflection, for transformation. When a musician walks away from their instrument, when a listener turns off a song mid-chorus, it is not necessarily an ending. It is often a pause, a necessary stillness before the next note can be played. The Eight of Cups teaches that stepping away is not failure, nor is it regret. It is an act of seeking, of trusting that something more meaningful lies ahead, even if it is not yet fully understood.

This card is a call to listen to intuition, to recognize when something no longer aligns with the soul. It is an invitation to walk away, not out of anger or despair, but out of the understanding that true artistry requires change. Some of the greatest musicians in history have embodied this energy, leaving behind genres, labels, and expectations to explore something new, even at the risk of alienating their audience. The Eight of Cups reminds us that true creative fulfillment cannot be found by staying in one place forever, there must be movement, even when that movement begins with a departure.

For those who listen, this card speaks to the way music evolves alongside us. The songs we love at sixteen may not be the songs we need at thirty. The music that once made us feel seen may eventually feel like a relic of a past self, something we listen to with fondness but no longer claim as our own. This is not a loss. It is growth. The Eight of Cups tells us that it is okay to walk away, to seek new sounds, to let go of the music that no longer holds us in the way it used to. It reminds us that there is always something more waiting beyond the familiar, something that will resonate with who we are now, rather than who we once were.

But this card also carries an element of longing. Walking away is never easy, even when it is necessary. There may be moments of doubt, of nostalgia, of wondering whether what was left behind was truly meant to be abandoned. A musician may question whether they should have stayed, whether they will ever find the same level of inspiration again. A listener may return to an old album, wondering if it will sound different this time, if it will feel like home once more. The Eight of Cups does not promise easy answers. It only promises that forward movement is necessary, even when the path is unclear.

This card reveals that music, like life, is a journey. There are moments of deep connection, of passion, of belonging but there are also moments of departure, of seeking, of stepping into the unknown. The Eight of Cups is not about turning away from music itself. It is about turning away from what no longer holds meaning in order to discover something that does. It is about knowing when to let go, when to be silent, when to trust that something more fulfilling awaits just beyond the horizon. And in that space, in the quiet between songs, in the absence of sound, something new begins to form: a melody not yet heard, a rhythm not yet felt, waiting for the moment when the time is right to begin again.

Nine of Cups

The Nine of Cups is a card of satisfaction, emotional fulfillment, and the deep joy that comes from seeing one's desires realized. It is the contented sigh at the end of a performance, the moment when a song reaches its perfect resolution, the feeling of hearing music that resonates so completely that it fills every empty space within. This card exists in the space where effort meets reward, where longing transforms into contentment, and where sound itself seems to embrace the listener in warmth and pleasure. The Nine of Cups is the moment when everything aligns, when the melody, the rhythm, and the emotion behind it merge into something undeniably satisfying.

This card represents the joy of creation, the feeling of writing a song that captures exactly what was meant to be expressed. It is the experience of playing music and being completely lost in it, no longer thinking, no longer doubting, just feeling. This is the energy of an artist who has found their voice, who is no longer searching but instead reveling in the ability to translate emotion into sound. It is the composer who, after endless revisions, finally hears the piece come together in perfect harmony. It is the singer who stands onstage, feeling the energy of the audience, knowing that the music has touched them in some unspoken way. The Nine of Cups is the reward for dedication, the moment of knowing that something truly meaningful has been created and shared.

Yet, this card is not just about personal achievement. It is also about the way music provides joy for others. Music, at its heart, is a gift, something that connects people across time and space. The Nine of Cups is the song that makes someone smile on a hard day, the melody that reminds a listener of a beautiful memory, the rhythm that makes a person want to dance. It is the artist who performs not just for themselves, but for the love of creating something that brings happiness to others. This card represents the moment when music is not just played, but received; when it becomes something more than sound, something deeply felt, something that lingers in the heart long after the last note fades.

For the listener, the Nine of Cups is the experience of finding the perfect song at the perfect time. It is the music that feels like it was made just for them, the lyrics that seem to articulate what could never quite be put into words. It is the album that plays on repeat because it feels like home, the song that makes everything feel right, even if only for a few minutes. There is a sense of gratitude in this card, an appreciation for the way music can provide exactly what is needed, whether it is comfort, excitement, inspiration, or pure enjoyment. The Nine of Cups reminds us that music is not just an escape, it is a source of deep, genuine fulfillment.

But while this card is often called the "wish fulfillment" card, it also carries a quieter lesson. The joy it represents is not fleeting pleasure, not the brief high of a passing moment, but something deeper, something that comes from knowing that what is desired has truly been attained. This means understanding that fulfillment does not come from chasing trends, from seeking validation, or from constantly striving for more. It comes from creating, playing, or listening with presence, with gratitude, with the knowledge that what exists in this moment is enough.

This is not to say that there is no room for ambition or growth. The Nine of Cups is not about complacency, it is about association. A musician who embodies this energy does not stop creating; rather, they create from a place of joy rather than from a place of lack. They do not make music because they feel they must prove something, but because they love the process, because it brings them happiness. A listener who embodies this energy does not constantly search for the next best thing; instead, they savor what they have, finding deep satisfaction in the music that already exists in their life. This card reminds us that fulfillment is not found in always looking ahead, but in truly embracing what is here now.

There is also an element of celebration in the Nine of Cups. This is the energy of a triumphant encore, of a record release party, of a moment when an artist looks out at the audience and sees nothing but smiling faces. It is the feeling of completion, of knowing that something meaningful has been accomplished. In this sense, the Nine of Cups encourages us to celebrate the music that brings us joy, to recognize its impact, to be present in the experience, to allow ourselves to feel the full depth of the pleasure it offers.

This card reveals that music, at its best, is a source of deep and abiding happiness. Whether as a creator or a listener, the Nine of Cups reminds us that fulfillment is not found in reaching for something just out of grasp, but in fully embracing the beauty of what already exists. It is the feeling of hearing a song that is so perfect it seems to complete something inside of us. It is the realization that music has the power to satisfy the soul in a way that nothing else can. And in that moment, there is nothing more to seek; only the sound, the feeling, the joy of being completely immersed in it.

Ten of Cups

The Ten of Cups is a card of deep emotional fulfillment, joy, and a sense of completion that extends beyond the self and into the realm of connection. It is not just personal satisfaction, but shared happiness, a feeling of wholeness that comes from being in harmony with those around us. This card embodies the kind of experience that transcends individual emotion and becomes something collective, something greater than the sum of its parts. It is the symphony that moves an entire audience to tears, the band that has played together for decades and still finds joy in every note, the moment when a song unites a crowd in pure, unfiltered elation.

Music, at its most powerful, is not just about the individual, it is about the way sound brings people together. The Ten of Cups is the energy of voices raised in harmony, of a choir filling a cathedral with a resonance so deep it seems to touch the soul. It is the feeling of standing in a concert crowd, thousands of strangers singing along to the same song, feeling as though, in that moment, they are all part of something singular and sacred. It is the connection between musicians who anticipate each other's movements without a word, whose instruments blend seamlessly because they are playing not just as individuals, but as one. This card is the embodiment of that unity, the reminder that music has the power to dissolve barriers, to remind us that joy is amplified when it is shared.

For a musician, the Ten of Cups is the culmination of years of practice, passion, and dedication. It is the realization that music is not just about techniques or success, but about the feeling it creates, the way it brings people together. This is the artist who plays not for fame or recognition, but because music is their lifeblood, because they know that what they create has the power to uplift, to heal, to bring light into the world. It is the band that stays together not out of necessity, but out of love for the craft and for each other. It is the composer who, after years of searching, finally hears their work performed in full, realizing that every struggle, every moment of doubt, was worth it for this one perfect moment. The Ten of Cups is the reassurance that the journey was not in vain, that the dream was worth chasing, that the fulfillment music brings is not fleeting, but lasting and real.

This card represents the way music becomes a part of life's happiest moments. It is the song played at a wedding, the lullaby sung to a child, the melody that reminds someone of home. It is the album that a family listens to together on road trips, the playlist of a summer that will always be remembered. The Ten of Cups is the music that accompanies celebration, the soundtrack to love, friendship, and belonging. It is the way a simple song can hold memories, carrying the emotions of a time and place long after the moment itself has passed.

There is something profoundly emotional about the way this card interacts with sound. It is the feeling of hearing a song and knowing, instinctively, that it carries meaning beyond words. It is the music that makes people laugh, dance, cry, and embrace. It is the reminder that, in a world that often feels fragmented, music has the power to remind us of what truly matters. The Ten of Cups is not about fleeting pleasure. It is about deep, resonant joy, the kind that lingers, that shapes the heart, that reminds us of who we are and who we love.

At its core, this card is about harmony. Not just musical harmony, though that is certainly part of it, but the kind of harmony that comes from being at peace with oneself, with others, with the world. It is the balance found in a perfectly constructed song, where every note serves a purpose, where nothing feels out of place. It is the way a melody can feel inevitable, as though it could exist no other way. The Ten of Cups suggests that this kind of harmony is not an accident, it is something that comes from love, from dedication, from an openness to the beauty that exists in the world.

But even in its happiness, the Ten of Cups carries a quiet lesson. Fulfillment is not something to be chased endlessly, nor is it something that comes from external validation. It is found in presence, in gratitude, in the ability to recognize that the most beautiful moments in life are often simple, unforced, and deeply personal. A song does not have to be complex to be powerful, and joy does not have to be extravagant to be real. The Ten of Cups reminds us that, in the end, what matters most is not perfection, but connection; the music, like love, is meant to be shared.

Ultimately, this card reveals that music is not just about sound; it is about feeling, about community, about the way melodies can weave people together in ways that words alone cannot. It is the love song that has been played at a thousand weddings, the folk tune passed down through generations, the anthem that unites people across cultures and backgrounds. The Ten of Cups reminds us that music has always been, and will always be, a source of joy, a celebration of life, a testament to the beauty of human connection. And, in that, there is something truly magical. Something worth holding onto, something worth singing about, forever.

Page of Cups

The Page of Cups is the dreamer, the artist at the beginning of their journey, the soul that feels deeply and expresses freely. I always think of this card as the kid that drops out of medical school to go to art school. It is the card of creative exploration, emotional vulnerability, and the willingness to embrace inspiration in its purest form. In music, the Page of Cups is the first song written late at night in a bedroom, the melody that seems to appear out of nowhere, the moment of sudden creative insight that leads to something beautiful. It is the openness to possibility, the willingness to play without fear, and the joy of discovering one's own artistic voice.

Music, like emotion, is fluid, and the Page of Cups understands this intuitively. This is the card of those who do not yet fully understand the technical aspects of their craft but who create anyway, driven by the simple desire to express what is in their heart. It is the songwriter who hums a tune into their phone while walking home, the child who picks up an instrument and plays instinctively, the person who, without ever having sung before, suddenly finds themselves carried away by a song. There is no pressure in this energy, no concern for perfection; only wonder, curiosity, and a willingness to let creativity unfold naturally.

For a musician, the Page of Cups represents the beginning of something new. It is the fresh idea that sparks excitement, the unexpected collaboration that opens new doors, the moment of artistic vulnerability that leads to real connection. This is the energy of someone who is willing to experiment, to explore different sounds, to follow their intuition rather than adhering to strict rules. There is something playful about this card, a reminder that music is meant to be enjoyed, that it is an act of creation that thrives on spontaneity. Some of the most memorable songs have been written in moments of sudden inspiration, when an artist allows themselves to be surprised by what emerges.The Page of Cups embraces this uncertainty, knowing that true artistry often begins with a single, unguarded note.

There is also a deep emotional sensitivity in this card, one that resonates with the way music has the power to move people. The Page of Cups does not shy away from feeling but embraces it fully, allowing emotion to flow into sound without reservation. This is the artist who writes from the heart, unafraid to be raw and real, unafraid to be seen. It is the songwriter who pens lyrics that feel deeply personal, only to discover that they resonate universally. The Page of Cups reminds us that music is not about technical mastery alone. It is about expression, about the ability to take something internal and share it with the world in a way that others can feel.

This card represents a sense of wonder, an openness to new experiences, and a deep emotional connection to sound. It is the person who hears a song and feels as though it was written just for them, who lets music guide them into uncharted emotional territory, who is willing to be vulnerable in the presence of sound. The Page of Cups is the person who puts on a song and lets themselves be carried away by it, who finds themselves crying over lyrics they had never noticed before, who feels as though music speaks in a language more truthful than words alone. There is something almost magical in this experience, a reminder that music is not just something we listen to, it is something we feel, something that moves through us, something that changes us.

There is also an element of surprise in the Page of Cups, a sense that inspiration can come from anywhere. This is the moment when a musician stumbles upon a new chord progression that feels right, even if they can't explain why. It is the listener who hears a new genre for the first time and falls in love instantly. It is the way a single song can unlock an entirely new world of sound, opening doors that had never been considered before. The Page of Cups reminds us that music is limitless, that creativity does not follow a linear path, that some of the most profound artistic discoveries happen by accident.

This card also carries a sense of innocence, a lack of cynicism, a belief that music is something magical and pure. It is the person who still believes in the power of a song to change the world, who still finds meaning in every note, who is not afraid to be moved. In a world that often values detachment and irony, the Page of Cups stands as a reminder that sincerity is powerful, that feeling deeply is not a weakness but a strength. Music is an emotional language, and the Page of Cups speaks it fluently, without hesitation, without self-doubt.

Yet, even in its joy, this card carries an important lesson. The Page of Cups reminds us that creativity must be nurtured, that inspiration alone is not enough. A melody may arrive like a gift from the universe, but it must be shaped, refined, turned into something tangible. The Page of Cups is the spark, the moment of insight, but it is up to the artist to turn that inspiration into something real. This card invites musicians and listeners alike to remain open to possibility but also to honor the creative process, to give their ideas the attention they deserve, to recognize that artistic expression is not just about inspiration, it is about devotion.

This card reveals that music, at its heart, is an act of love. A love for sound, for feeling, for connection, for the beauty of expression itself. The Page of Cups is the reminder that music is not just something to be understood but something to be felt, something to be experienced in its purest form. It is the invitation to listen with an open heart, to create without fear, to embrace the moments of unexpected inspiration that remind us why we fell in love with music in the first place. It is the reminder that every great song, every masterpiece, every life-changing piece of music begins with a single, simple note and the willingness to follow where it leads.

Knight of Cups

The Knight of Cups is the romantic, the idealist, the one who moves through life guided by emotion and intuition rather than logic or practicality. This card represents the artist who follows their heart wherever it leads, the songwriter who crafts melodies from deep wells of feeling, the performer who pours every ounce of their soul into their art. The Knight of Cups does not create for fame or recognition but for the pure pursuit of beauty, meaning, and emotional truth. There is something deeply poetic in this energy, a sense that music is not just sound but an expression of something greater, something transcendent.

This Knight is on a journey, not one of conquest or battle, but of discovery. In the realm of music, this means a relentless search for inspiration, for the perfect lyric, the perfect chord progression, the perfect song that captures an emotion too vast for words alone. The Knight of Cups is the musician who wanders from place to place, collecting stories and weaving them into melodies, never content to stay in one place for too long. There is a restless spirit in this card, a deep hunger to experience everything, to feel everything, and to translate those experiences into something meaningful. Music is not just a career or a pastime for this knight. It is a way of life, a calling, an unshakable force that drives them forward.

There is a sense of deep vulnerability in this card. The Knight of Cups does not hide behind a facade of detachment but instead embraces the full intensity of their emotions, allowing themselves to be moved, changed, and even broken by the beauty and pain of the world. This is the artist who writes love songs that feel as though they are bleeding onto the page, who sings with a voice that carries the weight of every heartbreak and every dream. Their music is not calculated or strategic; it is raw, honest, and deeply personal. This Knight does not create from a place of intellectual distance but from a place of deep feeling, allowing emotion to guide every note and every word.

This card represents the pursuit of artistry for its own sake, the willingness to chase inspiration wherever it may lead. It is the songwriter who follows their muse without questioning whether their work will be commercially viable, the performer who gets lost in the moment on stage, the composer who hears music in the rhythm of the rain and the whispers of the wind. The Knight of Cups does not measure success in terms of accolades or financial gain but in moments of pure artistic transcendence, in the feeling of having created something true and beautiful.

But there is also a shadow side to this relentless pursuit. The Knight of Cups can be so caught up in the dream that they lose sight of reality, so intoxicated by inspiration that they forget the discipline required to bring an idea to life. In music, this can manifest as an artist who begins a thousand songs but finishes none, always chasing the next wave of emotion, the next fleeting vision. It can be the musician who falls in love with the idea of their craft but struggles with the patience and dedication required to refine it. There is a danger to being so swept away by feeling that nothing ever solidifies, that the music remains a dream rather than a tangible creation.

For the listener, the Knight of Cups represents the ability to be completely transported by sound, to let music carry them away into new emotional landscapes. This is the person who hears a song and feels it in their bones, who listens to lyrics as if they were written specifically for them, who allows themselves to be swept up in the magic of melody and rhythm. Music, for them, is not just entertainment. It is a portal, a way of experiencing life more deeply. They do not listen passively but with their whole heart, allowing the sound to sink into them, to reshape them, to move them in ways they cannot explain.

This card is also a reminder that music is a form of romance, not just in the traditional sense of love songs, though it certainly includes those, but in the way music has the power to make life feel more vivid, more poetic, more meaningful. The Knight of Cups understands that a song can turn an ordinary moment into something unforgettable, that the right melody can make a simple drive feel like a journey through a dream. There is a cinematic quality to this energy, a sense that life is meant to be experienced fully, with a soundtrack playing in the background, elevating even the smallest moments into something sacred.

At its core, the Knight of Cups teaches that music is a quest, not a destination. There is no final achievement, no moment when an artist can say they have reached the peak of their creativity, no song that will ever fully capture everything they wish to express. Instead, there is only the journey, the endless pursuit of sound, emotion, and meaning. This card invites musicians and listeners alike to embrace that journey, to follow the music wherever it leads, to remain open to inspiration in all its forms. It is a reminder that the heart of music lies not in perfection but in passion, in the willingness to be vulnerable, in the courage to feel deeply and express freely.

The Knight of Cups is the embodiment of what it means to love music, not just as an art form but as a way of seeing the world. It is the reminder that music has the power to stir the soul, to ignite the imagination, to make us fall in love not just with a melody, but with life itself. It is the song that makes someone close their eyes and drift into memory, the chord progression that sends shivers down the spine, the lyrics that capture a feeling so perfectly that it feels like magic. And in the end, that is what this knight seeks, not fame, not fortune, but the pure, intoxicating magic of sound.

Queen of Cups

The Queen of Cups is the guardian of emotion, intuition, and artistic depth. She is the one who feels without boundaries, who understands the unspoken language of the heart, who lets herself dissolve into the currents of sensation and meaning. In music, this card embodies the artist who does not merely perform but channels something greater, something profound and unseen. The Queen of Cups does not approach music with calculation but with an open heart, allowing sound to flow through her like water, shaping itself into something luminous, something healing, something real.

Music under the influence of the Queen of Cups is not about technique or control, it is about surrender. It is about stepping into the vast ocean of feeling and allowing oneself to be carried by its tides. This is the artist who closes their eyes as they sing, not because they are unaware of their surroundings, but because they are somewhere else entirely, lost in the world the music has created. It is the instrumentalist who plays as though their soul is speaking through the strings, the pianist whose hands move across the keys as if in a trance, the composer who weeps as they write because the music is not just something they create, it is something they feel, something they live.

There is an intimacy to this card, a depth of connection that goes beyond mere performance. The Queen of Cups does not seek applause or validation; she creates because she must, because music is her language, her way of existing in the world. There is no separation between herself and the sound she makes.

She is the song, and the song is her. This is the singer who bares their soul in every note, the songwriter who draws from the deepest wells of memory and emotion, the musician who understands that music is not just about entertainment but about healing, about transformation, about the kind of catharsis that only melody and rhythm can provide.

The Queen of Cups represents the music that reaches into the most hidden places of the heart. This is the song that makes someone cry without understanding why, the melody that lingers in the mind long after it has ended, the album that feels like an old friend, holding space for emotions too vast to put into words. There is something deeply personal in this card, a reminder that music is not just something external, it is something internal, something that echoes the soul's own rhythms, something that reflects back the feelings we may not even know we are carrying.

This is also the music of nostalgia, of memory, of dreams. The Queen of Cups understands that a song is never just a song. It is a portal, a time machine, a thread that connects the past, present, and future. A melody can bring back a moment long forgotten, a voice can resurrect a love lost to time, a simple note can stir feelings that have lain dormant for years. This card reminds us that music is not linear; it exists outside of time, carrying with it the echoes of everything it has ever touched.

There is also an element of mystery in the Queen of Cups, an understanding that music, like emotion, is not always meant to be understood. Some songs do not have clear meanings, some melodies defy explanation, some harmonies feel like whispers from another world. This card does not demand logic; it does not ask for structure or analysis. Instead, it invites surrender, the willingness to feel without needing to explain. Music under the Queen of Cups is like a dream; it shifts, it flows, it moves through the listener in ways that cannot be grasped or contained. It is the song that feels like it belongs to another lifetime, the melody that haunts without reason, the lyric that arrives like a message from something unseen.

For a musician, the Queen of Cups is both a blessing and a challenge. She brings inspiration that is pure and boundless, but she also demands truth. She does not allow for empty words or hollow melodies. She asks for authenticity, for vulnerability, for the kind of music that strips away pretense and leaves only the raw beating heart of the artist. This is not the card of commercial success or catchy hooks; it is the card of depth, of artistry, of the kind of music that lingers in the soul long after the final note has faded.

There is a sacredness to the energy, a sense that music is not just an art form but a kind of magic, a ritual, a way of touching something beyond the physical world. The Queen of Cups understands that sound is vibration, that vibration is energy, and that energy has the power to heal, to shift, to transform. This is the music that soothes grief, that mends broken hearts, that brings peace in moments of despair. It is the lullaby sung to a child in the dark, the hymn that fills a cathedral with something unnameable, the song that feels like a prayer even if no god is named.

But there is also a warning in this card; the reminder that such depth can be overwhelming, that the ocean of feeling can sometimes become too vast, too consuming. The Queen of Cups feels everything, and in music, this can mean becoming lost in the very emotions that inspire the art. The artist who creates from such deep places must learn to navigate their own depths without drowning in them, must learn to channel feeling without being consumed by it. Music is a powerful force, but it must be held with care, with balance, with the understanding that even the most beautiful sound can become too much if it is not grounded.

The Queen of Cups teaches that music is not just something we hear, it is something we experience, something we absorb, something that changes us from the inside out. It is not a product, not a performance, not a means to an end. It is a force, a current, a tide that moves through the soul and leaves it altered. She reminds us that music is a mirror, reflecting our own depths back to us, showing us what we carry, what we long for, what we have lost and what we have yet to find.

She is the sound of rain against the window, the hum of a distant melody in the night, the song that feels like home even when we cannot explain why. She is the music that heals, that lingers, that speaks when words fail. And in her presence, we are reminded that some things in this world are meant to be felt rather than understood, that sometimes, the deepest truths come not in language, but in sound.

King of Cups

The King of Cups represents emotional wisdom, balance, and the ability to channel deep feelings with grace and control. He is the artist who has journeyed through the depths of emotion, experienced the highs and lows of creative passion, and emerged with the ability to shape that raw energy into something refined and powerful. This card signifies a profound connection to the emotional core of sound, but with a level of mastery that prevents the artist from being overwhelmed by their own intensity. The King of Cups does not simply feel, he understands, he guides, he directs emotion into something intentional, something lasting.

This is the musician who has learned that art is not just about inspiration but also about discipline. He knows that a song must be more than just a fleeting burst of passion; it must be crafted with care, with patience, with the knowledge that true artistry is about refining raw emotion into something that can stand the test of time. He does not let his emotions dictate his work blindly but instead uses them as a source of power, channeling them into music that carries both depth and structure.

There is an effortless quality to the King of Cups, a sense that he knows exactly what he wants to express and how to express it. His melodies do not meander, they flow with purpose. His lyrics are not indulgent, they are intentional, shaped by experience and insight. He does not create from a place of reckless abandon but from a place of knowing, from an understanding of the emotional weight that music carries and the responsibility that comes with wielding that power. His music is both deeply felt and carefully crafted, both spontaneous and deliberate, both intuitive and intellectual.

For the performer, the King of Cups represents a presence that is both magnetic and composed. He is the artist who stands on stage and commands attention, not through theatrics or excess, but through sheer emotional authenticity. His voice does not waver with nerves, yet it carries the full weight of every feeling behind it. He does not lose himself in the music, but he does not hold back either. There is a perfect balance, a knowing of when to let go and when to remain in control. He is the singer who can bring a room to tears with a single note, the instrumentalist who seems to speak through their instrument as though it were an extension of their soul, the composer who writes with such emotional clarity that the music feels inevitable, as though it has always existed.

The King of Cups is the moment when a song reaches deep into the heart and offers solace, guidance, or understanding. His music does not simply evoke emotion; it helps process it. This is the album that one turns to in times of heartbreak, not to wallow, but to make sense of the pain. It is the song that carries the weight of nostalgia but does not drown in it, the melody that brings peace rather than chaos. The King of Cups understands that music is a vessel for healing, for wisdom, for catharsis, and he ensures that his sound carries that purpose.

This card also speaks to the evolution of the artist, the moment when one moves beyond youthful infatuation with music and into a deeper, more sustained relationship with it. The King of Cups has seen the passionate highs and crushing lows of artistic life. He has known the intoxicating rush of inspiration and the quiet frustration of creative stagnation. He has experienced the doubt, the fear, the vulnerability that comes with pouring one's soul into art. But he has also learned how to navigate these challenges with grace. He no longer swings wildly between creative ecstasy and despair. He understands that music, like emotion itself, must be tended to with care, with patience, with wisdom.

There is a generosity in this energy, a sense that the King of Cups does not create music solely for himself, but for others. His songs are not just personal expressions, they are gifts. He understands the role that music plays in the lives of those who listen, the way it can become a refuge, a guide, a mirror. He doesn't create to impress or to prove himself; he creates because he knows that music is one of the most profound ways to connect. His music is not self-indulgent, even when it is deeply personal because he knows that the emotions he channels are universal.

In collaboration, this card represents an artist who brings emotional intelligence into every interaction. The King of Cups is not ruled by ego; he does not need to dominate a song, a performance, or a creative process. Instead, he listens, he adapts, he understands the unspoken rhythms of those around him. He knows how to give space when needed, how to lift others up, how to guide without controlling. In a band, he is the steady presence, the one who can diffuse tensions, who can see the bigger picture. He understands that music is about synergy, balance and creating something greater than the sum of its parts.

Yet, for all his mastery, the King of Cups has not lost touch with the raw emotion that fuels his art. He has not become cold or detached; he has not let his experience dull his passion. Instead, he has refined it. He still feels deeply but he does not let those feelings control him. He is not ruled by impulse, but he has not lost the spark of inspiration. His music still carries the full weight of emotion, but it does so with precision, with depth, with an understanding that makes it even more powerful.

This card is a reminder that the greatest artists are not those who burn out in a blaze of chaotic passion, nor those who harden themselves against feeling. The greatest artists are those who learn to hold both passion and discipline, both emotion and control, both inspiration and wisdom. The King of Cups is the embodiment of this balance, the master of the art of feeling, the musician who has found the perfect harmony between the wild ocean of emotion and the steady hand of craftsmanship.

He reminds us that music is more than an expression. It is a responsibility. To create sound is to shape the emotions of those who listen. To write lyrics is to speak into the hearts of others. To perform is to hold space for feeling, to allow others to experience something profound. To do this well, to do this with mastery, is not about losing oneself in the music, it is about understanding it, shaping it, guiding it and, in doing so, giving it the power to truly touch the soul.

The Minor Arcana: Swords

The suit of Swords is the realm of thought, intellect, communication, and the piercing clarity of truth. It is the suit of the mind, where music is not just an expression of emotion but a vehicle for sharp, unrelenting insight. Music under the influence of Swords is not passive; it is active, deliberate, cutting through illusions and exposing what lies beneath the surface. It is the song that forces a reckoning, the lyric that carries the weight of an idea, the melody that slices through silence like a blade.

The essence of Swords in music is both cerebral and visceral. There is a tension in this suit, an awareness that words and sound are not just forms of entertainment but instruments of power. The greatest protest songs, the most confrontational lyrics, the sharpest critiques of society all belong to the realm of Swords. This is the suit of the songwriter who wields language with precision, the artist who is unafraid to speak truth, even when it's uncomfortable. There is no softness here, no easy sentimentality, only the stark honesty of what must be said, what must be acknowledged, what can no longer be ignored.

The suit of Swords understands that music is an intellectual exercise as much as it is an emotional one. The mind is just as much a part of the creative process as the heart, and some of the most impactful music comes not from raw feeling but from the ability to articulate those feelings with clarity and intent. This is the music of analysis, of observation, of commentary. It is the carefully structured composition, the complex arrangement that challenges the listener to follow its intricacies, the lyric that lingers long after the song has ended, demanding to be examined, unpacked, understood.

Yet Swords are also the suit of conflict, of struggle, of the pain that comes with seeing too clearly. There is an edge to this music, a sharpness that can cut both ways. The artist who writes from the perspective of Swords is often one who has grappled with inner demons, who has wrestled with doubt, who has fought to understand the world and their place within it. This is the music of tension, of urgency, of the desperate need to express something that cannot remain unspoken. It is the song written in the aftermath of heartbreak, not to grieve, but to make sense of the wreckage. It is the album born out of existential questioning, each track a battle with meaning, with identity, with truth.

But the Suit of Swords is not just about struggle, it is also about clarity. Music in this realm has the power to bring order to chaos, to turn the fragmented thoughts of the mind into something structured, something articulate. This is where music becomes philosophy, where lyrics become poetry with razor-sharp precision. It is where the songwriter refines their voice, honing their message until it strikes with undeniable force. There is a discipline here, a refusal to settle for vague expression, an insistence on getting the words exactly right, on crafting melodies that carry not just feeling but thought, intention, depth.

This suit also speaks to the power of communication through music. It is the battle cry, the manifesto, the confessional monologue spoken in melody. The suit of Swords reminds us that music does not exist in a vacuum; it engages with the world, shapes it, critiques it, forces it to look at itself. Every song is a dialogue, a reflection of the time in which it was written, an argument being made, a point being driven home.

The performers who embody the energy of Swords are the ones who stand on stage with unwavering conviction, whose words cut through the noise and demand to be heard. Their music is not just about self-expression, it is about awakening something in those who listen. They do not simply perform; they challenge, they provoke, they leave the audience thinking long after the final note has faded.

But with this sharpness comes the potential for destruction. The suit of Swords warns of the double-edged nature of intellect and critique. The same clarity that allows music to illuminate truth can also be turned inward, leading to self-doubt, cynicism, even despair. This is the suit of the tortured artist, the one who sees too much, who thinks too much, who is caught in an endless loop of questioning, analyzing, breaking apart every lyric, every chord, until nothing feels real anymore. The artist under the weight of Swords may struggle to find peace, trapped in their own mind, unable to let go of the need to perfect, to understand, to control.

Yet even in its most difficult aspects, Swords offers something invaluable: perspective. Music in this realm does not simply stir emotion, it forces awareness. It is the song that wakes the listener from complacency, the melody that cuts through nostalgia and reveals the raw truth beneath. It is the artist who refuses to sugarcoat, who understands that music is not just a form of escape but a form of confrontation, a way of engaging with reality rather than retreating from it.

At its highest expression, Swords brings wisdom. The greatest artists in this realm are those who have learned to wield their intellect without being consumed by it, who have found the balance between clarity and compassion. They understand that music must not only dissect but also heal, must not only question but also offer understanding. These are the musicians who use their art to illuminate, to educate, to bring light even in the darkest corners.

The suit of Swords teaches that music is as much about thought as it is about feeling. It is the suit of the storyteller, the lyricist, the composer who builds intricate soundscapes with precision and intent. It is the realm of those who use music as a tool not just for beauty, but for truth. In that truth, no matter how sharp, there is always the possibility of transformation.

Ace of Swords

The Ace of Swords arrives like a blade through fog, slicing open the air with its clarity and force. It is the beginning of thought, the first flash of insight, the pure potential of the mind given shape and direction. The Ace of Swords represents the moment when an idea arrives so sharply, so undeniably, that it changes everything. It is not a gentle whisper of inspiration, but a strike, a sudden awareness that cuts through confusion, revealing exactly what must be said and how it must be said. It is the seed of musical truth, uncompromising and luminous, pulsing with the electricity of something newly born.

This card in the realm of sound is often experienced as that visceral jolt of clarity a musician or songwriter feels when the right phrase appears, or a melody forms with such precision it feels as though it already existed. The Ace of Swords is not hesitant or dreamy. It is urgent, exact, driven by purpose. It brings with it the hunger to express something essential, something that burns at the core of one's consciousness, something that has perhaps long been circling the edge of awareness but now emerges, unavoidably, like lightning.

The creative spark associated with this card is fiercely mental. The emotions might be secondary, or still catching up; what leads is the message, the idea, the clarity of intention. It is the song born from a sudden understanding, the track written after a revelation, the riff or beat that demands to be captured before it disappears. And when it strikes, there's no mistaking it, there's a sharpness, a velocity to it, as though the very air around the idea has shifted. A musician may feel possessed by it, unable to rest until the sound is formed, recorded, shaped into something tangible.

Yet the Ace of Swords is not just about inspiration, it's about truth. It is the uncompromising edge of honesty that certain music carries, the kind that refuses to flinch from reality. This is the song that names what others are too afraid to speak. This is the protest track, the breakup anthem that doesn't try to soften the blow, the raw verse that turns personal pain into universal clarity. The Ace of Swords does not care for comfort; it demands precision, and it slices through illusion with unapologetic force. Its power lies in its refusal to obscure or dilute. When channeled into music, it results in art that confronts, exposes, and elevates the truth.

For a listener, music under the influence of this card can feel like an awakening. It is the lyric that stops them in their tracks, the chord progression that unlocks a buried realization, the beat that stirs the mind even more than the body. It does not allow passivity. It stirs, provokes, activates. It does not bring comfort, but it does bring clarity. And sometimes, clarity is the most profound comfort of all. The relief of finally understanding something, even if that understanding hurts.

The Ace of Swords also relates to the intellectual structure of music. It reminds us that music is not only passion, not only instinct, but also a craft that requires thought and intention. It is the composer who studies the patterns of harmony to make them sing with new meaning. It is the producer who knows exactly when to cut a track to sharpen its impact. It is the wordsmith who carves lyrics with the precision of a scalpel, ensuring that every syllable strikes where it must.

In another sense, the card can mark the beginning of a new phase in a musician's creative life. It is the moment of choosing direction, of claiming a voice, of realizing what must be made and why. There may be a sense of release as the artist finally grasps their message, their vision, their path. There is a reason the sword is often raised upward in depictions of this card: it is a symbol of elevation, of rising above confusion, of seeing clearly and speaking with conviction. In music, this is the album that redefines a career, the single that changes everything, the shift from imitation to authenticity.

But the sword, as always, cuts both ways. The clarity of the Ace can also bring discomfort. To see clearly is to lose the illusions we may have clung to for safety. Music born of this card may not always be received easily. It may challenge, unsettle, or even offend. But that is its gift: it refuses to be small. It forces attention. It makes space for what has been silenced.

The Ace of Swords also reminds us of the power of the voice itself. Whether through lyrics, tone, or the sheer shape of a song, this card honors the force of articulation. It challenges artists to speak, not just to sing but to bring language to feeling, to give sound to silence, to turn the private into the public with courage and clarity. In this way, the Ace can be a call to use music as a tool for expression that matters. It asks, what are you trying to say? And more importantly, why aren't you saying it louder?

The Ace of Swords in music is a call to truth. It demands that artists rise to the clarity of their own minds, trust in the force of their insight, and use their craft as a conduit for that brilliance. It is the sound of awakening, of emergence, of a voice sharpened by awareness and ready to be heard. And while the journey it begins may not always be easy, it is always necessary because some songs are not written to soothe, but to change the world.

Two of Swords

The Two of Swords is a card of paradox, of stillness that conceals tension, of indecision that demands clarity, of opposing forces held in delicate balance. It represents the quiet before a choice, the space between knowing and acting, where the mind is caught between two competing truths. When this energy is translated into music, it takes on a unique resonance. The Two of Swords becomes the space between sound and silence, the emotional pause in a song, the internal conflict of the artist unsure of which way to go. It is a card of musical suspense, of listening inward before making a move, of holding one's breath just before the resolution.

This card represents the inner tension that precedes creative release. The Two of Swords is not about motion, it is about the weight of potential, the pull in opposite directions, and the burden of having to choose. In the musical realm, this may emerge during those moments when an artist feels caught between two sonic worlds, two creative identities, two messages. It is the point in the writing process where multiple ideas compete for dominance, where a song could go in many directions but hasn't yet found its true path. The artist sits at the crossroads, instrument in hand, listening not to what is already formed but to what is quietly asking to emerge.

Musically, the Two of Swords can be likened to the pregnant pause in a composition; the intentional use of silence, of restraint. It is the moment just before the beat drops, before the melody changes, before the lyric lands. In that space, there is immense power. Listeners lean forward, waiting, expecting, sensing that something is about to happen even though it hasn't arrived. Composers who understand the power of the pause know that music lives not only in sound, but in the air around it. The Two of Swords honors this truth. It is the breath held in a phrase, the unresolved chord that lingers just a moment too long, the refrain withheld until the exact moment it will make the greatest impact.

On a deeper level, The card also speaks to the emotional dissonance that music often reveals. A musician might be torn between expressing vulnerability and maintaining control, between giving voice to personal experience and crafting something that transcends the personal. This is the song that sits in the drafts folder, unfinished, not because it lacks inspiration, but because it's too close to something painful, or because its final form remains elusive. It may be that the artist does not yet feel ready to speak the truth the song requires. Or it may be that the song demands a level of clarity the artist has not yet reached. The Two of Swords is the space where emotion and intellect collide but do not yet reconcile.

This card can manifest in the way an artist holds back, consciously or unconsciously. There may be a guardedness, a tension beneath the surface of their delivery, a sense that something is being held in check. And yet, this restraint can be hauntingly powerful. It draws in the audience, makes them curious, invites them into the silence to wonder what lies beyond it. In this way, the Two of Swords becomes a kind of emotional suspense, where the absence of certainty or resolution is itself a form of expression.

For the listener, this card may reflect the personal process of interpreting music, especially when drawn to songs that mirror their own indecision or emotional complexity. These are the tracks that don't offer easy answers, that live in ambiguity, that refuse to spell out their messages too clearly. The lyrics might contradict themselves, or the tone may shift between moods without settling.

And yet, this reflects real human experience; the way we can feel joy and sorrow at once, or love and resentment, or hope and dread. The Two of Swords invites the listener to sit with that ambiguity, to let the song speak in riddles, to find solace not in resolution but in honest uncertainty.

This card can also appear in the life of a musician when they are facing a significant choice, perhaps a shift in genre, a question of authenticity versus marketability, a fork in the road between collaboration and solitude. The decision may not yet have a clear answer. The music being created during this time may carry that uncertainty, and that's not a flaw, it's a feature. Songs written from this space are often raw with potential. They may never be fully finished in the traditional sense, but they capture something that polished work sometimes misses: the beauty of becoming.

The Two of Swords highlights the role of intuition in the creative process. The figure in the card is often depicted blindfolded, suggesting that sight is not the guiding force here. Instead, the musician must rely on inner knowing, on subtle cues, on feeling their way forward through the dark. This is the songwriter who sets down their pen and listens. It is the composer who walks away from the piano for a moment and lets the melody find them instead of forcing it. It is the percussionist who trusts the moment of stillness, knowing that sometimes the most powerful beat is the one that comes after restraint.

In its highest expression, the Two of Swords teaches that stillness is not stagnation. It is a kind of sacred listening. It is the place where one waits for the right one, the right word, the right choice, not out of fear, but out of respect for the process. The mind may be caught in duality, but the soul is not rushed. Sometimes the most profound moments come not from certainty, but from the willingness to remain in that space of questioning, of waiting, of quiet.

Eventually, the swords must lower. The blindfold must come off. The silence will give way to sound. But the gift of the Two of Swords is in teaching that there is power in pause, truth in indecision, and beauty in the moment just before creation takes its final form. In music, this is where potential becomes possibility, where conflict becomes texture, and where the unspoken becomes the seed of something extraordinary.

Three of Swords

The Three of Swords is perhaps one of the most haunting cards in the tarot: a heart pierced cleanly by three blades, suspended in a stormy sky, drenched in rain. The imagery is stark, uncompromising, and deeply emotional. In music, this card resonates as the aching ballad, the devastating verse, the soft unraveling of the soul made audible. It represents heartbreak in its purest form, not just romantic loss but emotional pain in all its raw, internalized intensity. When this card appears in the context of music, it speaks to those songs that come not from the desire to entertain or uplift but from the aching need to release sorrow that would otherwise consume the body from within.

The Three of Swords carries with it the sound of mourning, of lament, of vulnerability cracked wide open. It is the moment after everything changes. This isn't the kind of grief that passes quickly; it's the kind that lingers in the bones, reshapes the self, and demands to be witnessed. In the hands of a musician, this pain becomes a tool not to exploit or exaggerate, but to understand and transform. Music under the influence of this card is not polished or perfectly composed; it is often stripped down, trembling at the edges, raw with a truth that doesn't need to be pretty to be powerful.

This card does not arrive during moments of stability. It enters when the heart has been fractured, when words have failed, and when silence itself feels too loud. And in that space of devastation, music becomes the only way forward. The Three of Swords is the song written at three in the morning when sleep is impossible and everything feels too heavy to hold. It is the melody hummed through tears, the journal scrawled into lyrics, the voice cracking in the middle of the verse because it hurts too much to sing clearly. But the break in the voice, the off-key tremor, the silence between phrases, these things are not flaws. They are the soul speaking.

Music connected to the Three of Swords often carries the kind of beauty that wounds you gently. It might be sparse, acoustic, slow-moving. It might be furious, wailing, unfiltered. But always, there is truth. This card demands an honesty that can't be denied. It refuses to look away from suffering. It honors the reality that sometimes love ends, sometimes trust is broken, sometimes hope dissolves into memory. And it tells us that the expression of this pain is not only valid, it is necessary. Without it, we might drown. But through music, we can surface.

The artists who work with this card's energy are often not afraid to bleed a little onto the page or into the microphone. They know that there is a kind of sacredness in pain, not because it is noble, but because it is universal. They reach for the aching chord progressions, the echoing reverb, the verses that speak of loss without metaphor. They write not to be heard, but to survive. And in doing so, they offer listeners the chance to feel seen in their own pain. A song birthed from the Three of Swords may not solve anything, but it doesn't have to. Sometimes it is enough to say, "I know what it's like to hurt, too."

There is also an important aspect of catharsis here. The Three of Swords is the pain that transforms; not immediately, but eventually. When felt fully, heartbreak clears the way for something new. It strips away illusions. It demands that we confront what we've lost, but it also shows us what we are made of. In music, this becomes the album that marks a turning point, the single that signals a breakup or a breakdown, the shift in tone that suggests someone has truly lived through something. It is not an aesthetic, it is a reckoning. The songs born from this place are often among the most memorable, not because they are grand or technically perfect, but because they say exactly what the listener didn't know they needed to hear.

Listeners gravitate toward music of the Three of Swords when they, too, are carrying something heavy. These are the songs played on repeat after loss, the ones that accompany long walks at dusk, the ones turned up loud to drown out an inner scream. They don't offer answers. They offer companionship. They say, "You're not alone in this." And that is a powerful medicine. Not a cure, but a balm.

For the artist, working with this energy may not be comfortable, but it is essential. There is a temptation, often, to bypass pain; to spiritualize it or intellectualize it. But the Three of Swords resists this. It requires the musician to go to the core of the feeling, to sit in the ruins, and to listen. Not just to the inner voice, but to the silence that comes after the heartbreak. There is music in that silence, too. Music waiting to be born not in spite of the pain, but because of it.

And even when the worst has passed, the songs remain. Music has a way of preserving emotion, freezing it in time. A track written in the depths of grief can still bring tears years later, not because the wound hasn't healed, but because the memory of the wound is honored in the notes. The Three of Swords teaches that pain can be transformed, not erased. It can become part of the architecture of who we are, and through music, it becomes part of something larger than the self.

This card does not promise a happy ending, but it does promise truth. And in music, truth, however painful, is sacred. The Three of Swords reminds us that to feel deeply is not a weakness. To break is not to fail. To write and sing and scream from the heart's most wounded place is an act of extraordinary courage. And in doing so, we do not only express our own heartbreak, we give voice to a universal song, one that echoes through every broken heart, every solitary night, and every morning that comes after.

Four of Swords

The Four of Swords is a card of stillness, retreat, and restoration. It comes after the upheaval of the Three of Swords, offering a moment to breathe and gather strength before the journey continues. This card resonates deeply as the space where silence becomes as essential as sound, where pauses allow for reflection, and where retreat creates the conditions for renewal. The Four of Swords is the rest in the measure, the moment when the musician steps away from the instrument, the quiet introspection that informs creative expression. It is the sound of stillness, the power of restraint, and the wisdom of knowing when to pause.

Music is often perceived as a continuous flow of melody and rhythm, but the Four of Swords reminds us that silence is an integral part of its language. In the same way that the card represents the need to step back from external pressures, Without these moments of quiet, music would lose its shape and impact. The Four of Swords teaches us that stillness is not absence; it is presence in a different form.

For a musician, this card often appears during times of creative exhaustion or emotional overwhelm. It signals the importance of stepping back, not out of defeat, but as an act of self-preservation and preparation. The Four of Swords is the sanctuary after the storm, a reminder that periods of rest are not indulgent but necessary. After a period of intense creative output or emotional turmoil, the artist must retreat to recover their strength. This is not the emptiness of a creative block but the fertile silence where new ideas are quietly brewing.

The relationship between the Four of Swords and music also lies in the act of listening. When the mind is quiet, when external noise is set aside, the musician can truly hear, not only the sounds around them but the rhythms of their own thoughts and feelings. This card invites the artist to reconnect with their inner voice, to find inspiration not through frantic activity but through peaceful introspection. It is the moment when the songwriter sits in an empty room, not writing, but simply being, letting melodies drift in and out of consciousness like whispers. It is the space where intuition is sharpened, where the seeds of new music are planted.

Music connected to the Four of Swords offers solace and calm. These are the tracks that feel like sanctuary, the kind you turn to when the world feels too loud. They may be slow, ambient, minimalist, or meditative. They don't demand attention; they invite you to sink into their atmosphere. Listening to this kind of music is like stepping into a quiet chapel or lying down in a sunlit field. It creates a space for reflection, for emotional processing, for simply being. In this way, the Four of Swords reminds us that music doesn't always have to be energetic or confrontational. Sometimes its greatest power lies in its ability to hold us gently.

This card also speaks to the role of restraint in musical composition. A piece that honors the Four of Swords is one that understands the value of simplicity. It doesn't try to fill every space with sound; it allows moments of stillness to carry their own weight. Think of a sparse piano melody where the notes seem to hover in the air, or a singer's voice that trails off into silence, leaving the listener suspended in the pause. These choices are not empty, they are deliberate. They reflect an understanding that music, like life, needs space to breathe.

In the creative process, the Four of Swords can be a reminder to embrace cycles of rest and renewal. Artists often push themselves to keep producing, fearing that stillness will lead to stagnation. But this card offers a different perspective: that stepping away can be an essential part of the journey. A musician who honors the Four of Swords knows when to set down their instrument, not because they are uninspired, but because they trust that inspiration will return when the time is right. In these moments of pause, the subconscious has room to process, to dream, to find connections that might be missed in the rush of constant activity.

The Four of Swords also highlights the importance of retreat in a broader sense. For an artist, this might mean withdrawing from external expectations or the pressures of an audience to focus on their inner world. It is the act of creating not for others, but for oneself. This might manifest as an intimate home recording session, a journal of fragmented lyrics written in solitude, or the quiet exploration of a new sound without the weight of needing to perfect it. In this retreat, the artist reconnects with the pure joy of making music, free from the need for validation.

This card reminds us that music itself can act as a form of rest. A listener turning to music during times of stress or fatigue is often seeking the energy of the Four of Swords. The right song can feel like a deep exhale, a moment of calm in the chaos, a chance to recharge. This is why so many people turn to music as a form of healing. It provides a space to retreat inward, to reflect, to feel held. In this way, the Four of Swords represents not only the act of making music but also its capacity to provide sanctuary for those who listen.

The Four of Swords also teaches patience. It is not a card of immediate action or resolution. It doesn't promise quick answers or instant inspiration. Instead, it invites a slower rhythm, one that honors the natural ebb and flow of creativity and life. In music, this might mean allowing a composition to evolve over time, trusting that the pauses and quiet moments are as important as the crescendos. It might mean sitting with unfinished work, letting it rest until it's ready to emerge. This patience is not passive, it is active trust in the process.

The Four of Swords is a card of quiet power. It reminds us that music, like life, is not a constant crescendo. It has peaks and valleys, sound and silence, action and rest. To honor the Four of Swords in music is to embrace these cycles, to find beauty in stillness, and to trust that even in moments of retreat, the soul is still singing.

Five of Swords

The Five of Swords is a card steeped in conflict, both external and internal. Its imagery consists of a figure holding swords while others walk away in defeat under a stormy sky and reflects a complex web of victory, loss, and the costs of ambition. In music, the Five of Swords emerges as a representation of discord, tension, and the unresolved dynamics that can exist within the creative process, performance, and the music industry itself. It is the sound of fractured harmonies, strained relationships, and the relentless pursuit of success that leaves collateral damage in its wake. This card does not shy away from uncomfortable truths; instead, it confronts the darker aspects of human and artistic endeavor, urging musicians and listeners alike to reflect on the cost of their actions and ambitions.

In the context of music, the Five of Swords often manifests in the tension between collaboration and competition. Bands, orchestras, and creative partnerships can be fertile ground for conflict, as egos clash and differing visions pull in opposite directions. The Five of Swords asks: what happens when the desire to "win" overrides the unity of the group? In a band setting, this might be the member who dominates creative decisions without regard for others, or the disputes over credit that fracture once-cohesive dynamics. The resulting music might still carry brilliance, but it often comes with an undertone of unease, a tension audible in the final product. The Five of Swords reminds us that even the most harmonious compositions can carry the weight of discord beneath their surface.

This card also speaks to the individual artist's internal battles. For a songwriter or composer, the Five of Swords can represent the push and pull between creative integrity and commercial pressures. An artist might feel compelled to compromise their vision in order to appeal to a wider audience, but at what cost? The Five of Swords poses this question with an edge: is the fleeting satisfaction of external success worth the internal dissonance it creates? The songs written under this energy might carry traces of this conflict. Lyrics that seem at odds with the music, melodies that feel forced, or a sense of disconnection between artist and audience.

On a deeper level, the Five of Swords embodies the struggles that arise when art becomes entangled with ambition. In the competitive world of music, the drive to succeed can sometimes overshadow the joy of creation. This card captures the shadow side of ambition: the sacrifices made, the relationships strained, and the self-worth tied too tightly to external validation. It's the artist who burns bridges in pursuit of their goals, only to find themselves standing alone with their victories. These stories are not uncommon in the music industry, where fame and success are often built on fragile foundations. The Five of Swords serves as a cautionary reminder that even the most glittering achievements can feel hollow if they come at too great a cost.

Musically, the energy of the Five of Swords often find expression in pieces that feel unresolved or intentionally dissonant. Compositions that embrace sharp, jarring notes, irregular rhythms, or unpredictable shifts in tone reflect the conflict inherent in this card. Think of genres like punk, with its raw, rebellious edge, or avant-garde music that challenges conventional notions of harmony. These are the sounds that provoke, unsettle, and demand attention. They embody the Five of Swords by refusing to conform, even if it means alienating some listeners. The music born from this energy doesn't seek to soothe. It seeks to confront. It asks the audience to sit with discomfort and to consider what lies beneath the surface.

For listeners, the Five of Swords can be an invitation to explore music that challenges them emotionally or intellectually. These might be songs that speak to personal struggles or societal issues, forcing the listener to confront truths they'd rather avoid. The lyrics might cut deep, revealing the complexity of human relationships, the pain of betrayal, or the weight of moral ambiguity. These are not songs of resolution or peace; they leave threads hanging, questions unanswered, and emotions raw. Yet, in their honesty, they offer a kind of catharsis. The Five of Swords reminds us that music doesn't always have to heal, it can also illuminate the wounds.

This card also highlights the power dynamics that exist within the music industry. It brings to mind the stories of exploitation, manipulation, and inequity that often lurk behind the scenes. Artists who feel taken advantage of by labels, producers, or even their peers may resonate with the Five of Swords. It represents the uneasy victories where one party's gain comes at another's expense. These stories are woven into the history of music, from disputes over songwriting credits to the systemic inequities that favor profit over artistry. The Five of Swords calls attention to these imbalances, urging reflection on how they shape the music we hear and the lives of those who create it.

At its core, the Five of Swords is a card of reckoning. It asks artists and audiences alike to confront the ways in which conflict, ambition, and power shape the creative process. For musicians, it might signal a need to evaluate their motives and relationships, whether they are creating from a place of connection or competition, whether they are honoring their truth or sacrificing it for external gain. For listeners, it offers a lens through which to examine the music they consume: what stories are being told, and whose voices are being amplified or silenced?

The beauty of the Five of Swords lies in its complexity. While it's undeniably a card of challenge and discord, it also holds the potential for growth and awareness. In music, this might look like an artist confronting their own shortcomings, repairing fractured relationships, or using their platform to address injustice. It might be the band that reunites after years of estrangement, finding a deeper connection through their shared history. Or it could be the listener who, through a difficult song, gains insight into their own emotions or experiences. The Five of Swords doesn't promise an easy resolution, but it does offer the possibility of transformation through honesty and reflection.

The Five of Swords reminds us that music, like life, is not always harmonious. It carries dissonance, tension, and unresolved questions. But within these challenges lies the opportunity for growth, understanding, and connection. Whether we are creating, performing, or listening, this card invites us to engage with the complexities of the human experience, to face the shadows as well as the light, and to find meaning in the discord. Music under the influence of the Five of Swords might not be easy to hear, but it is profoundly necessary. It tells the truths that need to be told, even when they are difficult.

Six of Swords

The Six of Swords is a card of movement, of leaving behind the troubled waters of the past to journey toward calmer shores. In its imagery, a small boat carries figures across a river, their backs turned to what lies behind. It is a card of quiet transformation, marked by the bittersweet recognition that leaving is necessary, even if it comes with grief. This card represents the songs that guide us through transitions, the compositions that mirror journeys of healing and growth, and the moments when music becomes both the vessel and the destination.

Music has long been a companion to transition. It is there when we pack our lives into boxes and drive to a new city, when we sit in the stillness of an airplane hurtling us toward an unknown future, or when we close a door one last time, carrying only the memories of what was. The Six of Swords lives in these moments. It is the song playing softly in the background as we say goodbye, the melody that gives us the courage to face the uncertainty ahead. In these instances, music becomes a bridge, a way to hold both the pain of leaving and the hope of arriving.

The essence of the Six of Swords is movement, not in haste, but with intention. Musically, this can be reflected in pieces that evoke a sense of journey. Think of a song that starts with a melancholy tone but gradually lifts, as if carrying the listener from one emotional state to another. The transitions within the music mirror the emotional journey of the card. These are not abrupt or jarring changes; they flow naturally, much like the slow, steady movement of a boat across water. The Six of Swords reminds us that healing and change take time, and music has a unique way of capturing this gradual process.

This card speaks to the act of creating music as a form of processing and release. After periods of upheaval, many artists turn to their craft as a way to make sense of what they've experienced. The songs born from this space often carry a deep sense of introspection. They are not necessarily about resolution but about the act of moving forward, even when the path is unclear. A songwriter might sit down with their instrument, not to craft a polished masterpiece, but to let their emotions flow into sound. These moments of raw expression become a form of self-guided therapy, a way to navigate the waters of change.

The Six of Swords also reflects the role of music as a guide. In times of uncertainty or emotional turbulence, music often serves as a source of comfort and direction. It can be the song that reminds us we're not alone, the lyrics that articulate feelings we struggle to name, or the melody that gives us the strength to keep going. In this way, the Six of Swords represents the musicians and artists who create these lifelines for others. They may not know the full impact of their work, but their music becomes the boat that carries countless listeners through their own difficult journeys.

There is also a sense of community within the Six of Swords. In the card's imagery, the journey is not undertaken alone; the figures in the boat move together. Similarly, music often creates a shared experience, even among strangers. A song can unite people who are navigating their own transitions, providing a sense of collective understanding. At a concert, for example, thousands of individuals might sing along to a song that holds personal meaning for each of them, yet in that moment, they are bound by the shared act of expression. The Six of Swords reminds us that while transitions are deeply personal, they are also universal, and music has the power to bridge these individual and collective experiences.

This card also resonates with the idea of emotional release. Just as the figures in the boat leave behind the weight of their past, music often helps us release what no longer serves us. A song can bring tears that cleanse, laughter that lightens the load, or simply a sense of peace that makes the journey ahead feel less daunting. The Six of Swords suggests that while the process of letting go can be painful, it is also freeing. Music becomes the soundtrack to this release, helping us to honor what we're leaving behind while gently guiding us toward what lies ahead.

The water in the Six of Swords is significant. It symbolizes emotion, depth, and the subconscious. In music, water often appears as a metaphor for these same themes. Songs evoke the imagery of rivers, seas, or storms often carry the energy of the Six of Swords, exploring themes of movement, change, and emotional depth. These songs remind us that transitions are not just external, they are deeply internal as well. The currents of emotion that carry us forward are reflected in the melodies and rhythms that speak to our hearts.

For the listener, encountering music tied to the Six of Swords can be a profoundly healing experience. These are the songs that feel like a safe harbor in times of distress, the ones that remind us it's okay to grieve, to hope, to move forward. They don't deny the pain of transition; They acknowledge it while offering the promise of something better on the horizon. A song under the influence of the

Six of Swords doesn't try to fix everything. It simply sits with you in the boat, accompanying you on the journey.

The Six of Swords also challenges us to embrace the unknown. In music, this might look like exploring new genres, instruments, or styles. A musician navigating a personal or professional transition may use this energy to reinvent themselves, leaving behind what no longer feels authentic and venturing into uncharted territory. This is not always an easy process; it requires courage and trust. But the Six of Swords reminds us that every journey begins with a single step or a single note. And within that step lies the potential for transformation.

The Six of Swords teaches us that music, like life, is a series of transitions. It carries us from one emotional state to another, from one chapter to the next. It provides a way to process, to heal, and to grow. Whether we are creating, performing, or listening, music becomes the vessel that helps us navigate the waters of change. And though the journey may be uncertain, the Six of Swords assures us that we are moving toward calmer, brighter shores. Through music, we find the strength to keep going, one note, one step, one breath at a time.

Seven of Swords

The Seven of Swords is a card that embodies cunning, strategy, and subversion. Its imagery, a figure sneaking away with a handful of swords, looking back to assess if their actions have gone unnoticed, carries with it themes of secrecy, deception, and independence. Yet, the card is not limited to moral judgments; it also speaks to the necessity of unconventional thinking and the courage to carve one's own path. When applied to music, the Seven of Swords represents the complex interplay of authenticity, ambition, and the sometimes-hidden dynamics of creation. It is the spirit of rebellion, the craft of reinvention, and the quiet truths that lie beneath the surface of what we hear and create.

In the world of music, the Seven of Swords often manifests as the unspoken strategies behind artistic success. Artists rarely arrive at their creative destination by following a straightforward path. Instead, they navigate the often treacherous terrain of their careers with ingenuity, taking risks that others might shy away from. This might be the musician who reinvents their style in the face of declining relevance, risking alienation from their audience in order to remain true to their evolving self. It could also be the songwriter who creates under a pseudonym, seeking the freedom to explore themes they feel unable to address under their public persona. In these acts of strategy and subversion, the energy of the Seven of Swords is present.

This card also calls attention to the dynamics of power and ownership within the music industry. The Seven of Swords may reflect the artist who feels compelled to "take back' their creative power in a world that often commodifies it. This might involve reclaiming rights to their music, circumventing exploitative contracts, or finding alternative ways to distribute their work. The card's association with secrecy and cunning suggests that these actions are not always overt; they may occur behind the scenes, in quiet negotiations or unpublicized decisions. For the artist, these strategies are necessary for survival, but they also raise questions about the broader systems that necessitate such actions.

Musically, the Seven of Swords is the sound of defiance. It is found in genres that challenge the status quo, from protest songs to experimental compositions that defy conventional structures. These pieces often carry an undercurrent of rebellion, a refusal to adhere to the rules. Think of punk rock's raw energy, hip-hop's incisive commentary, or the avant-garde works that intentionally disrupt listeners' expectations. These forms of music align with the Seven of Swords in their willingness to question, to subvert, and to provoke. They invite listeners to confront uncomfortable truths, whether about society, relationships, or themselves.

The Seven of Swords represents the artist's inner conflict between authenticity and the pressures of external expectation. Musicians may feel the need to hide parts of themselves in order to fit into certain molds, while simultaneously longing to express their truth. This tension can lead to music that feels layered and complex, with hidden meanings embedded in lyrics or compositions. The Seven of Swords asks what is being concealed, and why? It challenges both artists and listeners to dig deeper, to uncover the motivations and fears that influence the creative process.

For the listener, encountering music under the influence of the Seven of Swords can be a deeply introspective experience. These are songs that resonate on a subconscious level, revealing their full meaning only after multiple listens. They might include cryptic lyrics, unexpected shifts in tone, or melodies that linger in the mind long after the song has ended. Such music mirrors the card's themes of mystery and revelation, encouraging listeners to look beyond the surface and engage with the hidden layers of the work.

The Seven of Swords also speaks to the act of borrowing and reimagining within music. Throughout history, musicians have drawn inspiration from one another, incorporating elements of existing works into their own creations. This process, while essential to artistic evolution, is not without its controversies. The line between homage and appropriation, between innovation and theft, can be blurry. The Seven of Swords invites us to examine these dynamics with honesty acknowledging both the creative ingenuity and the ethical questions they raise. In doing so, it highlights the duality of the card: the potential for brilliance, as well as the shadows that often accompany it.

Collaboration, too, can fall under the purview of the Seven of Swords. While music is often celebrated as a collective endeavor, it is not immune to the complexities of human relationships. Egos, competition, and differing visions can lead to hidden agendas or power struggles within groups. The Seven of Swords reflects the unspoken dynamics that can arise in these situations, whether it's the band member who feels overshadowed, the producer who subtly steers the project in their preferred direction, or the songwriter who withholds their best material for a solo venture. These undercurrents may not always be visible, but they shape the music in profound ways.

On a more personal level, the Seven of Swords resonates with the solitary aspects of creativity. It reflects the moments when an artist retreats from the world, working quietly and independently to bring their vision to life. This might involve breaking away from traditional methods or defying expectations in order to pursue a unique idea. For some, solitude is necessary for creative freedom; for others, it can be isolating. The card acknowledges both the empowerment and the challenges that come with forging one's own path.

The Seven of Swords reminds us that music, like life, is rarely straightforward. It is shaped by hidden stories, strategic decisions, and the interplay of light and shadow. For musicians, this card serves as a reminder to embrace their ingenuity, to navigate challenges with courage and resourcefulness, and to remain true to their creative vision, even when the path is unclear. For listeners, it invites a deeper engagement with the music they love, encouraging them to explore the layers of meaning and intention that lie beneath the surface.

The Seven of Swords is not a card of easy answers or simple truths. It reflects the complexities of human nature and the ways in which these complexities manifest in art. Yet within its shadowy energy lies a powerful invitation: to think critically, to act boldly, and to approach the creative process with both honesty and imagination. Music under the influence of the Seven of Swords may not always offer comfort, but it does offer insight, transformation, and the opportunity to connect with the hidden depths of ourselves and the world around us.

Eight of Swords

The Eight of Swords is a card that captures the feeling of being trapped, bound by unseen forces or self-imposed limitations. In its imagery, a blindfolded figure stands surrounded by swords, seemingly unable to move or escape. While the scene suggests imprisonment, it also hints at a deeper truth: the swords form an incomplete barrier, and the bindings appear loose, suggesting the possibility of freedom. This duality, the tension between perceived restriction and the potential for release, resonates deeply in the realm of music. The Eight of Swords speaks to the struggles that musicians and listeners face in moments of creative or emotional paralysis, and it illuminates music's unique ability to break through such barriers.

The Eight of Swords often emerges during periods of stagnation or creative block. These are the times when inspiration seems distant, and the tools that once brought joy feel like heavy burdens. This paralysis can be exacerbated by external pressures: deadlines, criticism, or the relentless demands of the music industry. Yet, as the Eight of Swords reminds us, the barriers that seem insurmountable are often rooted in perception. The blindfold of the card symbolizes the internal doubts and fears that prevent progress. For the artist, this might take the form of perfectionism, imposter syndrome, or the fear of failure. The challenge lies in recognizing these inner obstacles and confronting them head-on.

Music itself can embody the energy of the Eight of Swords, offering a mirror to the listener's own experiences of entrapment and liberation. Songs that explore themes of confinement, whether physical, emotional, or psychological, allow listeners to confront their own feelings of restriction. These compositions often carry a sense of yearning, a desire to break free, even as they dwell within the constraints of their subject matter. A somber ballad might describe a love that feels suffocating, while a driving rhythm could evoke the restless energy of someone pushing against their limits. Such music becomes a cathartic experience, offering an outlet for emotions that might otherwise remain unspoken.

For many artists, the act of creating music under the influence of the Eight of Swords can be a way of navigating their own struggles. When words fail, melodies often speak, allowing musicians to process their emotions in a language that transcends logic. The repetitive structure of certain genres, like blues or minimalist compositions, mirrors the cyclical thoughts that often accompany feelings of entrapment. In these works, the repetition itself becomes a form of expression, conveying the sense of being caught in an endless loop. Yet even within this structure, subtle variations hint at the possibility of change, echoing the card's message that freedom is always within reach.

The Eight of Swords also speaks to the limitations imposed by societal norms and expectations, particularly in the music industry. Artists often find themselves confined by the industry. Artists often find themselves confined by the demands of their audience or the market, pressured to conform to trends or adhere to a particular image. This can be especially challenging for those who wish to experiment or evolve beyond the style that initially brought them success. The card's energy reminds musicians of the importance of questioning these external pressures and finding ways to reclaim their creative autonomy. This act of defiance is not always easy, but it is necessary for true artistic growth.

On a broader level, the Eight of Swords invites us to consider the ways in which music can both reflect and challenge systems of oppression. Throughout history, music has served as a voice for the voiceless, giving expression to the struggles of marginalized communities. Spirituals, protest songs, and freedom anthems often carry the energy of the Eight of Swords, speaking to the experience of living within systems that seek to limit or silence. These songs are not just laments; they are acts of resistance, embodying the hope and determination needed to break free from chains, both literal and figurative.

Engaging with music under the influence of the Eight of Swords can be a deeply introspective experience. These are the songs that hold up a mirror to our own feelings of confinement, inviting us to explore the sources of our discomfort. They might feel uncomfortable at first, stirring emotions we would rather avoid. Yet in doing so, they also open a path toward healing. The Eight of Swords teaches us that the only way to move forward is to confront what binds us, and music becomes a powerful guide in this process.

In moments of personal struggle, music often provides a way to reclaim a sense of agency. A single song can become a lifeline, reminding us that we are not alone in our experiences. The lyrics might articulate emotions we have struggled to name, or the melody might offer a sense of calm in the midst of chaos. Even in the darkest moments, music has the ability to create a space of possibility, where the first steps toward freedom can be imagined.

The energy of the Eight of Swords also challenges musicians and listeners alike to consider the role of silence. In a culture that often prioritizes constant output and consumption, silence can feel like a void, an absence of meaning. Yet the card suggests that within silence lies the potential for transformation. For the musician, this might mean stepping away from their craft temporarily, allowing space for new ideas to emerge. For the listener, it might involve sitting with the silence between songs, allowing the emotions stirred by the music to fully resonate. In both cases, the absence of sound becomes an integral part of the journey.

The Eight of Swords reveals the transformative power of perspective. The swords that appear to trap the figure in the card are not insurmountable barriers; they are challenges that can be overcome with awareness and effort. Similarly, music reminds us that even in the face of adversity, there is always a way forward. Whether through the act of creating, listening, or simply being present with sound, music becomes a tool for breaking through the blindfolds of fear and doubt.

Music is not just an escape; it is a means of liberation. It offers a way to confront and transcend the limitations that hold us back, whether they come from within or not. Through its rhythms, melodies, and silences, music carries us beyond the confines of our own minds, showing us that freedom is always closer than it seems. It is the breath of fresh air after a long period of suffocation, the spark of hope in a moment of despair. In this way, the Eight of Swords reminds us that while we may feel trapped, we are never truly without the tools to set ourselves free.

Nine of Swords

The Nine of Swords is a card steeped in the imagery of anguish and sleepless nights. It depicts a figure sitting upright in bed, head in hands, surrounded by the ominous presence of nine swords looming above. This is a card of mental and emotional struggle, of anxieties that whisper in the dark and fears that feel insurmountable. Yet within its shadowy depths, the Nine of Swords also carries the potential for release, for finding solace through understanding and expression. In music, this card's energy resonates profoundly, reflecting the ways in which sound and song can articulate despair, confront the darkness, and ultimately offer a path to healing.

Music has long been a medium for exploring the human experience of pain and fear. The Nine of Swords reminds us of the universality of these feelings, even when they are isolating in the moment. Songs born from this energy often feel deeply personal, as though the artist has opened a window into their soul. These pieces resonate because they give voice to emotions that many struggle to articulate: grief, regret, guilt, and the haunting specter of what might have been. The rawness of these compositions can be overwhelming, yet their honesty offers a sense of connection, reminding listeners that they are not alone in their suffering.

The Nine of Swords often manifests during moments of deep inner turmoil. These are the times when creation feels less like a choice and more like a necessity, a way to process the intensity of their emotions. Writing or performing under this card's influence can be an act of catharsis, a way of externalizing what might otherwise remain trapped within. The result is music that feels unflinchingly real, unafraid to delve into the depths of despair. Whether it is a mournful ballad, a thunderous cry in heavy metal, or the haunting strains of a minor key melody, this music carries the weight of the artist's vulnerability.

The Nine of Swords also speaks to the way music interacts with the human psyche during moments of distress. For the listener, encountering music that reflects their own pain can be both confronting and comforting. It provides a mirror to their emotions, allowing them to feel seen and understood. Yet this mirror is not passive; it invites transformation. A song that captures the essence of sorrow can also offer a way through it, guiding the listener toward a place of acceptance or release. The Nine of Swords teaches that facing the darkness is a necessary step toward finding light, and music often serves as a companion on this journey.

This card's energy can also be found in the darker themes of certain musical genres. Gothic rock, doom metal, and melancholic folk often dwell in the emotional landscapes of the Nine of Swords, using sound to evoke the weight of despair. These genres embrace the shadows, weaving narratives of loss, fear, and existential uncertainty. Yet even in their darkest moments, they often carry a thread of beauty, a reminder that there is value in exploring these emotional depths. In this way, the Nine of Swords encourages us to confront the parts of ourselves we might prefer to avoid, using music as a bridge to understanding and integration.

The Nine of Swords also reflects the pressures and anxieties that many musicians face in their creative lives. The industry itself can be a source of intense stress, with its relentless demands for success, innovation, and visibility. Artists may wrestle with feelings of inadequacy or the fear of failure, their minds racing with self-doubt in the quiet hours of the night. These internal struggles often bleed into their work, creating music that feels charged with tension and vulnerability. Yet the act of creating under such conditions can also be a way of reclaiming agency, transforming fear into something tangible and meaningful.

Listeners, too, engage with the energy of the Nine of Swords through the act of interpretation. A deeply emotional song can feel like an invitation to explore one's own inner world, to sit with the feelings that arise and allow them to unfold. This is not always a comfortable process. The Nine of Swords reminds us that healing often requires moving through discomfort, facing the shadows that lurk at the edges of our consciousness. Music becomes a tool for this exploration, offering a structure within which emotions can be safely navigated.

This card also highlights the interplay between silence and sound. In the stillness of a sleepless night, when the mind is loudest and the world feels most empty, music can fill the void. A single note, a hushed melody, or a whispered lyric can cut through the silence, offering a sense of presence and grounding. For some, the act of listening in these moments becomes a ritual, a way of connecting with something larger than themselves. The Nine of Swords suggests that even in our darkest hours, there is something to hold onto, and music often embodies that lifeline.

The card's imagery also brings to mind the idea of unresolved tension, both emotionally and musically. In composition, tension is often used to evoke a sense of unease or anticipation, keeping the listener on edge. Dissonant chords, unresolved progressions, and haunting melodies can all reflect the restless energy of the Nine of Swords. Yet just as the card implies the possibility of release, music, too, often moves toward resolution. The shift from tension to harmony mirrors the emotional journey of facing one's fears and emerging stronger on the other side.

The Nine of Swords reminds us of the transformative power of vulnerability. In music, as in life, it is often through embracing our fears and anxieties that we find a path forward. For the artist, this might mean creating work that feels deeply personal, even if it risks exposure or criticism. For the listener, it might mean allowing oneself to fully feel the emotions that a song evokes, trusting that the process will lead to healing. The card teaches us that darkness is not something to be avoided but something to be understood and integrated.

In the end, the Nine of Swords and music share a common purpose: to illuminate the complexities of the human experience and to remind us that even in our darkest moments, we are not alone. The shadows may feel overwhelming, but they are not insurmountable. Music, with its unique ability to convey emotion and connect us to one another, becomes a beacon in the night, a reminder that hope is always within reach. The Nine of Swords may dwell in the realm of fear, but it also points toward the power of expression, understanding, and ultimately, liberation

Ten of Swords
The Ten of Swords is perhaps one of the most striking and sobering cards in the tarot. Its imagery, typically a figure lying prone with ten swords piercing their back, evokes an undeniable finality. This is a card of painful endings, betrayal,

and rock-bottom moments, but also one of transformation and renewal. The darkest night carries within it the promise of dawn, and the Ten of Swords invites us to contemplate the cyclical nature of endings and beginnings. When applied to music, this card becomes a profound metaphor for creative collapses, the catharsis of loss, and the way sound can rise from silence, carrying the seeds of rebirth.

The energy of the Ten of Swords often manifests during times of artistic or personal crisis. These moments might include the end of a significant creative project, the dissolution of a band, or the loss of inspiration. Such experiences can feel devastating, as though the very foundation of one's identity has been torn apart. Yet the Ten of Swords reminds us that these moments, while painful, are not without purpose. They create space for transformation, for the emergence of something new and perhaps even greater. For a musician, this might mean reinventing their sound, starting anew with fresh collaborators, or stepping away from music entirely before returning with a renewed sense of purpose.

The Ten of Swords also resonates with the themes of heartbreak and betrayal, both of which are frequent subjects in music. Songs that channel the energy of this card often feel raw and unflinching, capturing the depth of human pain in a way that is both poignant and universal. These are the ballads of endings, the laments of broken trust and shattered dreams. They do not shy away from the devastation of their subject matter, instead embracing it fully. In doing so, they provide listeners with a space to process their own grief, to feel seen and understood in their most vulnerable moments.

Yet the Ten of Swords is not only about endings; it is also about what comes after. In music, the collapse of one structure often gives rise to another. This is evident in the evolution of genres, where the end of one era leads to the birth of a new movement. Consider the way punk rock emerged from the perceived stagnation of 1970s mainstream rock, or how grunge rose from the disillusionment of the 1980s glam-metal scene. These shifts are marked by a willingness to confront the failures and limitations of what came before, to embrace destruction as a necessary prelude to creation. The Ten of Swords reminds us that in music, like life, endings are not final; they are fertile ground for innovation and growth.

The Ten of Swords often appears in the music that accompanies moments of personal loss or despair. These are the songs that seem to articulate the unspeakable, giving form to feelings of hopelessness and defeat. They might be steeped in melancholy, with minor keys and haunting melodies that evoke the weight of sorrow. Yet even in their darkest moments, these pieces often carry a subtle thread of hope. A quiet shift in tone, a gentle resolution in the final notes, these details suggest that the end is not the end, that something still awaits beyond the horizon. The Ten of Swords teaches us to find solace in this ambiguity, to trust in the inevitability of renewal even when it cannot yet be seen.

The Ten of Swords challenges musicians to confront their fears of failure and imperfection. The card's energy invites a kind of surrender, a willingness to let go of what no longer serves. This might mean abandoning a project that has become a source of frustration, or releasing the need for a piece of music to meet certain expectations. In this context, the Ten of Swords becomes a liberating force, clearing the way for authentic expression. By accepting the collapse of one idea, the artist creates space for the emergence of something truer and more resonant.

The card's imagery also speaks to the way music can capture the collective experience of endings. In times of societal upheaval or tragedy, music often becomes a means of processing shared grief. Protest songs, elegies, and requiems all carry the energy of the Ten of Swords, bearing witness to moments of collective loss while also pointing toward the possibility of collective healing. These compositions serve as both a record of pain and a call to move forward, reminding us that even in the face of devastation, the human spirit endures.

The Ten of Swords also finds expression in the themes of finality and closure that appear in music. Some songs and albums are explicitly designed as farewells, marking the end of an era for the artist or listener. These works often carry a sense of gravity, as though they are bearing the weight of everything that came before. They might be reflective, looking back on past struggles and triumphs, or they might be resolute, embracing the end with a sense of peace. In either case, they honor the importance of endings, treating them not as failures but as integral parts of the creative energy.

One of the most profound lessons of the Ten of Swords is the idea that pain can be a source of wisdom and growth. In music, this is reflected in the way artists transform their most challenging experiences into works of beauty and meaning. A heartbreak becomes the seed of a timeless love song; a personal loss inspires a symphony of remembrance. These creations do not erase the pain from which they arose, but they give it a purpose, allowing it to resonate in ways that uplift and connect. The Ten of Swords reminds us that even the darkest moments can be transmuted into something powerful and transformative.

The Ten of Swords invites us to consider the role of music in the cycles of life, death, and rebirth. It teaches us that while endings are inevitable, they are never the final word. Music, with its infinite capacity for reinvention, becomes a metaphor for this truth. A melody may fade, but its echoes linger; a silence may fall, but it is always followed by sound. The Ten of Swords reminds us that in music, as in life, every ending carries within it the promise of a new beginning. Through the shadows, it points us toward the light, encouraging us to embrace the transformative power of creation, destruction, and the eternal rhythm of renewal.

Page of Swords

The Page of Swords stands as a symbol of youthful curiosity, intellectual pursuit, and an eagerness to explore new ideas. This card often represents the beginnings of a journey toward understanding, a restless energy that seeks knowledge and clarity, even if the path is uncertain. The Page of Swords embodies the spark of discovery, the bold experimentation that drives artistic evolution, and the courage to question conventions. It is the archetype of the musician or listener who approaches sound with an open mind, a sharp intellect, and a willingness to push boundaries.

The Page of Swords represents a stage of exploration and inquiry. For a composer, songwriter, or producer, this might manifest as an insatiable curiosity about techniques, genres, or technologies. The energy of this card drives the artist to ask, "What if?" What if I blend these seemingly incompatible styles? What if I use this unusual instrument or effect? What if I abandon traditional structures altogether? The Page of Swords thrives on questions like these, on the thrill of discovery and the possibility of uncovering something entirely new.

This card often appears during moments of artistic experimentation, when a musician is more concerned with exploration than perfection. It's the stage where ideas are tested, boundaries are pushed, and failure is embraced as a necessary part of growth. In music, this might translate into improvisation, where spontaneity and intuition take precedence over polished execution. Jazz, for instance, is a genre that often embodies the energy of the Page of Swords, with its emphasis on innovation and the interplay of ideas in real time. Similarly, avant-garde and experimental music channels this card's spirit, challenging listeners to question their assumptions about sound and meaning.

For the listener, the Page of Swords encourages an active engagement with music. Rather than passively consuming what is familiar or popular, this card invites exploration and discovery. It's the energy that leads someone to dive into obscure playlists, attend experimental performances, or learn about the cultural and historical contexts of the music they love. The Page of Swords reminds us that music is not just an experience but a dialogue, a space where curiosity can lead to profound insights.

The Page of Swords also speaks to the way music can function as a tool for intellectual engagement. While many associate music primarily with emotion, this card highlights its capacity to provoke thought and stimulate the mind. Certain compositions invite listeners to engage with complex ideas, challenging them to think critically or see the world in a new way. For example, the intricate counterpoint of a Bach fugue or the layered production of a modern electronic track can be as intellectually stimulating as they are aesthetically pleasing. Similarly, politically charged lyrics or concept albums often carry the energy of the Page of Swords, using music as a medium for communication and inquiry.

The Page of Swords is often associated with communication, and music, as a universal language, embodies this concept beautifully. It allows for the exchange of ideas and emotions that transcend words, creating connections across cultures and generations. The youthful, inquisitive nature of the Page of Swords aligns with the way music often serves as a bridge between different worlds. This is particularly evident in fusion genres, which combine elements from diverse traditions to create something entirely new. Whether it's jazz blending with hip-hop, classical merging with electronic, or folk intertwining with rock, these musical hybrids reflect the Page of Swords' embrace of curiosity and dialogue.

This card also emphasizes the importance of learning and growth, particularly for musicians honing their craft. The Page of Swords represents the student's mindset, an openness to study and practice that fosters mastery over time. A guitarist experimenting with unusual chord voicings, a producer learning the nuances of a new software plugin, or a vocalist training to expand their range; all of these endeavors reflect the Page's dedication to knowledge and improvement. This energy encourages a mindset of continual growth, reminding us that the journey of musical discovery is never truly complete.

In the broader landscape of music history, the Page of Swords can be seen in the figures who challenge norms and forge new paths. From composers like Igor Stravinsky, who shocked audiences with his bold innovations in "The Rite of Spring," to contemporary artists experimenting with AI-generated soundscapes, the Page of Swords embodies the spirit of those who are unafraid to ask questions and defy expectations. These trailblazers are not content to remain within established boundaries; they push music forward, often provoking both admiration and controversy in the process.

The Page of Swords is a seeker of truth, and music, too, often serves as a medium for uncovering deeper truths about ourselves and the world around us. A songwriter grappling with personal revelations, a composer inspired by the mysteries of the cosmos, or a producer exploring the frontiers of sound design: all are engaging with the essence of the Page of Swords. This card teaches us that while the pursuit of understanding may be fraught with uncertainty, it is a journey worth undertaking, one that leads to growth, insight, and transformation.

The Page of Swords also reminds us of the importance of balance in our creative and intellectual pursuits. While its energy is undeniably invigorating, it can also be restless and scattered, prone to overthinking or spreading oneself too thin. In music, this might manifest as an artist becoming so caught up in experimentation that they lose sight of their original vision, or a listener becoming overwhelmed by the sheer volume of new material to explore. The Page of Swords teaches us to temper curiosity with focus, to channel its energy into purposeful exploration rather than aimless wandering.

The Page of Swords invites us to approach music with a sense of wonder and openness. It challenges us to question what we think we know, to embrace the unknown, and to see every note, rhythm, and lyric as an opportunity for discovery. Whether we are creating, performing, or listening, this card reminds us that music is a vast and ever-changing landscape, one that rewards those who are willing to explore its depths with an open heart and a curious mind. In this way, the Page of Swords becomes a guide, encouraging us to continually seek, learn, and grow through the transformative power of sound.

Knight of Swords

The Knight of Swords is a card of swift action, intellectual determination, and boundless energy. Representing a quest for truth and an unstoppable drive toward a goal, this card is often seen as a symbol of courage, passion, and the relentless pursuit of one's ambitions. The Knight of Swords speaks to the urgency and intensity that propels creativity forward, the audacity to tackle bold ideas, and the fervor that can transform sound into a revolutionary force. It is the archetype of the musician who charges ahead fearlessly, determined to leave a lasting impact on the world.

The Knight of Swords often represents the raw, unfiltered momentum that accompanies the birth of a powerful idea. This is the energy of an artist struck by inspiration, driven to translate that spark into sound as quickly and forcefully as possible. It's the frenzied writing of lyrics in the middle of the night, the unrelenting focus of a composer pouring their soul into a score, or the marathon recording sessions that push the boundaries of endurance. The Knight of Swords is not one for hesitation or second-guessing. When this energy takes hold, there is no time to pause; the idea must be realized, no matter the obstacles.

This card also embodies the spirit of ambition and the desire to challenge norms. In music, it reflects the artist who pushes against boundaries, striving to make a mark through innovation or rebellion. Punk rock, with its raw energy and defiant attitude, carries the essence of the Knight of Swords, as do genres like rap and heavy metal, where intensity and a relentless pursuit of truth often take center stage. The artists in these spaces are not afraid to confront uncomfortable realities, delivering their messages with an urgency that demands attention.

The Knight of Swords also represents the technical precision and intellectual rigor that music can require. While the card is often associated with passion and intensity, it also highlights the mental clarity and focus needed to achieve mastery. A jazz musician navigating complex improvisations, a conductor bringing a symphony to life, or a producer crafting intricate soundscapes all channel the Knight of Swords' ability to marry intellect with action. This card reminds us that true mastery often requires not just raw talent but also discipline, study, and a relentless commitment to one's craft.

For a listener, the Knight of Swords might manifest in the way music can inspire action or awaken a sense of purpose. Songs with driving rhythms, forceful melodies, and lyrics that demand change often carry this card's energy. These are the anthems that rally movements, the soundtracks to revolutions, and the pieces that ignite a spark of determination in the heart of the listener. The Knight of Swords does not call for passive enjoyment; it demands engagement, challenging us to consider how music can be a catalyst for personal or societal transformation.

However, the Knight of Swords is not without its challenges. The same qualities that make this card so powerful (its speed, intensity, and singular focus) can also lead to recklessness or burnout. In music, this might manifest as an artist pushing themselves too hard, sacrificing their well-being in pursuit of their vision. It might also appear in the tendency to prioritize speed over depth, rushing to create without fully considering the emotional or artistic weight of the work. The Knight of Swords teaches us that while ambition is essential, it must be tempered with self-awareness and care.

The energy of the Knight of Swords is particularly resonant during times of creative breakthrough or transition. This card often appears when a musician is embarking on a bold new project, taking risks, or moving in an entirely new direction. It encourages the artist to trust their instincts and charge forward, even if the path ahead is uncertain. In this way, the Knight of Swords becomes a symbol of courage and resilience, reminding us that great achievements often require boldness and determination.

The Knight of Swords can be seen in the figures who have reshaped the landscape through sheer force of will. Artists, like Beethoven, whose stormy compositions broke with classical conventions, or Jimi Hendrix, whose groundbreaking guitar work redefined the possibilities of rock, embody the fearless and transformative energy of this card. These individuals were not content to follow the paths laid out for them; they forged their own, driven by a vision that demanded to be realized.

The Knight of Swords also speaks to the way music can capture the urgency of the human experience. In times of crisis or upheaval, songs often become vehicles for expression and resistance, channeling the collective energy of a moment into sound. Protest songs, revolutionary anthems, and works created during moments of great cultural change all carry the spirit of the Knight of Swords. They remind us of music's power not just to reflect the world but to shape it, to drive action and inspire courage in the face of adversity.

At its core, the Knight of Swords is about momentum, about seizing the moment and moving forward with conviction. In music, this energy can be both exhilarating and transformative. It pushes artists to take risks, to explore uncharted territory, and to pour their passion into every note and rhythm. It also challenges listeners to engage with music in a deeper, more active way, to let it inspire and motivate rather than simply entertain.

The Knight of Swords reminds us that music is not just a medium of expression but a force of action. It has the power to challenge, to disrupt, and to inspire change, both within the individual and in the broader world. This card calls on us to embrace that power, to channel the drive and determination it represents into our creative and personal endeavors. Whether we are making music, listening to it, or using it as a tool for transformation, the Knight of Swords encourages us to act boldly and with purpose, trusting in the strength of our vision and the clarity of our truth.

Queen of Swords

The Queen of Swords represents a unique blend of intellect, emotional clarity, and wisdom. She is a figure of truth and discernment, capable of understanding the complexities of life without being overwhelmed by them. Her energy manifests as the ability to communicate profound truths through sound and lyrics while maintaining a balance between intellect and emotion. The Queen of Swords embodies the artist, listener, or thinker who approaches music with both critical insight and heartfelt authenticity, allowing it to serve as a bridge between thought and feeling.

At the heart of the Queen of Swords is clarity. This card speaks to the ability to cut through the noise, distilling complexity into simplicity without losing depth. In music, this might manifest in a songwriter's ability to articulate deeply personal or universal experiences with poignant precision. Think of the way a single line of lyric can encapsulate an entire world of emotion or the way a melody can strike directly at the core of human experience. She reminds us that music does not have to be grandiose or overly complex to be meaningful; sometimes, its greatest power lies in its ability to express the inexpressible with elegant simplicity.

The Queen of Swords also highlights the intellectual side of music. She values structure, technique, and the art of communication, understanding that music is not just an emotional outlet but also a language with its own grammar and rules. A composer working with intricate counterpoint, a producer layering tracks to create a precise emotional arc, or a lyricist crafting words with poetic precision all channel the energy of this card. The Queen of Swords encourages artists to think deeply about their work, to approach their craft with intention and mastery, and to ensure that every note and word serves a purpose.

Despite her intellectual focus, the Queen of Swords is far from cold or detached. She is deeply attuned to emotion, but she approaches it with a sense of balance and discernment. In music, this is reflected in works that marry emotional depth with intellectual rigor. A song can be deeply moving without being sentimental, and a composition can be intellectually stimulating without being inaccessible. The Queen thrives in this middle ground, where thought and feeling coexist in harmony. She reminds us that music's power lies not just in its ability to make us feel but also in its capacity to make us think and understand.

The Queen of Swords represents the moment when an artist achieves clarity of vision. This is not the chaotic inspiration of the Knight of Swords or the exploratory curiosity of the Page of Swords; it is a calm, focused understanding of what needs to be expressed and how to express it. For a musician, this might mean finding the perfect arrangement for a song, choosing the right words to convey a message, or knowing when to strip a piece down to its bare essentials. The Queen of Swords reminds artists to trust their judgment and to honor their truth, even if it means making difficult decisions.

The energy of the Queen of Swords can also be found in music that addresses hard truths or confronts uncomfortable realities. She does not shy away from pain or complexity; instead, she examines them with clarity and grace, finding meaning in even the darkest moments. Many powerful songs and compositions carry this energy, whether they explore themes of loss, injustice, or resilience. Think of a mournful ballad that brings catharsis through its honesty or a protest song that speaks truth to power with unwavering conviction. The Queen of Swords reminds us that music can be a tool for facing reality, not escaping it, and that its greatest strength often lies in its ability to illuminate the truth.

The Queen of Swords encourages a thoughtful and discerning approach to music. She invites us to engage with sound not just as entertainment but as a source of insight and understanding. This might mean delving into the meanings behind lyrics, appreciating the craftsmanship of a composition, or considering the cultural and historical context of a piece. The Queen of Swords teaches us to listen with both our hearts and our minds, finding deeper connections and truths through the music we love.

The Queen of Swords is also a figure of independence and self-reliance, qualities that resonate deeply in the world of music. She represents the artist who stands firm in their vision, unafraid to make bold choices or to challenge conventions. This might be the independent musician who forges their own path without the support of a major label, or the composer who creates work that defies traditional expectations. The Queen of Swords values authenticity above all else, encouraging artists to stay true to themselves even when it's difficult.

In the broader context of music history, the Queen of Swords can be seen in figures who have used their craft to express clarity and truth. Artists like Joni Mitchell, whose introspective lyrics cut to the heart of human experience, or Nina Simone, whose music combined emotional depth with incisive social commentary, embody the energy of this card. These artists understood the power of music to communicate complex ideas and emotions, and they used it with precision and purpose.

The Queen of Swords also reminds us of the transformative power of music as a means of understanding and healing. While her energy is often associated with intellect and clarity, she also recognizes the importance of addressing emotional wounds. Music that resonates with the Queen of Swords often provides solace and perspective, helping listeners process their own experiences through the lens of sound and storytelling. Whether it's a deeply personal song that feels like a conversation with the artist or a sweeping symphony that offers a sense of transcendence, these works reflect her ability to guide us toward insight and resolution.

The Queen of Swords teaches us that music is both an art and a discipline, a means of expression and a tool for understanding. She challenges us to approach it with both passion and thoughtfulness, to honor its emotional power while also appreciating its intellectual depth. Whether we are creating, performing, or listening, the Queen of Swords reminds us to seek truth, embrace clarity, and approach music as a path toward wisdom and connection. In her presence, sound becomes more than an experience; it becomes a profound act of communication and understanding, one that bridges the gap between intellect and emotion, self and other, thought and feeling.

King of Swords

The King of Swords is a figure of intellect, authority, and strategic clarity. As a master of logic and communication, he wields his power with precision, embodying wisdom gained through experience. The King of Swords signifies the synthesis of technical expertise, deep understanding, and the ability to shape sound with both intellect and purpose. His presence is a call to engage with music as an art form that balances creativity with discipline, emotion with rationality, and spontaneity with structure.

When the King of Swords appears in connection with music, he represents the pinnacle of mastery and control. He is the composer who can weave complex musical themes into a cohesive whole, the producer who orchestrates every detail of a recording session with confidence, and the performer who delivers each note with precision and intention. The King of Swords approaches music not just as an act of creation but as an act of leadership, where vision, discipline, and expertise come together to create something extraordinary.

In music, the King of Swords is often associated with the intellectual aspect of the art. While music is deeply emotional, it is also a highly structured and mathematical medium. The King of Swords reminds us that understanding the rules and frameworks of music such as harmony, rhythm, and form can open the door to greater creative freedom. He is the one who has studied the mechanics of sound, internalized its principles, and uses that knowledge to craft works that resonate on both an intellectual and emotional level.

This card also speaks to the role of music as a form of communication. The King of Swords understands the power of words, melodies, and rhythms to convey meaning and evoke response. His presence suggests that music can be a tool for articulating ideas, sparking dialogue, or even leading movements. The protest songs of Woody Guthrie or Bob Dylan, with their incisive lyrics and deliberate messages, reflect the King of Swords' ability to use music as a force for clarity and change.

The King of Swords often represents the journey toward mastery. It is not enough to have talent or passion; one must also cultivate skill, discipline, and a deep understanding of the craft. This card challenges artists to think critically about their work, to refine their techniques, and to approach music with a sense of purpose and vision. The King of Swords is not swayed by trends or fleeting emotions; his work is deliberate, intentional, and grounded in a profound understanding of his art.

The King of Swords also speaks to leadership within music. He is the conductor who commands an orchestra with authority, the bandleader who guides their group with clear direction, or the producer who oversees every aspect of an album's creation. His role is not just to create but to inspire and organize others, ensuring that the collective effort results in something greater than the sum of its parts. This card reminds us of the importance of collaboration and the value of a clear and guiding vision in any musical endeavor.

The King of Swords can also represent the influence of music critics, scholars, and historians who analyze and interpret the art. These individuals, like the King of Swords, engage with music on an intellectual level, offering insights that deepen our understanding and appreciation of its nuances. Their role is to provide context, draw connections, and help audiences navigate the vast landscape of sound with clarity and purpose.

At its core, the King of Swords challenges us to think about the ways music can be both structured and transcendent. He reminds us that creativity doesn't exist in opposition to discipline but can be enhanced by it. The intricate compositions of Johann Sebastian Bach, for instance, reflect this balance; works of breathtaking beauty that are also feats of technical precision and intellectual depth. The King teaches us that greatness in music often comes from this intersection of heart and mind.

For listeners, the King of Swords invites a more analytical engagement with music. He encourages us to think critically about what we hear, to pay attention to the details of a composition, and to seek out the underlying messages and meanings. His energy is present in the moments when we notice the subtle interplay between instruments, the clever twists in a song's structure, or the layered themes in a set of lyrics. He reminds us that music, like any art form, rewards close attention and thoughtful reflection.

The King of Swords also symbolizes music's ability to bring order to chaos. In times of uncertainty or emotional upheaval, music can serve as an anchor, providing structure and clarity. This might take the form of a carefully composed piece that brings a sense of calm, or a song with a clear and steady rhythm that grounds the listener. The King of Swords understands that while music often arises from emotion, its form and structure are what allow it to communicate effectively and resonate deeply.

However, the King of Swords also serves as a cautionary figure. His emphasis on intellect and precision can sometimes lead to a detachment from emotion. In music, this might manifest as work that is technically brilliant but lacks soul, or as an over-reliance on theory at the expense of spontaneity. The King of Swords reminds us that while mastery and discipline are essential, they must be balanced with vulnerability and emotional authenticity.

In the history of music, the King of Swords can be seen in the figures who have not only mastered their craft but also shaped the field through their intellect and vision. Artists like Leonard Bernstein, who combined his talents as a composer, conductor, and educator, embody this energy. Bernstein's ability to communicate complex ideas through music, whether on the stage of Carnegie Hall or in a classroom, reflects the King of Swords' commitment to clarity, wisdom, and purposeful leadership.

This card reminds us that music is a form of knowledge as much as it is a form of expression. It is a medium that can teach, inspire, and transform, offering both beauty and insight. Whether we are creating, performing, or simply listening, this card challenges us to engage with music thoughtfully and intentionally, to seek out its deeper truths, and to approach it with the respect and discipline it deserves.

The King of Swords stands as a testament to the power of music when wielded with wisdom and clarity. He encourages us to hone our skills, to think critically about our work, and to approach music not just as an art but as a tool for communication, connection, and transformation. In his presence, we are reminded that music has the power to cut through the noise, to illuminate the complexities of the human experience, and to bring order and understanding to a chaotic world.

The Minor Arcana: Pentacles

The suit of Pentacles is tied to the element of earth, representing material things, practicality, and the tangible aspects of life. It is associated with work, resources, physical manifestation, and the connection between effort and reward. When applied to music, the Pentacles highlight the ways in which this ethereal art form is rooted in the physical world, dependent on resources, effort, and structure to thrive. Music may feel divine and transcendent, but it is also built from human labor, physical instruments, and the structures that make its production and sharing possible.

The Pentacles remind us that while music can be a purely creative pursuit, it also requires a foundation of practicality and material support to exist. Instruments must be made, maintained, and played. Performances need venues, whether a concert hall, a street corner, or a digital platform. Musicians often rely on careful planning, financial resources, and steady effort to bring their visions to life. The

Pentacles bring attention to this grounded side of music, showing how dreams are turned into reality through discipline, craftsmanship, and perseverance.

The cards in the Pentacles suit encourage musicians to approach their work with a practical mindset. This means not only focusing on the creative aspects of music but also considering how to sustain it as a craft or profession. A musician may be bursting with ideas, but without the necessary tools, time, or money, those ideas may remain unfulfilled. The Pentacles urge the artist to cultivate a balance between inspiration and material stability, to build a foundation that allows creativity to flourish without undue stress or hardship.

Pentacles are deeply connected to the concept of value, both in terms of personal worth and external exchange. In music, this value can be seen in the relationship between the artist and their audience. The Pentacles prompt musicians to think about how their work is received and valued by others, whether through applause at a performance, downloads on a streaming platform, or even financial compensation. These cards remind musicians that their art holds worth, not just as an intangible expression but as something that can impact and enrich the lives of others in measurable ways.

The Pentacles also invite reflection on the labor and skill that go into music. Every note played, every song written, every performance delivered is the result of hours, often years, of dedicated practice. The Pentacles honor this effort, celebrating the craftsmanship that transforms raw talent into artistry. Just as a gardener tends to the earth to grow something beautiful and nourishing, musicians tend to their skills, their instruments, and their creative processes to bring their visions to life. This suit acknowledges the rewards that come from this steady, patient work.

When considering music as a profession, the Pentacles speak to the intersection of creativity and commerce. They address the realities of sustaining oneself through music, whether as a performer, composer, teacher, or producer. This may involve negotiating contracts, managing finances, or marketing one's work. While these tasks may seem mundane compared to the act of creating music, the Pentacles teach that these practical considerations are not separate from the art itself, they are essential components of a sustainable musical career.

The Pentacles also reflect the tangible, physical aspects of music. While music is often thought of as intangible (vibrations carried through the air), it is deeply rooted in the physical world. The strings of a guitar, the keys of a piano, the vocal cords of a singer, all are physical mechanisms through which sound is created. The Pentacles remind us to honor these tools and the craftsmanship behind them. A well-made instrument, a well-tuned voice, or a well-designed recording studio are all reflections of the Pentacles' energy, showing how material resources and care can enhance the quality of musical expression.

Another layer of the Pentacles' meaning in music involves the grounding effect of sound. Music has the power to root us in the present moment, to connect us to our bodies and the earth. Rhythms can mimic the heartbeat, melodies can soothe or energize, and harmonies can evoke a sense of balance and stability. The Pentacles remind us that music is not only an art of the spirit but also one of the body, capable of grounding us in physical sensation and aligning us with the natural rhythms of life.

This suit also speaks to the community aspect of music, emphasizing the importance of shared resources and collaboration. A symphony orchestra, for instance, requires not only the individual skills of its musicians but also the cooperation and coordination of the group as a whole. Similarly, a music festival relies on organizers, technicians, sponsors, and audiences to come together and create something larger than any single contributor. The Pentacles remind us that music is often a collective effort, sustained by networks of support and shared purpose.

The Pentacles also highlight the rewards that come from the intersection of music and materiality. These rewards are not solely financial, they can also take the form of a tangible sense of accomplishment, a deep connection with an audience, or the fulfillment of seeing a creative vision come to life. The Pentacles teach that these rewards are earned through effort and persistence, and they encourage musicians to celebrate their successes while continuing to nurture their craft.

At the same time, the pentacles caution against becoming too focused on material concerns. While it is important to consider the practicalities of music, the Pentacles remind us not to lose sight of the deeper purpose of the art. Music is not simply a product to be sold or a skill to be perfected; it is a means of expression, connection, and transcendence. The Pentacles encourage a balanced approach, where the material and the spiritual aspects of music coexist in harmony.

This suit underscores the importance of grounding creativity in the realities of the physical world. It highlights the labor, skill, and resources required to bring music into being, while also celebrating the tangible rewards and connections it can create. Whether as a reminder to honor the tools of the trade, a call to approach music with discipline and purpose, or an encouragement to find value in one's work, the Pentacles guide us to see music not just as an abstract art form but as a grounded, vital part of life.

Ace of Pentacles

The Ace of Pentacles is a card of new beginnings, fresh opportunities, and the manifestation of potential in the material world. Representing the earth element in its purest form, this card embodies the promise of growth, abundance, and stability. When applied to music, the Ace of Pentacles invites us to explore the ways in which creativity can take root in tangible, practical ways. It represents the moment when inspiration meets opportunity, setting the stage for something lasting and meaningful to grow.

The Ace of Pentacles often signifies the initial spark of a project or idea that has the potential to manifest into something significant. This is the moment when a melody comes to mind, an instrument is picked up for the first time, or a new collaboration is proposed. It is not just the fleeting inspiration of a thought or feeling; it is the kind of inspiration that carries with it a sense of groundedness, a belief that it can be nurtured into something real and substantial.

The card's connection to the earth element underscores the importance of physicality and practicality in music. The Ace of Pentacles reminds us that every grand symphony or heartfelt song begins with the first note, the first strum, or the first beat. It celebrates the moment when an idea is given form: when a musician moves from thought to action, committing to bring their vision into reality. This card honors the tools of the trade, whether they are instruments, voices, or recording equipment, and it emphasizes the role these physical objects play in shaping the creative process.

The Ace of Pentacles also speaks to the opportunities that arise when we align ourselves with our musical passions. It might appear in the life of a musician when they receive their first instrument, secure their first gig, or find themselves in a space that encourages their creativity to flourish. These opportunities are gifts from the universe, but they require action and commitment to bring them to fruition. The Ace of Pentacles is not a guarantee of success but an invitation to plant seeds of potential and nurture them with care.

This card can symbolize the foundation of a new musical partnership or project. It suggests that the energy is ripe for building something solid and enduring with others. This could be the formation of a band, the beginning of a mentorship, or the establishment of a music studio. Whatever the specifics, this card indicates the groundwork is being laid for something that has the potential to grow into a source of abundance and fulfillment for all involved.

The Ace of Pentacles also draws attention to the financial and material aspects of music. While music is often seen as a deeply spiritual or emotional art form, it also exists within the realm of commerce and practicalities. The Ace of Pentacles may point to the beginning of a career in music, a financial investment in an instrument or recording equipment, or even the first paycheck earned from a performance. These tangible manifestations of musical effort are a reminder that creativity, when paired with practicality, can lead to material stability and success.

The Ace of Pentacles is a card of potential, and this potential can manifest in countless ways within the world of music. It might represent the discovery of a new genre that resonates deeply, the realization of a unique sound or style, or the development of a technique that becomes a signature. This card encourages musicians to remain open to possibilities, to explore their craft with curiosity and a willingness to learn, and to trust that their efforts will lead them toward their goals.

The Ace of Pentacles invites an appreciation for the material aspects of music: the craftsmanship of an instrument, the acoustics of a performance space, or the tangible experience of holding a vinyl record or ticket stub. It reminds us that while music can transport us to other realms, it is also deeply rooted in the physical world. This card encourages listeners to engage with music not just as a fleeting experience but as something that can leave a lasting impression, grounding us in the present moment while enriching our lives in meaningful ways.

The Ace of Pentacles also holds a message about abundance and gratitude. It reminds us to appreciate the resources and opportunities that allow us to create, share, and experience this art form. Whether it is the gift of a supportive community, access to education or technology, or simply the time to devote to one's craft, the Ace of Pentacles encourages a spirit of thankfulness for these blessings. It reminds us that when we approach music with gratitude and care, we cultivate the conditions for even greater abundance to flow into our lives.

The imagery often associated with the Ace of Pentacles, a hand emerging from the clouds, offering a golden coin, can be seen as a metaphor for the way music itself often feels like a gift from beyond. This card suggests that the seeds of musical inspiration are always present, waiting to be noticed and nurtured. Whether we are creating or listening, the Ace of Pentacles reminds us to remain receptive to these gifts and to recognize their potential to bring beauty, joy, and stability into our lives.

Ultimately, the Ace of Pentacles is a card of hope and promise. It encourages us to take the first step, to invest in our dreams, and to trust that our efforts will lead to growth and fulfillment. It celebrates the intersection of creativity and practicality, showing us that the most extraordinary music is often born from a combination of inspiration, skill, and grounded action. Whether we are musicians, listeners, or simply lovers of sound, the Ace of Pentacles reminds us that music has the power to enrich our lives in profound and tangible ways.

Two of Pentacles

The Two of Pentacles is a card of balance, adaptability, and the art of managing competing priorities. In the imagery of this card, a figure skillfully juggles two pentacles, often depicted as connected by an infinity symbol. This dynamic image captures the perpetual motion and effort required to maintain harmony amidst the chaos of life. When applied to music, the Two of Pentacles symbolizes the delicate interplay between creativity and practicality, inspiration and discipline, and the myriad demands that come with engaging in the world of sound.

Music, by its very nature, is an exercise in balance. It is built on the interplay of rhythm and melody, tension and release, sound and silence. The Two of Pentacles serves as a reminder that music thrives in this state of equilibrium, where different elements coexist and complement each other. It asks us to consider how musicians manage their time, energy, and resources to sustain their craft, and how listeners find balance in their emotional responses to music. The card highlights the dynamic process of maintaining stability in the ever-shifting landscape of musical creation and appreciation.

For musicians, the Two of Pentacles often represents the challenge of juggling multiple aspects of their lives and careers. Many artists face the reality of having to balance their passion for music with other responsibilities, such as work, family, or education. This card acknowledges the difficulty of this task, while also offering encouragement. It suggests that, with adaptability and focus, it is possible to navigate these competing demands without losing sight of one's creative goals. The infinity symbol connecting the two pentacles serves as a reminder that this balancing act is not static but an ongoing process, one that requires continuous adjustment and effort.

The Two of Pentacles also speaks to the balancing act within the creative process itself. Musicians often find themselves navigating the tension between innovation and tradition, experimentation and structure. This card encourages artists to embrace these contrasts, recognizing that they are not opposites but complementary forces. For example, a songwriter might experiment with unconventional chord progressions while still adhering to a familiar verse-chorus structure, or a producer might blend digital effects with acoustic instruments to create a unique sound. The Two of Pentacles celebrates the creativity that emerges from this interplay, reminding us that some of the most compelling music arises from the fusion of seemingly disparate elements.

On a more practical level, this card addresses the financial and logistical challenges of sustaining a musical career. The Two of Pentacles often appears when resources are stretched thin or when difficult choices must be made about where to invest time and energy. For a musician, this might mean deciding between taking on more gigs to pay the bills or dedicating time to a passion project that might not bring immediate financial rewards. The card suggests that while these decisions can be challenging, they also offer an opportunity to develop resilience and resourcefulness. It encourages musicians to approach these challenges with a sense of play and adaptability, finding creative solutions to maintain balance in their lives.

The imagery of the Two of Pentacles, with its sense of motion and rhythm, also resonates with the physicality of music. Whether it's a drummer keeping time, a conductor guiding an orchestra, or a dancer moving to the beat, music is deeply rooted in the body and its ability to maintain balance and coordination. This card invites us to consider the physical demands of making music, from the precision of a guitarist's fingers on the strings to the breath control of a vocalist. It reminds us that music is not just an intellectual or emotional experience but also a deeply embodied one, requiring physical skill and discipline.

The Two of Pentacles can reflect the ways in which music helps us navigate the complexities of life. Music often provides a sense of balance, offering comfort in times of stress or energy in moments of fatigue. It can help us process conflicting emotions, creating a space where joy and sorrow, excitement and calm, can coexist. The Two of Pentacles reminds us that music has the power to bring harmony to our inner worlds, helping us find stability amidst life's uncertainties.

In collaborative settings, the Two of Pentacles emphasizes the importance of flexibility and communication. Whether in a band, an orchestra, or a songwriting partnership, musicians must learn to balance their individual voices with the collective vision of the group. This card highlights the give-and-take required to create something greater than the sum of its parts, as well as the need for adaptability when challenges arise. It suggests that successful collaboration is not about erasing differences but about finding a way to weave them together into a cohesive whole.

The Two of Pentacles also invites reflection on the cyclical nature of music. Just as the infinity symbol suggests an endless loop, music often operates in cycles such as repeating melodies, recurring motifs, and rhythmic patterns that anchor a piece while allowing for variation and improvisation. This card reminds us that music, like life, is a dynamic process, constantly shifting and evolving while maintaining a sense of community. It encourages us to embrace this ebb and flow, finding joy in the moments of harmony and grace in the moments of discord.

The Two of Pentacles is a card of resilience and adaptability. It acknowledges the challenges inherent to balancing the many facets of a musical life, while also celebrating the creativity and growth that can emerge from these efforts. Whether we are musicians striving to harmonize our artistic vision with the demands of everyday life, or listeners seeking solace and inspiration in the music we love, the Two of Pentacles reminds us that balance is not a fixed state but an ongoing dance, a dance that, when approached with grace and determination, can lead to profound beauty and fulfillment.

Three of Pentacles

The Three of Pentacles is a card that celebrates collaboration, mastery, and the shared effort required to create something incurring and meaningful. Often depicted as a craftsman working alongside others in a sacred or purposeful space, this card emphasizes the importance of teamwork, the blending of skills, and the recognition of each individual's contribution to a larger vision. The Three of Pentacles reminds us of the collective energy that underpins the creation, performance, and appreciation of music. It speaks to the artistry, effort, and unity that transform an idea into a resonant, harmonious reality.

At its heart, the Three of Pentacles is about the convergence of diverse talents and perspectives. In the world of music, this often manifests in the form of collaborations. A songwriter brings lyrics to life, a producer layers sounds to craft a sonic landscape, and a performer delivers the emotion that connects the music to its audience. Each participant plays a vital role, and the card underscores the beauty of these combined efforts. It suggests that when musicians come together with mutual respect and shared purpose, they can achieve something far greater than any could accomplish alone.

This card also reflects the practical side of music-making. While inspiration and passion are essential, the Three of Pentacles reminds us that the craft of music requires discipline, skill, and attention to detail. It honors the work that goes into refining a piece, whether it's perfecting a guitar riff, fine-tuning a vocal performance, or meticulously editing a track in the studio. This is not the solitary act of creation but the communal process of honing, improving, and elevating the music to its fullest potential. It is about recognizing that mastery comes not only from individual talent but also from the willingness to engage with others, learn from them, and build something together.

In a performance setting, the Three of Pentacles comes alive in the interplay between musicians. Picture a jazz trio, where each player listens intently to the others, responding in real time to create an improvised masterpiece. Or consider an orchestra, where dozens of musicians work in unison under the guidance of a conductor to bring a composer's vision to life. In these moments, the energy of the Three of Pentacles is palpable, the synergy that arises when individuals pool their skills, knowledge, and passion to create something extraordinary.

The card also speaks to the role of guidance and mentorship in music. The imagery often includes a figure who offers direction or approval, symbolizing the importance of teachers, producers, and other mentors who help musicians grow and develop their craft. This dynamic is not about hierarchy but about shared learning and the willingness to receive constructive feedback. For a musician, this might mean working with a vocal coach to expand their range, collaborating with a producer to refine their sound, or even learning from the input of bandmates. The Three of Pentacles celebrates these relationships as essential to the creative process, reminding us that growth often comes through collaboration.

On a broader level, the Three of Pentacles highlights the communal nature of music itself. Music is rarely created or experienced in isolation; it thrives on connection and interaction. Even a solo artist depends on an audience to complete the circle of creation, as the energy of their performance is reflected back in the responses of those who listen. This card invites us to consider the myriad ways in which music connects people, how a shared rhythm can unite a crowd, how a lyric can resonate with countless individuals, or how a piece of music can serve as a bridge between cultures, generations, or experiences. The Three of Pentacles reminds us that music is, at its core, a collective endeavor.

For those who work behind the scenes in music, this card is especially relevant. The sound engineers who mix tracks, the designers who create album covers, and the promoters who plan concerts all contribute to the larger ecosystem of music. The Three of Pentacles acknowledges their roles as essential to the success of any musical project. It honors the unsung heroes who ensure that the final product is polished, accessible, and impactful, showing that their contributions are just as vital as those of the performers.

The Three of Pentacles also carries a message about the importance of recognizing and valuing each participant's role. In music, as in any collaborative effort, egos can clash, and misunderstandings can arise. This card reminds us that true success comes from mutual respect and the understanding that every contribution matters. It calls for a spirit of humility and cooperation, encouraging musicians to set aside personal agendas and focus on the shared goal of creating something meaningful and enduring.

For listeners, the Three of Pentacles can be a reminder to appreciate the layers of effort and collaboration that go into the music they enjoy. A song may seem effortless in its beauty, but it is often the result of countless hours of practice, planning, and teamwork. This card invites listeners to engage more deeply with the music, to consider the stories behind its creation, and to honor the individuals who brought it to life. It reminds us that music is not just a product but a process, a testament to the shared human experience of creating and connecting.

The card's emphasis on craftsmanship also resonates with the physical aspects of music. The construction of instruments, the acoustics of a performance space, and the technology used in recording and production are all examples of the material foundation that supports musical expression. The Three of Pentacles invites us to appreciate these tangible elements, recognizing that they are integral to the magic of music. It reminds us that even the most transcendent art form is rooted in the physical world, shaped by human hands and minds.

The Three of Pentacles is a celebration of collaboration, effort, and shared purpose. It teaches us that music is not a solitary pursuit but a communal one, enriched by the contributions of many. Whether we are creating, performing, or listening, this card encourages us to honor the collective energy that brings music to life. It reminds us that through collaboration, respect, and dedication, we can create something that resonates deeply and endures beyond the moment of its creation.

Four of Pentacles

The Four of Pentacles is a card of stability, boundaries, and sometimes the tension between holding on and letting go. Often depicted as a figure clutching tightly to a pentacle, with two more at their feet and one balanced atop their crown, this card speaks to the human need for security and the fear of losing what has been gained. The Four of Pentacles invites a reflection on ownership, control, and the interplay between preservation and innovation. It raises questions about what we value, how we protect it, and whether we allow room for growth and evolution.

At its core, the Four of Pentacles addresses the desire for stability, which is a critical concern in the world of music. For musicians, this can manifest as a focus on establishing a career that provides both financial and creative security. The card recognizes the challenges artists face in navigating a field where success is often unpredictable and fleeting. It validates the instinct to safeguard one's hard-earned accomplishments, whether that means securing a stable income, building a loyal fan base, or holding on to creative control in an industry that often pressures artists to conform to commercial demands.

However, the Four of Pentacles also serves as a cautionary reminder that excessive attachment to stability can stifle creativity. Music, by its very nature, is a fluid and ever-changing art form. The need to maintain control, whether over one's artistic direction, intellectual property, or public image, can sometimes lead to rigidity, limiting the potential for growth and experimentation. A musician who becomes too focused on preserving their current success may hesitate to take risks, fearing the loss of what they have built. The card asks us to consider how much we might sacrifice by holding on too tightly and whether true stability lies in adaptability rather than resistance to change.

The theme of possession is central to the Four of Pentacles, and this extends to the idea of ownership in music. This can include the ownership of songs, rights, and recordings, which has long been a contentious issue in the music industry. The card highlights the importance of protecting one's creative work while also exploring the potential pitfalls of prioritizing ownership above all else. It raises questions about how the desire for control can sometimes lead to conflict between artists and record labels, among collaborators, or even within oneself. The Four of Pentacles challenges us to strike a balance between valuing what we have created and being open to sharing it with the world in a way that fosters connection and collaboration.

The Four of Pentacles might also reflect a tendency to cling to familiar music, reluctant to explore new genres or artists. This can be a natural response to the emotional connections we form with the music we love. Songs and albums often become anchors, reminding us of specific moments or feelings in our lives. Yet, the card gently encourages us to consider whether holding on too tightly to the past might prevent us from discovering new sounds and experiences. It asks us to examine the ways in which music can be both a source of comfort and a gateway to new horizons.

The Four of Pentacles also speaks to the balance between material success and artistic integrity. Many musicians grapple with the tension between creating music that is true to their vision and producing work that is commercially viable. This card acknowledges the pressure to prioritize financial stability, especially in a profession where income can be inconsistent. It suggests that while it is essential to secure one's livelihood, it is equally important not to lose sight of the deeper purpose of making music. The Four of Pentacles asks artists to reflect on what truly drives them and whether their actions align with their values.

In the context of collaboration, this card can illuminate issues of control and contribution. When multiple individuals come together to create music, questions of authorship, decision-making, and division of labor often arise. The Four of Pentacles encourages open communication and a willingness to share responsibilities and rewards. It warns against allowing a fear of losing control to overshadow the collective effort, reminding us that music is often at its best when it is a product of shared energy and vision.

The imagery of the card, with its focus on a solitary figure clutching their treasures, also invites a reflection on isolation. For musicians, the pursuit of security and control can sometimes lead to a sense of disconnection, from their audience, from their peers, or even from their own creativity. The Four of Pentacles asks us to consider whether our desire for stability might be creating barriers that limit our ability to connect and grow. It suggests that true abundance comes not from hoarding what we have but from engaging with others and allowing our work to flow freely into the world.

On a broader level, the Four of Pentacles can speak to the cultural and societal forces that shape the music industry. Issues such as gatekeeping, exclusivity, and the commodification of art are all reflected in this card. It invites a critique of the systems that prioritize profit and control over accessibility and innovation, challenging us to imagine a musical landscape that values creativity and collaboration over competition and scarcity.

Despite its associations with limitation, the Four of Pentacles also holds the promise of empowerment. It reminds musicians and listeners alike of the importance of valuing their contributions and protecting their creative energy. It celebrates the sense of accomplishment that comes from building something meaningful and encourages us to honor the work we have done. At the same time, it challenges us to consider how we can use that foundation as a springboard for further exploration and growth.

In the end, the Four of Pentacles is a card of reflection and balance. It asks us to consider what we hold dear, why we hold on to it, and whether we are willing to let go when the time is right. It celebrates the achievements and stability that come from dedication and hard work, while also reminding us that music, like life, is a dynamic and evolving force. It encourages us to find the courage to release what no longer serves us, to share what we have created, and to trust that in doing so, we make room for new opportunities, connections, and inspiration to flow into our lives.

Five of Pentacles

The Five of Pentacles is a card steeped in imagery of struggle, often showing two figures braving the cold as they pass by a glowing window of sanctuary. It speaks of hardship, scarcity, and the human need for connection and hope in the face of adversity. The Five of Pentacles reflects not only the trials and tribulations faced by musicians and listeners but also the transformative power of music to address, process, and ultimately transcendent these difficulties. This card embodies the idea that music can arise from even the most barren circumstances, serving as both a solace and a testament to resilience.

Music has long been a medium through which individuals and communities express their pain and seek understanding during times of loss and hardship.

The Five of Pentacles resonates deeply with the blues, a genre born out of suffering and oppression, where each note and lyric tells a story of endurance. Similarly, folk songs, protest anthems, and spirituals often emerge from a place of scarcity and struggle, giving voice to those who are marginalized or silenced. This card reminds us that music does not always arise from joy or abundance but can grow from the cracks of despair, becoming a means of survival when all else seems lost.

The Five of Pentacles reflects the challenges that often accompany a life dedicated to art. Financial instability is a reality for many artists, who may struggle to make ends meet while pursuing their passion. The card captures the sense of vulnerability and uncertainty that can come with this path, where success is elusive, and recognition can be fleeting. Yet, it also speaks to the perseverance required to continue creating in the face of such difficulties. Musicians often channel their hardships into their work, transforming personal pain into something universal and cathartic. The Five of Pentacles honors this resilience, showing that even in the darkest moments, there is the potential for beauty and connection.

The card also invites reflection on the communal nature of struggle and the ways in which music can serve as a bridge during times of isolation. The figures on the card walk together, suggesting that even in hardship, companionship and solidarity can provide warmth and hope. In music, this is reflected in the shared experiences of both creators and listeners. A song about loss can resonate with millions, reminding each listener that they are not alone in their suffering. Music becomes a kind of sanctuary, offering a space where grief can be expressed, understood, and ultimately transformed. The glowing window in the card, though distant, suggests that hope is never entirely out of reach, and music often serves as the light guiding us toward it.

The Five of Pentacles speaks to the role of music as a source of comfort during personal trials. A song can become a lifeline, articulating emotions that feel too heavy to bear alone. It can provide a sense of validation, as if the artist understands and shares in the listener's pain. The card reminds us that music has the power to accompany us through our darkest hours, offering solace even when the world seems cold and unwelcoming. It is a testament to the way art can connect us to something greater, even when we feel disconnected from ourselves or our surroundings.

In the broader context of the music industry, the Five of Pentacles highlights the inequities and challenges faced by those who create and share music. It asks us to consider the ways in which systemic barriers can marginalize certain voices, preventing them from reaching the sanctuary of recognition and support. The card invites a critique of an industry that often prioritizes profit over artistry, leaving many talented musicians out in the cold. At the same time, it celebrates the tenacity of those who continue to make music despite these challenges, finding ways to survive and thrive outside traditional systems.

The Five of Pentacles also reflects the emotional vulnerability inherent in both creating and experiencing music. To write a song, to perform it, or even to listen deeply is to expose oneself to a kind of rawness. This card acknowledges the courage it takes to confront that vulnerability, to open oneself to the possibility of rejection or misunderstanding in pursuit of something meaningful. It honors the bravery of those who face their own struggles and transform them into art, offering their truth to the world with the hope that it might resonate with others.

Yet, the card's imagery also reminds us that hardship is not permanent. The figures in the card are in motion, suggesting that their journey, though difficult, is not without progress. Music, too, is inherently dynamic, capable of shifting and evolving with time. A song that once reflected a moment of despair can become a source of strength, reminding us of how far we have come. The Five of Pentacles invites us to consider music as a chronicle of resilience, a record of not only what has been lost but also what has been overcome.

The interplay of scarcity and abundance is central to the Five of Pentacles, and this extends to the creative process itself. Many artists find that limitations, whether financial, emotional, or situational, can spur innovation, forcing them to think creatively and make the most of what they have. The card suggests that even in times of scarcity, there is potential for growth and expression. It challenges us to see hardship not only as an obstacle but as a catalyst for transformation, encouraging us to look for the seeds of possibility within the barren landscape.

Ultimately, the Five of Pentacles is a card of resilience and the human capacity to find light in darkness. It acknowledges the pain and challenges that are often part of the artistic journey, while also celebrating the strength and creativity that emerge from these experiences. It reminds us that music, like life, is not always easy, but it is always worth pursuing. Whether we are creating, performing, or listening, the Five of Pentacles encourages us to honor the role of music as a source of solace, connection, and hope. A reminder that even in the harshest winters, the warmth of creativity and human connection can guide us toward sanctuary.

Six of Pentacles

The Six of Pentacles is a card deeply rooted in the principles of giving, receiving, and the delicate balance of exchange. It often depicts a benefactor distributing coins to those in need, with scales held in one hand as a symbol of fairness and justice. This card evokes the themes of generosity, collaboration, and the interconnected flow of resources, knowledge, and inspiration. It explores how music itself can be both a gift and a need, a shared currency that circulates between artists, audiences, and the larger cultural landscape.

The Six of Pentacles reminds us that music is a form of generosity. To create music is to offer something of oneself to the world, such as a melody, a lyric or a rhythm. Musicians pour their emotions, experiences, and thoughts into their work, creating something that has the power to resonate far beyond their own lives. This act of creation is inherently generous, as it involves making something deeply personal accessible to others. The Six of Pentacles celebrates this giving, acknowledging the vulnerability and courage required to share one's art and the potential it has to enrich the lives of those who receive it.

Yet, the card also highlights the importance of balance in this exchange. Just as the benefactor in the image distributes wealth with care, musicians must navigate the balance between giving and sustaining themselves. In an industry where artists are often expected to give endlessly through constant touring, creating new content, and engaging with fans, the Six of Pentacles serves as a reminder that giving must be balanced with receiving. Musicians, like anyone else, need support, recognition, and resources to continue their work. This card asks us to consider how we can ensure that this balance is maintained, creating a system where generosity flows in both directions.

The Six of Pentacles represents the role of reciprocity in the relationship between listener and artist. While music is often freely available, it is important to recognize and honor the effort that goes into its creation. This can take many forms, from purchasing albums and attending concerts to simply sharing an artist's work with others. The card invites listeners to consider how they can give back to the musicians whose work has touched them, creating a cycle of support that sustains both artist and audience. It also emphasizes the non-material ways in which this exchange can occur, such as the emotional connection and energy that an audience brings to a live performance.

The Six of Pentacles also speaks to the collaborative nature of music. In many ways, creating music is an act of shared generosity, where each participant contributes their skills and ideas to a common goal. Whether it's a band working together to write a song, a producer shaping an album, or a songwriter collaborating with a lyricist, the card reminds us of the importance of mutual support and respect in these relationships. It celebrates the beauty of what can be achieved when individuals come together with a spirit of generosity, each offering their unique gifts for the benefit of the whole.

The Six of Pentacles raises questions about equity and the distribution of resources. It challenges us to consider who has access to opportunities and support, and how we can create a more just and balanced system. The card reminds us that generosity is not only about individual acts but also about creating structures that allow everyone to thrive. This might involve advocating for fair pay for artists, supporting emerging talent, or addressing systemic barriers that prevent certain voices from being heard. The Six of Pentacles calls for a music industry that values reciprocity and fairness, ensuring that the flow of resources benefits everyone involved.

The card's imagery of giving and receiving also resonates with the way music is experienced and shared. A song, once created, becomes a gift that can be passed from one person to another, spreading its influence and meaning across time and space. The Six of Pentacles honors this ripple effect, acknowledging the ways in which music can inspire, comfort, and connect people. It reminds us that the act of sharing music, whether by playing a record for a friend, teaching someone to play an instrument, or introducing an artist to a new audience, is itself an act of generosity, one that keeps the cycle of exchange alive.

On a personal level, the Six of Pentacles encourages musicians to reflect on their own relationship with giving and receiving. It asks, "Are you giving too much without replenishing yourself? Are you open to receiving the support and recognition you need?" The card suggests that true generosity comes not from a place of depletion but from abundance, a sense of balance and wholeness that allows one to give freely without sacrifice. For musicians, this might mean setting boundaries, seeking mentorship, or allowing themselves to be vulnerable enough to accept help and collaboration. For listeners, the card invites a similar reflection. How do you engage with music? Do you take it for granted, or do you honor the effort and emotion behind it? The Six of Pentacles encourages a mindful approach to music, one that recognizes it as a gift and responds with gratitude and support. It asks listeners to consider how they can contribute to the cycle of exchange, not only by supporting artists materially but also by engaging deeply with their work and allowing it to shape their lives.

The Six of Pentacles is a celebration of connection and interdependence. It reminds us that music is not created or experienced in isolation but is part of a larger web of relationships and exchanges. It teaches us that generosity and reciprocity are not one-sided acts but ongoing cycles that sustain and enrich everyone involved. Whether we are creating, performing, or listening, this card invites us to approach music with a spirit of balance and gratitude, recognizing it as both a gift and a responsibility. It calls on us to give freely, receive openly, and honor the flow of energy and creativity that music brings into our lives.

Seven of Pentacles

The Seven of Pentacles is a card of pause, assessment, and measured growth. It often depicts a figure standing contemplatively beside a flourishing plant, one that bears fruit after careful tending. In the realm of music, this card resonates with the slow and steady process of creation, the cultivation of a career, and the art of trusting in time and effort. It acknowledges the musician's journey as one that demands patience, perseverance, and the ability to reflect on progress without succumbing to frustration or doubt.

At its heart, the Seven of Pentacles asks us to consider the relationship between effort and outcome. For musicians, this can take many forms such as writing a song, recording an album, honing a craft, or building an audience. The card reflects the hours spent practicing an instrument, perfecting lyrics, or tweaking the mix of a track, all with no immediate promise of success. Music, like the growing plant in the card, often requires a significant investment of energy and care before it begins to bear fruit. The Seven of Pentacles reminds musicians that their work is not wasted, even if the results are not yet visible. It speaks to the value of dedication and trust in the process, encouraging artists to continue nurturing their art, knowing that growth takes time.

This card also invites reflection, urging musicians to step back and assess their progress. In the fast-paced and competitive world of music, it can be tempting to push forward relentlessly, always seeking the next achievement or milestone. The Seven of Pentacles offers a different perspective, encouraging a moment of pause to consider what has been accomplished and where adjustments might be needed. This is not a card of complacency but of intentional evaluation. It asks musicians to think critically about their goals, their methods, and whether their current path aligns with their vision. It's an opportunity to realign and refine, ensuring that energy is directed toward what truly matters.

For many, the Seven of Pentacles represents the challenge of delayed gratification. In a culture that often prioritizes instant results, the slow unfolding of a musical career or the painstaking process of creating a masterpiece can be discouraging. The card acknowledges this frustration, validating the weariness that can accompany long-term effort. Yet it also offers reassurance: the work is not for nothing. Each step, each rehearsal, each decision contributes to the larger picture. The Seven of Pentacles teaches musicians to embrace the journey as much as the destination, finding fulfillment in the act of creation itself, even before the results manifest.

Listeners, too, can find meaning in the Seven of Pentacles when it comes to their relationship with music. In an age of streaming and algorithmic playlists, where music is consumed rapidly and often passively, this card invites a more intentional approach. It encourages listeners to take the time to delve deeply into an album, to appreciate the layers of effort and artistry that went into its creation. The Seven of Pentacles reminds us that music, like any art form, reveals its richness fully only to those who are willing to engage with it patiently and thoughtfully.

Collaboration in music also carries the energy of the Seven of pentacles. Whether in a band, a production team, or a songwriting partnership, creating something together often involves a process of trial, error, and growth. The card acknowledges the challenges of collaboration, the need for compromise, the balancing of different ideas and egos and the patience required to see a shared vision through to fruition. It celebrates the moments when perseverance pays off, when the collective effort yields something greater than any individual could have achieved alone.

The Seven of Pentacles highlights the tension between artistry and commerce. It asks musicians and industry professionals alike to consider how they measure success. Is it about chart positions and financial returns, or is it about the depth and authenticity of the work? The card suggests that true value lies in the integrity of the process and the impact of the music itself, rather than in immediate or superficial markers of success. It challenges the industry to support long-term artistic growth rather than chasing fleeting trends, fostering an environment where musicians can thrive on their own terms.

The Seven of Pentacles also speaks to the cyclical nature of a musical career. Just as the figure in the card tends to a plant that will eventually bear fruit and then begin the cycle anew, so too does a musician's journey involve phases of creation, release, and reflection. An album might take years to write, record, and produce, only to be followed by the equally demanding tasks of promotion and performance. The card encourages musicians to honor each phase of this cycle, recognizing that growth and renewal are ongoing processes. It's a reminder that success is not a single event but a continuous unfolding, shaped by persistence and care.

Emotionally, the Seven of Pentacles asks musicians to stay connected to their purpose, even during times of doubt. It's easy to lose sight of the passion that first drew someone to music when progress feels slow or uncertain. This card invites a return to that passion, encouraging artists to reconnect with the joy and meaning of their work. It suggests that even in moments of stagnation or frustration, there is value in simply showing up and continuing to create. The act of tending, of investing time and energy into something meaningful, is itself a form of growth.

The Seven of Pentacles is a card of hope and perseverance. It acknowledges the challenges of the journey while celebrating the quiet triumphs along the way. It reminds us that music, like any meaningful pursuit, is not about instant gratification but about the steady and deliberate cultivation of something enduring. It calls on musicians and listeners alike to honor the process, to trust in the unfolding, and to find beauty in the act of creation, even when the harvest feels far away. In this way, the Seven of Pentacles becomes a testament to the resilience and patience that lie at the heart of every musical endeavor.

Eight of Pentacles
The Eight of Pentacles is a card of labor, focus, and the pursuit of mastery. It often depicts a figure diligently working, carving pentacles with precision and care, surrounded by the tools of their craft. This card symbolizes the process of refining one's skills, the discipline required to create something meaningful, and the satisfaction that comes from immersing oneself in a passionate endeavor. It celebrates the artist's journey from novice to expert, emphasizing the importance of dedication, hard work, and an unyielding commitment to improvement.

At its core, the Eight of Pentacles is about the daily grind of practice and creation. For musicians, this card evokes the hours spent perfecting scales, experimenting with chord progressions, or rehearsing a challenging piece until it feels seamless. It reminds us that while inspiration may strike suddenly, true artistry is built on the foundation of consistent effort. The Eight of Pentacles honors the invisible hours behind every polished performance. The times when a musician wrestles with frustration, hones their technique, and pushes through the monotony of repetition to achieve something extraordinary.

This card also speaks to the transformative power of dedication. The act of committing oneself to a craft can be as meaningful as the outcome itself. The process of creating, whether writing lyrics, composing a melody, or producing a track is deeply personal, requiring not only technical skill but also emotional investment. The Eight of Pentacles celebrates this interplay of head and heart, where precision meets passion, and where the artist's identity becomes inseparable from their work. It suggests that music, like the pentacles in the image, is both an expression of individuality and a tangible product of labor.

The Eight of Pentacles can also represent the pursuit of growth and learning. No matter how skilled one becomes, there is always more to explore, new genres to delve into, new techniques to master, new collaborations to embark upon. This card encourages humility and curiosity, reminding musicians that the path to mastery is never truly complete. It invites them to embrace the role of the eternal student, finding joy in the act of discovery and improvement. The Eight of Pentacles assures artists that their efforts are worthwhile, even if the progress feels slow or incremental.

In the context of collaboration, the Eight of Pentacles reflects the collective effort required to bring a musical vision to life. From the precision of a recording engineer to the subtle artistry of a session musician, every role in the creation of music demands focus and dedication. This card celebrates the interconnectedness of these efforts, showing how individual contributions combine to create something greater than the sum of its parts. It emphasizes the importance of respect and trust in collaborative relationships, where each person's craftsmanship is valued and nurtured.

Listeners, too, can resonate with the energy of the Eight of Pentacles. While the act of listening may seem passive, truly engaging with music requires a kind of active dedication. It involves paying attention to the nuances of a composition, allowing oneself to be moved by its emotional depth, and perhaps even revisiting it to uncover new layers of meaning. The Eight of Pentacles reminds us that music is not only created with care but deserves to be received with care as well. It invites listeners to approach music with an open mind and a willingness to immerse themselves fully, treating each song as a crafted work of art.

The Eight of Pentacles also reflects the reality of the music industry as a space of relentless effort and ambition. It speaks to the hours spent refining a demo, negotiating contracts, or building a fanbase from the ground up. For emerging artists, this card acknowledges the struggle of balancing artistic integrity with the demands of a commercial landscape. It offers encouragement, reminding them that success is often the result of sustained effort rather than overnight recognition. For established artists, the Eight of Pentacles suggests a return to fundamentals, urging them to continue challenging themselves and refining their craft, even after achieving success.

This card's emphasis on craftsmanship extends to the tools and environments that shape music. Just as the figure in the card works within a workshop, musicians rely on their instruments, recording studios, and creative spaces to bring their ideas to life. The Eight of Pentacles invites artists to honor these tools and spaces, treating them as extensions of their creative process. It suggests that the act of creating music is as much about the environment and materials as it is about the artist's vision, highlighting the interconnectedness of all aspects of the craft.

Emotionally, the Eight of Pentacles is a card of fulfillment through effort. It acknowledges that the path to mastery can be challenging, filled with moments of doubt, fatigue, and self-criticism. Yet, it also celebrates the deep satisfaction that comes from seeing one's progress and knowing that each step forward is earned. For musicians, this card is a reminder that their dedication is not only shaping their art but also shaping who they are. It suggests that the process of creating and refining music is as much about personal growth as it is about the final product.

On a symbolic level, the Eight of Pentacles represents the alchemy of transformation. Just as the figure in the card turns raw materials into something beautiful and meaningful, musicians take intangible emotions and ideas and give them form through sound. This act of creation is both magical and methodical, requiring both inspiration and discipline. The Eight of Pentacles encourages musicians to honor this duality, recognizing that their work is both an art and a craft, both intuitive and deliberate.

The Eight of Pentacles is a celebration of dedication, growth, and the joy of creation. It honors the time and effort that musicians pour into their craft, acknowledging the challenges and rewards of pursuing mastery. It reminds us that music is not only the finished product but also about the journey of creating, learning, and refining. Whether we are musicians or listeners, this card invites us to approach music with care and respect, recognizing it as a labor of love that requires both heart and skill. Through the lens of the Eight of Pentacles, music becomes a testament to the power of focus and perseverance, a reminder that true artistry is forged in the fires of commitment and passion.

Nine of Pentacles

The Nine of Pentacles is a card of self-sufficiency, refinement, and the satisfaction that comes from hard-earned success. Often depicted as a figure standing amidst a lush garden, this card symbolizes the rewards of discipline and perseverance. It carries an air of confidence and grace, a quiet celebration of accomplishments and the freedom they bring. The Nine of Pentacles speaks to the sense of mastery, independence, and fulfillment that can emerge from a life dedicated to the craft. It reminds musicians of the beauty of self-reliance, the power of their artistry, and the richness of a life shaped by music.

At its essence, the Nine of Pentacles is about arriving at a moment of achievement after a long journey of effort. In music, this card reflects the experience of reaching a point where the skills, vision, and determination invested in one's work have begun to bear fruit. It might be the release of an album that feels true to one's artistic voice, the completion of a difficult piece of music, or the quiet satisfaction of mastering a challenging technique. The Nine of Pentacles acknowledges the work that has gone into these moments, celebrating not only the outward success but also the inner growth and confidence that accompany it.

This card is particularly resonant for musicians who have chosen to carve their own path. In an industry often dominated by commercial pressures and trends, the Nine of Pentacles encourages artists to remain true to their vision, valuing their independence above external validation. It honors the decision to prioritize authenticity, even when it requires taking risks or making sacrifices. For independent musicians, the card can serve as a powerful affirmation of their journey, a reminder that success is not always about fame or fortune but about creating a life that feels aligned with their values and passions.

The imagery of the Nine of Pentacles also evokes a sense of harmony and balance. The figure in the garden suggests a life where creative work and personal fulfillment coexist, where the fruits of one's labor are not only tangible but also deeply nourishing. For musicians, this card highlights the importance of cultivating a sustainable relationship with their art. It suggests that success is not merely about achieving goals but also about finding joy and meaning in the process. The Nine of Pentacles invites artists to take pride in their accomplishments while remaining grounded, creating space for both ambition and gratitude.

In many ways, the Nine of Pentacles celebrates the artistry and refinement that come from dedication to craft. It speaks to the subtlety and sophistication that emerge over time, as a musician's skills deepen and their voice matures. This card honors the elegance of restraint, the ability to create music that is not only technically impressive but also emotionally resonant. It suggests that true mastery lies not in showing off but in creating work that feels effortless and natural, a reflection of the artist's confidence and grace.

For listeners, the Nine of Pentacles offers an opportunity to reflect on the role of music in their own lives. It encourages them to seek out and appreciate music that feels authentic and meaningful, music that resonates on a deeper level. Just as the figure in the card is surrounded by beauty and abundance, listeners are invited to cultivate their own "garden" of musical experiences, curating a collection of songs, albums, and performances that enrich their lives. The card also encourages an attitude of gratitude, reminding listeners to honor the effort and dedication that go into creating the music they love.

Collaboration in music can also carry the energy of the Nine of Pentacles, particularly when it involves mutual respect and shared independence. This card speaks to partnerships where each individual brings their own unique strengths to the table, creating something greater together while maintaining their distinct identities. It suggests a balance between unity and individuality, where collaboration enhances rather than diminishes the artist's voice. The Nine of Pentacles celebrates these relationships, showing how they can lead to work that is both cohesive and deeply personal.

The Nine of Pentacles raises questions about the nature of success and fulfillment. It challenges the conventional metrics of fame, wealth, and popularity, suggesting that true success lies in the ability to create and live on one's own terms. This card encourages both musicians and industry professionals to prioritize integrity and sustainability, fostering an environment where artists can thrive without compromising their vision. It invites a shift in perspective, from chasing external validation to cultivating a sense of inner accomplishment and pride.

Emotionally, the Nine of Pentacles is a card of confidence and self-worth. It reflects the satisfaction that comes from knowing one has worked hard and earned their place, whether as a musician, a performer, or a listener deeply engaged with their craft. This card encourages artists to embrace their achievements without hesitation, celebrating the strength and resilience that have brought them to this point. It also invites a sense of gratitude, recognizing the support, inspiration, and opportunities that have shaped the journey.

The symbolism of the garden in the Nine of Pentacles is particularly powerful when applied to music. Just as a garden requires care, patience, and attention to flourish, so too does a musical career or a body of work. This card reminds us that the beauty and abundance of music are not accidental but the result of consistent effort and love. It invites musicians to take pride in the "garden" they have cultivated, finding joy in its richness and knowing that it reflects their unique vision and dedication.

The Nine of Pentacles is a card of empowerment, celebrating the independence and fulfillment that come from a life shaped by passion and effort. It honors the musician's journey, from the struggles of learning and growing to the moments of triumph and satisfaction. It reminds us that music is not only a means of expression but also a source of personal strength and identity. Whether we are creating, performing, or listening, the Nine of Pentacles invites us to approach music with a sense of pride and gratitude, recognizing it as both a reflection of our inner selves and a gift to the world. Through the lens of this card, music becomes a symbol of what is possible when we commit ourselves fully to our craft, creating a life that is as rich and harmonious as the melodies we bring to life.

Ten of Pentacles

The Ten of Pentacles represents completion, abundance, and the enduring connections that define a meaningful life. It often depicts a family gathered together, surrounded by symbols of wealth, stability, and generational harmony. This card speaks to the power of music to create legacies, unite people across time, and build something lasting. It celebrates the culmination of efforts, the richness of shared experiences, and the profound ways in which music can transcend the boundaries of individual lives, weaving a collective story of connection and fulfillment.

The Ten of Pentacles is about legacy, what we create, share, and leave behind. In music, this legacy can take many forms: a song that becomes an anthem for generations, a body of work that inspires future artists, or a family tradition of musical work that inspires future artists, or a family tradition of musical talent passed down through the years. The card reflects the enduring impact of music, its ability to echo beyond its moment of creation and resonate with people long after the final note has been played. It invites musicians to consider the long-term significance of their work, not just in terms of personal achievement but as a contribution to a larger cultural tapestry.

For musicians, the Ten of Pentacles can symbolize the culmination of a career or the realization of a long-held vision. It represents the satisfaction of reaching a point where one's efforts have come to fruition, creating a sense of stability and accomplishment. This might manifest as a release of a definitive album, the establishment of a successful band, or the creation of a personal archive of music that feels complete. The card celebrates these moments of achievement, encouraging artists to take pride in what they have built and to recognize the ways in which their work contributes to the broader musical landscape.

The imagery of the Ten of Pentacles also evokes the idea of music as a unifying force. Just as the family in the card gathers together in harmony, music has the power to bring people together, creating bonds that transcend differences in age, culture, and background. Whether it's a family singing together at home, a community choir, or a concert that unites thousands of strangers, music fosters a sense of belonging and shared experience. The Ten of Pentacles honors these moments, showing how music can create a sense of home and connection, even in the most diverse and far-reaching contexts.

The Ten of Pentacles speaks to the strength of collective effort. Bands, orchestras, and production teams all embody the spirit of this card, working together to create something greater than any individual could achieve alone. It highlights the importance of trust, respect, and mutual support in these partnerships, celebrating the richness that emerges when diverse talents and perspectives come together. The card suggests that music, like a family or community, thrives on collaboration and shared purpose, growing stronger through the contributions of each member.

This card invites listeners to reflect on the ways music shapes their own lives, from the songs that evoke memories of loved ones to the albums that define significant moments. It suggests that music is not only a personal experience but also a shared heritage, passed down from one generation to the next. The Ten of Pentacles encourages listeners to honor this legacy, appreciating the connections music creates and the ways it enriches life on both an individual and collective level.

The Ten of Pentacles also speaks to the idea of music as a cultural and historical archive. Songs and compositions are not only artistic expressions but also reflections of the times and places in which they were created. They carry stories, emotions, and values across generations, preserving a sense of identity and continuity. This card highlights the responsibility of musicians to contribute to this archive thoughtfully, creating work that honors the past while also speaking to the present and future. It reminds us that music is both a personal expression and a collective inheritance, shaped by and shaping the world around it.

Emotionally, the Ten of Pentacles is a card of fulfillment and gratitude. It reflects the joy of knowing one's efforts have contributed to something lasting and meaningful, whether that's a career, a family tradition, or a connection with an audience. For musicians, this card offers reassurance that their work has value, even beyond what they may immediately see. It encourages artists to embrace the richness of their journey, celebrating not only their own achievements but also the relationships, memories, and experiences that have been woven into their music.

On a symbolic level, the Ten of Pentacles represents the cyclical and timeless nature of music. Just as the family in the card spans multiple generations, music connects the past, present, and future in a continuous flow. A song written decades ago can feel as fresh and relevant as one written today, while a new composition might draw inspiration from centuries-old traditions. This card honors the way music transcends time, creating a bridge between eras and allowing each generation to find its voice within a shared heritage.

The Ten of Pentacles challenges the emphasis on short-term success and fleeting trends. It advocates for a perspective that values sustainability, integrity, and long-term impact over immediate gratification. This card encourages both musicians and industry professionals to think about what they are building, not just for themselves, but for the future of music as a whole. It suggests that true success lies in creating something enduring, something that will continue to resonate and inspire for years to come.

The Ten of Pentacles is a card of celebration and connection. It honors the richness of a life shaped by music, the joy of shared experiences, and the power of art to create lasting legacies. It reminds musicians and listeners alike that music is more than just sound, it is a thread that weaves together individuals, families, and communities, creating a tapestry of meaning and belonging. Whether through a timeless song, a family tradition, or a powerful performance, the Ten of Pentacles invites us to recognize the enduring beauty and significance of music, embracing it as a source of abundance, harmony, and love.

Page of Pentacles

The Page of Pentacles represents the energy of curiosity, youthful ambition, and the desire to lay the groundwork for future growth. Often depicted as a figure holding a pentacle, gazing at it with focus and wonder, this card symbolizes the beginning stages of learning and mastery. The Page of Pentacles embodies someone to pick up an instrument, compose their first melody, or explore the boundless world of sound. It is a card of potential, offering a reminder that even the most accomplished musicians were once beginners, driven by a simple love for their craft.

The Page of Pentacles is about exploration. For musicians, this card captures the magic of trying something new such as plucking the strings of a guitar for the first time, discovering how to shape a note on a wind instrument, or piecing together the elements of a beat on a computer. These moments are not about perfection or polish but about the joy of the process, the thrill of creating sound from silence. The Page of Pentacles invites musicians to embrace this sense of wonder, treating music not as a task but as an opportunity to learn, grow, and express themselves.

The card also speaks to the importance of grounding one's aspirations in practice and effort. While the Page of Pentacles is filled with enthusiasm and vision, it also carries a sense of responsibility. It reminds musicians that growth requires dedication, that each small step builds the foundation for greater achievements. This energy is especially resonant for beginners, who may be overwhelmed by the vastness of what lies ahead. The card reassures them that progress is made one note, one chord, one rhythm at a time, and that every moment of effort brings them closer to their goals.

For seasoned musicians, the Page of Pentacles can serve as a call to reconnect with their beginner's mindset. It encourages them to approach their craft with the same curiosity and openness that first drew them to music. This might involve experimenting with a new genre, trying out an unfamiliar instrument, or collaborating with someone who brings a fresh perspective. The card suggests that even the most experienced artists can benefit from returning to the fundamentals, finding new inspiration in the simplicity and purity of the creative process.

In the realm of education, the Page of Pentacles holds particular significance. It reflects the dynamic relationship between teacher and student, where knowledge is passed down with patience and care. For music educators, this card highlights the importance of fostering curiosity and confidence in their students, creating an environment where they feel free to explore and make mistakes. For students, it emphasizes the value of persistence and openness, encouraging them to embrace the challenges of learning as opportunities for growth. The Page of Pentacles celebrates the act of teaching and learning as a shared journey, where both parties are enriched by the exchange.

The Page of Pentacles also resonates with the idea of music as a lifelong pursuit. It reminds us that there is always more to learn, regardless of age or experience. This card speaks to the joy of discovery at any stage, whether it's a young child mastering their first scales, an adult returning to an instrument after many years away, or a seasoned musician delving into a new style. The Page of Pentacles assures us that it is never too late to start, or to start again, and that every moment spent engaging with music is valuable and rewarding.

For listeners, this card invites a deeper engagement with music. It encourages them to explore beyond their usual preferences, seeking out new genres, artists, and styles. Just as the figure in the card studies the pentacle with curiosity, listeners are urged to approach music with an open mind, treating it as a source of discovery and inspiration. The Page of Pentacles suggests that music has the power to expand our horizons, offering not only enjoyment but also new ways of thinking and feeling.

The Page of Pentacles reflects the early stages of a musical project. It might signify the first draft of a song, the initial sketches of a composition, or the brainstorming phase of a collaborative effort. This card acknowledges the uncertainty and excitement of these beginnings, when ideas are still taking shape and possibilities feel endless. It encourages musicians to nurture these seeds of creativity, giving them the time and attention they need to grow. The Page of Pentacles reminds us that every masterpiece begins as an idea, and that the journey from inspiration to completion is as important as the final result.

The card's connection to the Earth element further emphasizes the importance of grounding and focus in the creative process. While the Page of Pentacles is filled with curiosity and ambition, it also understands the need for patience and perseverance. In music, this translates to the discipline of practice, the care taken in crafting a composition, and the attention given to refining one's skills. The card suggests that success in music is not achieved through shortcuts or quick fixes but through steady, mindful effort. It celebrates the satisfaction that comes from building something meaningful, one step at a time.

Emotionally, the Page of Pentacles carries a sense of optimism and possibility. It reflects the excitement of embarking on a new journey, the confidence that comes from seeing one's progress, and the hope that the future holds even greater achievements. For musicians, this card is a reminder to celebrate their growth, no matter how small, and to trust in their ability to keep moving forward. It invites them to approach their craft with joy and curiosity; letting go of self-doubt and embracing the adventure of learning.

The Page of Pentacles is a card of potential and promise. It honors the beginnings of a musical journey, whether it's a young artist finding their voice, a seasoned musician exploring new territory, or a listener discovering a song that changes their perspective. It reminds us that music is not only about the destination but also about the process of getting there. Through the lens of the Page of Pentacles, music becomes a symbol of growth, resilience, and the endless possibilities that await those who are willing to explore.

Knight of Pentacles

The Knight of Pentacles is a card of steadfastness, responsibility, and methodical progress. In contrast to the fiery passion of the Knight of Wands or the emotional charge of the Knight of Cups, the Knight of Pentacles approaches his journey with patience and unwavering commitment. This card embodies the disciplined artist, the one who understands that mastery is not achieved overnight but through consistent effort and careful attention to detail. The Knight of Pentacles invites musicians to focus on the process, valuing persistence and craftsmanship over immediate results.

The Knight of Pentacles represents a deliberate approach to growth and achievement. For musicians, this means embracing the daily grind of practice, refining their skills, and honing their craft over time. While other tarot cards may celebrate the bursts of inspiration that fuel creativity, the Knight of Pentacles reminds us that inspiration alone is not enough. It takes hours of repetition, the slow building of muscle memory, and a commitment to steady improvement to transform raw talent into artistry. This card speaks to the quiet but profound satisfaction that comes from putting in the work, knowing that each small step is part of a larger journey.

The Knight of Pentacles is not flashy, nor does he seek recognition for his efforts. Similarly, this card encourages musicians to focus on their own path rather than comparing themselves to others. In a world where social media and industry metrics often measure success in terms of visibility and popularity, the Knight of Pentacles advocates for a different kind of success, one rooted in personal growth, integrity, and the pursuit of excellence. For the musicians, this means valuing the quality of their work over external validation, trusting that their dedication will yield results in its own time.

This card also speaks to the importance of routine and structure in a musical practice. The Knight of Pentacles thrives on consistency, understanding that progress is made not through bursts of energy but through sustained effort. For musicians, this might mean setting aside regular time for practice, adhering to the creative schedule, or establishing habits that support their artistic goals. While this discipline may seem mundane compared to the thrill of performance or the rush of inspiration, the Knight of Pentacles assures us that it is the foundation upon which lasting success is built. His energy reminds us that the work we do in private is what allows us to shine in public.

The Knight of Pentacles represents reliability and teamwork. He is the band member who shows up to every rehearsal prepared, the producer who meticulously polishes every track, or the songwriter who patiently refines their lyrics until they capture the desired emotion. This card values the contributions of those who may not seek the spotlight but whose dedication ensures that the final product is strong and cohesive. The Knight of Pentacles honors the unsung heroes of music, the technicians, the engineers, the session musicians, whose steady work supports the success of others. It encourages a spirit of respect and gratitude for all those who contribute to the musical process, reminding us that every role is vital.

Emotionally, the Knight of Pentacles represents a grounded and stable approach to music. While the creative process can sometimes be fraught with doubt, frustration, or elation, this card offers a reminder to stay balanced and focused. For musicians who feel overwhelmed by the challenges of their craft, the Knight of Pentacles provides reassurance that progress is possible, even if it comes slowly. His presence encourages patience and perseverance, helping artists to trust in their own abilities and the process of growth.

For listeners, the Knight of Pentacles invites an appreciation for the craftsmanship behind the music they enjoy. It encourages a deeper engagement with the work, recognizing the time and effort that go into creating each note, lyric, and arrangement. Just as the Knight values the details of his labor, listeners are invited to pay attention to the nuances of a song, the subtle shifts in dynamics, the precision of the rhythm, the layers of harmony, and to honor the artistry behind them. This card fosters an attitude of mindfulness, encouraging listeners to approach music not as a product to consume but as an art form to savor.

The Knight of Pentacles serves as a reminder of the value of long-term thinking. While the industry often prioritizes quick results and fleeting trends, this card advocates for sustainable growth and careful planning. It suggests that success in music is not about chasing the next big thing but about building a foundation that can support a lasting career. For independent artists, this might mean investing in their craft, cultivating a loyal audience, and making decisions that align with their values rather than succumbing to pressure. The Knight of Pentacles encourages artists and industry professionals alike to think beyond the present moment, focusing on what will stand the test of time.

Creatively, the Knight of Pentacles represents the phase of refinement and execution in a musical project. While other cards may capture the excitement of brainstorming or the joy of completion, this card is about the work that happens in between: editing, adjusting, and perfecting. It speaks to the discipline required to turn an idea into a finished piece, whether it's a song, an album, or a performance. The Knight of Pentacles encourages musicians to approach this process with care and intention, trusting that their effort will result in something worthwhile.

On a symbolic level, the Knight of Pentacles resonates with the rhythm of the Earth, the steady pulse that underlies all things. This rhythm is reflected in the metronome's ticking, the drummer's beat, or the bassline that anchors a song. The Knight of Pentacles reminds us that music is built on foundations, on patterns and repetitions that create structure and coherence. He invites musicians to honor these foundations, finding strength and inspiration in the steadiness they provide.

The Knight of Pentacles is a card of dedication and resilience. It celebrates the quiet work of creating, the persistence required to overcome challenges, and the joy of building something meaningful over time. It honors the musician's journey from the first tentative steps to the steady rhythm of a life devoted to art. Through this card, music becomes a symbol of what is possible when we commit ourselves fully to our craft, trusting in the process and embracing the power of patience, effort, and love for the art form.

Queen of Pentacles

The Queen of Pentacles is a figure of balance, nurturing, and abundance. She holds a deep connection to the Earth and its rhythms, embodying the fusion of practicality with creativity. As she sits gracefully on her throne, gazing at the pentacle in her hands, her energy reflects care, resourcefulness, and the ability to manifest dreams into tangible realities. The Queen symbolizes the profound ways in which creativity can be nurtured, supported, and cultivated into something meaningful. She represents the artist who is not only deeply connected to their craft but also mindful of the environment in which it flourishes.

Music under the influence of the Queen of Pentacles takes on a grounded and holistic quality. She is the mother of melodies, tending to her compositions and performances with care and intention. Her presence is a reminder that music, like all forms of art, requires nurturing, not just in its creation but also in its sharing and sustenance. The Queen of Pentacles encourages musicians to cultivate their craft with patience and love, understanding that their work is not separate from the life they live but deeply intertwined with it.

The Queen of Pentacles' connection to the Earth element is particularly significant in music. She invites artists to root themselves in their personal experiences and to draw inspiration from the natural world. For a songwriter, this might mean crafting lyrics that reflect the cycles of life, the beauty of the seasons, or the quiet strength of nature. For a composer, it could be creating pieces that evoke the ebb and flow of tides or the rustling of leaves. The Queen's influence suggests that music can be a reflection of the world around us, a mirror of the energies that sustain and ground us.

She also represents the importance of creating a supportive environment for musical growth. Just as the Queen of Pentacles tends to her garden, ensuring that each plant has the resources it needs to thrive, she encourages musicians to build a foundation for their art. This might mean creating a physical space for practice and creativity, cultivating a supportive community, or ensuring that their emotional and physical well-being is cared for. The Queen understands that music cannot flourish in isolation; it needs a fertile ground, a safe space where ideas can be explored and developed. She reminds musicians that self-care and stability are not distractions from their craft but essential components of their ability to create.

The Queen of Pentacles also emphasizes the value of music as a gift to be shared. Her nurturing energy extends beyond herself, encompassing her community and those she loves. In this sense, she reflects the musician who creates not only for personal fulfillment but also to connect with others. Whether through a performance, a recording, or a single song shared with a friend, music becomes an act of giving under her influence. The Queen encourages artists to see their work as a contribution to the greater good, a way of spreading joy, comfort, and understanding to those who hear it.

For those who teach music, the Queen of Pentacles embodies the essence of mentorship and guidance. She is the teacher who patiently supports her students, tailoring her approach to their individual needs and strengths. Her focus is not solely on technical mastery but also on nurturing a love for music and an appreciation for its power. She understands that each student is unique, and she takes the time to help them discover their own voice. The Queen of Pentacles reminds educators that their role is not just to impart knowledge but to create an environment where their students can grow and thrive.

In the creative process, the Queen of Pentacles represents the integration of inspiration with practicality. She understands that while dreams and ideas are important, they must be grounded in reality to take shape. This might mean balancing the creative freedom of writing and performing with the logistical aspects of recording, rehearsing, and organizing projects. The Queen's energy encourages artists to approach their work with both passion and discipline, ensuring that their vision is brought to life in a way that is sustainable and achievable.

Her connection to abundance also plays a significant role in music. The Queen of Pentacles is not about excess or indulgence but about recognizing and appreciating the resources available to her. For musicians, this might mean valuing the instruments they have, the opportunities they're given, or the simple act of creating sound. She teaches us to find richness in what we already possess, to see the potential in small beginnings, and to approach our craft with gratitude. Her influence fosters an attitude of contentment and resourcefulness, reminding us that true abundance comes not from having everything but from making the most of what we have.

The Queen of Pentacles is also a deeply emotional figure, though her emotions are expressed through care and action rather than overt display. In music, this translates to a focus on creating work that resonates on a soulful level. She encourages musicians to infuse their art with sincerity and depth, to craft pieces that speak to the heart. Her energy is not about grand gestures or dramatic performances but about the quiet power of authenticity. Under her influence, music becomes a medium for connection and healing, a way of expressing emotions that words alone cannot capture.

In the realm of performance, the Queen of Pentacles embodies grace and presence. She is the artist who commands attention not through force or showmanship but through the authenticity of her expression. Her performances are marked by a sense of groundedness, a connection to her audience that feels genuine and unforced. She reminds musicians that their power lies not in perfection but in their ability to connect, to share a part of themselves with those who listen.

The Queen of Pentacles also encourages musicians to consider the long-term impact of their work. She is a steward of the future, mindful of how her actions today shape the world tomorrow. This might mean creating music that is timeless, that continues to resonate long after its initial release. It could also involve mentoring younger musicians, supporting their development, and ensuring that the art form is carried forward. The Queen of Pentacles reminds us that music is a legacy, a gift that can inspire and uplift for generations to come.

The Queen of Pentacles is a card of care, connection, and commitment. She celebrates the artist who approaches their craft with love and integrity, who nurtures their talent and shares it generously. She honors the balance between creativity and practicality, reminding us that music is both an art and a discipline. Through her influence, music becomes a source of sustenance and joy, a reflection of the beauty and abundance of life itself. The Queen of Pentacles invites us to see music not only as a pursuit but as a way of living, a way of connecting to ourselves, to others, and to the world around us.

King of Pentacles

The King of Pentacles is the embodiment of abundance, stability, and accomplishment. He sits on his throne as a figure of authority, success, and wisdom, surrounded by symbols of prosperity and rooted firmly in the material world. As a culmination of the Pentacles suit, the King represents the mastery of resources and the ability to create a legacy. He speaks to the harmony between artistry and the material structures that sustain it. His presence reminds us that music, while deeply creative and emotional, also benefits from discipline, financial stability, and long-term vision.

The King of Pentacles teaches that music is not just a fleeting act of inspiration but also an endeavor that can be cultivated into a sustainable craft. He represents the musician who has mastered their art through years of dedication and hard work, who has built a career with both creativity and practicality in mind. The King's influence encourages musicians to think strategically about their art, not as a compromise of creativity but as a way to ensure its longevity. He is the planner, the provider, and the protector of musical dreams, guiding the artists to balance their passion with the realities of the world.

The King of Pentacles represents a musician's moment of achievement in their journey. He is the artist who has worked tirelessly to reach a level of mastery, who has honed their skills to the point where they can confidently create and share their work. But his success is not defined solely by fame or wealth; it is also rooted in the respect he commands and the stability he has cultivated. The King of Pentacles values quality over quantity, understanding that true artistry lies in depth and substance rather than superficial appeal. His energy encourages musicians to take pride in their work, knowing that their dedication and effort have built something enduring.

This card also highlights the importance of financial stability in the creative process. The King of Pentacles understands that art flourishes when it is supported by a strong foundation. For musicians, this might mean finding ways to make their craft financially sustainable, whether through smart business decisions, diversifying their income streams, or investing in tools and resources that enhance their work. The King's presence serves as a reminder that there is no shame in valuing the material aspects of a musical career. Instead, it is a mark of wisdom and foresight to recognize that stability allows for greater freedom and creativity.

The King of Pentacles also speaks to the role of mentorship and leadership in music. As a figure of authority, he represents the seasoned artist who shares their knowledge and experience with others. He is the producer who nurtures new talent, the teacher who inspires their students, and the mentor who guides young musicians through the challenges of the industry. His approach is patient and supportive, valuing the development of others as much as his own success. In this way, the King of Pentacles reminds us that true mastery is not just about personal accomplishment but about uplifting and empowering others.

The card's connection to abundance is particularly significant in music. The King of Pentacles embodies the idea that prosperity is not limited to material wealth but also includes a richness of experience, relationships, and creative expression. For musicians, this might mean valuing the joy of making music, the connections formed with collaborators and audiences, and the satisfaction of creating something meaningful. The King encourages artists to appreciate the abundance already present in their lives and to build on it with gratitude and intention. He reminds us that music is both a gift and a legacy, something to be cherished and shared.

Creatively, the King of Pentacles represents a phase of refinement and execution. He is the artist who has moved beyond experimentation and exploration to focus on perfecting their craft. His energy is deliberate and meticulous, emphasizing the importance of attention to details and a commitment to excellence. This might mean taking the time to polish a piece, or ensuring that a performance is executed with precision and passion. The King of Pentacles values the process of creation as much as the final product, understanding that every step contributes to the overall success of the endeavor.

In the realm of collaboration, the King of Pentacles is a symbol of reliability and support. He is the bandleader who ensures that everyone is heard and valued, the producer who creates a stable environment for creativity, and the manager who handles the practical aspects of a project so that the artists can focus on their work. His energy fosters trust and cooperation, reminding us that music is often a collective effort and that success is built on strong relationships and mutual respect.

The King of Pentacles invites an appreciation of music's craftsmanship. His energy encourages us to look beyond the surface and to recognize the effort, skill, and thought that go into creating a piece of music. He reminds us that every note, rhythm, and lyric is the result of dedication and care. By honoring the work of musicians, listeners can deepen their connection to the art and the artists who create it.

On a symbolic level, the King of Pentacles resonates with the rhythm of life itself. His connection to the Earth element is reflected in the steady beat of a drum, the grounding bassline of a song, or the predictable cycles of harmony and melody. He reminds us that music, like life, is built on patterns and structures that provide stability and coherence. The King's influence encourages musicians to honor these foundations, finding strength and inspiration in the steady pulse that underlies their art.

The King of Pentacles is a card of mastery, generosity, and legacy. He celebrates the artist who has dedicated themselves to their craft, who has built a stable foundation for their creativity, and who shares their work with others in a spirit of abundance and gratitude. His presence reminds us that music is both a personal journey and a communal experience, a way of connecting to ourselves, to others, and to the world around us. Through the lens of this card, music becomes a symbol of what is possible when passion, discipline, and wisdom come together to create something lasting and meaningful.

Self-Reflection and Emotional Balance

Tarot, with its evocative imagery and deep symbolic language, provides a framework for exploring emotions in ways that bypass the rational mind, for exploring emotions in ways that bypass the rational mind, delving into the subconscious where feelings often reside unexamined. Music, too, has this power; it can evoke, express, and transform emotions that words alone might struggle to capture. When musicians use tarot as a tool for emotional processing, they engage in a creative dialogue that can lead to profound self-discovery and artistic growth.

At its core, tarot is a mirror, reflecting back the inner world of the person seeking its wisdom. Each card functions as a gateway to a specific emotional or psychological state, inviting exploration of themes such as joy, grief, hope, and fear. For musicians, this reflective quality is particularly valuable. Music often arises from the depths of emotion, but the process of translating those feelings into sound requires clarity and intention. Tarot can help illuminate the emotional terrain, giving musicians a map to navigate their inner world and identify the stories they wish to tell.

For example, a musician grappling with heartbreak might turn to the Three of Swords, a card that poignantly captures the pain of loss. The stark imagery of the pierced heart can serve as a focal point for exploring the layers of their sorrow, from the initial sting of betrayal to the quiet ache of longing. Through this exploration, the musician might begin to identify the nuances of their experience and translate these feelings into their music. The tarot becomes a tool for distillation, helping the musician shape raw emotion into something tangible and meaningful.

Tarot also provides a safe space for confronting difficult emotions. Cards like the Tower or the Moon may evoke feelings of upheaval or confusion, but they also offer a sense of structure and narrative. The Tower's image of destruction and collapse is tempered by its underlying promise of renewal, reminding the musician that even the most chaotic emotions have a purpose. This perspective can be deeply healing, allowing the musician to engage with their feelings without fear of being overwhelmed. In turn, this emotional engagement can lead to music that is honest and cathartic, resonating with listeners who recognize their own struggles in the artist's work.

Another way tarot supports emotional processing is through its encouragement of introspection. Cards like the Hermit invite the musician to step away from external distractions and listen to their inner voice. This inward focus can be especially helpful during creative blocks, which often arise when unresolved emotions are ignored or suppressed. By spending time with the cards, musicians can uncover hidden feelings or patterns that may be hindering their creative flow. For instance, drawing the Eight of Swords might reveal a sense of self-imposed limitation, prompting the musician to examine how fear or doubt is affecting their work. This awareness can then inform the music they create, imbuing it with a sense of liberation and self-empowerment.

The transformative power of tarot lies not only in its ability to bring emotions to the surface but also in its capacity to shift perspectives. Cards like the Hanged Man encourage a reframing of circumstances, inviting the musician to see their experiences in a new light. A period of sadness, when viewed through the lens of the Hanged Man, might be understood as a necessary pause, a time of gestation before renewal. This shift in understanding can inspire music that moves beyond simple expression of emotion to explore themes of resilience, growth, and transformation. The musician becomes both the observer and the creator of their emotional journey, using the tarot as a guide to navigate and reframe their experiences.

The collaborative nature of tarot also fosters a sense of co-creation that can be deeply empowering. Unlike traditional forms of emotional processing that might feel passive or linear, tarot invites active participation. The musician shuffles the cards, lays them out, and interprets their meanings, engaging directly with their emotions at every step. This sense of agency can be particularly valuable for artists, who often channel their emotions into their work as a way of asserting control over their inner world. By working with the tarot, musicians reclaim their role as storytellers of their own lives, crafting narratives that honor their feelings while transforming them into art.

Tarot's emphasis on archetypes also enriches emotional processing by connecting personal experiences to universal themes. A musician working through feelings of betrayal might draw the Seven of Swords, a card that speaks to deceit and cunning. While the musician's immediate response might be tied to their specific circumstances, the card's broader symbolism invites reflection on the nature of trust and vulnerability. This connection to the universal can be profoundly validating, reminding the musician that their emotions are part of the shared human experience. It also deepens the emotional resonance of their music, allowing listeners to see themselves in the artist's story.

Tarot's ability to illuminate the interplay of emotions is another key benefit for musicians. Many cards, like Temperance, speak to balance and integration, encouraging the musician to explore how seemingly opposing feelings coexist. A song inspired by Temperance might weave together themes of joy and sorrow, creating a rich tapestry that mirrors the complexity of human emotion. Similarly, the interplay of light and shadow in cards like the Sun and the Moon can inspire music that embraces contrast, capturing the tension and beauty of duality.

Tarot encourages musicians to see emotions as dynamic and evolving. Just as the cards move through cycles of challenge and resolution, so too do feelings shift and transform. A musician might begin their journey with the despair of the Five of Cups but find themselves drawn to the hope and renewal of the Star as they process their emotions. The cyclical perspective fosters a sense of flow, reminding the musician that no feeling is permanent and that every emotion has a role to play in the creative process. The music that emerges from this understanding is often layered and multidimensional, reflecting the richness of the emotional journey.

In this way, tarot becomes more than a tool for self-reflection; it becomes an active partner in the musician's creative process. By engaging with the cards, musicians gain insight into their inner world, find new ways of understanding and expressing their emotions, and create music that resonates on a deeply human level. Tarot's ability to hold space for both the personal and the universal makes it an invaluable resource for artists seeking to process their feelings and transform them into something meaningful. Through the fusion of tarot and music, emotions find their voice, becoming stories that heal, inspire, and connect.

Tarot as an Emotional Gateway in Music

Music is a calling, a profound expression of the soul's need to create, communicate, and connect. For many musicians, the journey toward understanding their purpose and rekindling their passion is as complex and transformative as the music they create. Tarot, with its archetypal symbols and intuitive wisdom, offers a powerful tool for navigating this journey. By engaging with the cards, musicians can explore their inner world, confront doubts, and reconnect with the core of their artistic identity. Tarot becomes not only a reflective practice but a guide, illuminating the path toward authentic creative expression.

The journey begins with the understanding that purpose and passion are not fixed states; they are dynamic forces that ebb and flow, shaped by experience and self-awareness. Musicians often face periods of uncertainty, such as times when the spark of inspiration feels distant, or when the demands of the outside world cloud their sense of why they create in the first place. Tarot's ability to uncover hidden truths and provide clarity makes it an ideal companion in these moments. The cards act as a mirror, reflecting the musician's internal landscape and revealing the deeper motivations and desires that drive their art.

At the heart of this process is the Major Arcana, which charts a universal journey of self-discovery and growth. The Fool, the first card of the tarot, is a natural starting point for any musician seeking to reconnect with their purpose. The Fool represents the essence of pure potential, the willingness to take risks and embrace the unknown. For a musician, this card might evoke memories of the first time they picked up an instrument, wrote a song, or performed in front of an audience. It reminds them of the unfiltered joy and curiosity that first drew them to music. By meditating on the Fool, musicians can strip away the layers of doubt, fear, or expectation that may have accumulated over time, reconnecting with the childlike wonder that lies at the heart of their passion.

As the journey unfolds, other cards offer additional insights into the musician's relationship with their craft. The Magician, with its tools of creation laid out on the table, speaks to the musician's potential for mastery and self-expression. This card challenges the artist to consider how they can harness their skills and resources to align with their higher purpose. It also invites a sense of empowerment, urging the musician to see themselves as an active participant in their own creative journey. The Magician reminds them that they already possess everything they need to create something meaningful. The challenge is to trust in their ability and take action.

The High Priestess, in contrast, draws the musician inward, encouraging them to listen to their intuition and explore the subconscious forces that shape their artistry. This card often appears when a musician feels disconnected from their inner voice, when external pressures or self-doubt have drowned out the quiet whispers of inspiration. The High Priestess invites the musician to embrace stillness and introspection, to trust that their passion for music is a reflection of something deeper within. Through this connection to the inner self, musicians can rediscover a sense of authenticity in their work, creating music that feels true to their essence.

Tarot also helps musicians confront and move through obstacles that may be blocking their sense of purpose. Cards like the Devil and the Tower often symbolize moments of struggle or upheaval, but they also hold the promise of liberation and transformation. The Devil may reveal patterns of self-sabotage, such as perfectionism or fear of failure, that stifle creative expression. The Tower, with its imagery of destruction and renewal, reminds musicians that breaking free from these patterns often requires a willingness to let go of old beliefs or habits. While these cards may be challenging, they offer invaluable insights into the forces that hold musicians back, providing a roadmap for overcoming them.

One of the most powerful aspects of tarot is its ability to connect the personal with the universal. Musicians often create from a deeply personal place, but the act of making music is also a means of connecting with others and contributing to something greater than oneself. Cards like the Star and the World emphasize this interconnectedness, reminding musicians that their work has the power to inspire, heal, and unite. The Star, with its message of hope and renewal, encourages musicians to see their passion as a guiding light, not just for themselves, but for their listeners. The World, representing completion and unity, speaks to the musician's role in the larger fabric of humanity, where their unique voice contributes to a collective symphony.

Tarot's archetypes also help musicians explore the relationship between their purpose and their identity. Cards like the Emperor and the Empress offer contrasting perspectives on how musicians can embody their creative role. The Emperor emphasizes structure, discipline, and leadership, encouraging musicians to take control of their artistic vision and build something lasting. The Empress, on the other hand, celebrates creativity, nurturing, and flow, inviting musicians to embrace the organic, intuitive aspects of their craft. By reflecting on these archetypes, musicians can gain a deeper understanding of how they approach their work and where they might need to find balance.

Beyond individual cards, tarot spreads can be tailored to explore specific questions about purpose and passion. A musician might use a spread to examine the roots of their creative calling, the challenges they face, and the steps they can take to move forward. Each card in the spread becomes a piece of a larger puzzle, offering insights that, when woven together, create a cohesive narrative. This process of storytelling mirrors the act of making music, where disparate elements come together to form a harmonious whole.

Tarot also fosters a sense of ritual and intentionality, which can be deeply grounding for musicians. The act of drawing cards, reflecting on their meanings, and applying their insights to one's life is itself a creative practice, one that mirrors the process of composing or performing music. This ritual creates space for musicians to pause, reflect, and reconnect with their purpose, even in the midst of a busy or chaotic life. It becomes a moment of alignment, where the musician can tune in to their inner world and reignite their passion for their craft.

Perhaps most importantly, tarot reminds musicians that their purpose and passion are ever-evolving. Just as the cards move through cycles of growth, challenge, and renewal, so too does the creative journey. Tarot encourages musicians to embrace this fluidity, to see each phase of their journey as a valuable part of their story. Whether they are riding the highs of inspiration or navigating the lows of creative block, the cards offer guidance and reassurance, reminding them that their purpose is not a destination but a path.

In the end, tarot serves as both a compass and a companion, guiding musicians toward a deeper understanding of themselves and their art. By engaging with the cards, musicians can uncover the truths that lie at the heart of their passion, overcome the obstacles that obscure their purpose, and create music that is rich with meaning and authenticity. Through this process, they not only reconnect with their calling but also discover new ways of sharing their unique voice with the world. Tarot becomes a bridge between the inner and outer realms, a source of inspiration and clarity that fuels the creative fire.

Interpreting Chords and Cards

Music and tarot share a common language of patterns, archetypes, and emotional resonance, making the alignment of musical theory with tarot symbolism a compelling exploration. Both systems are deeply rooted in structure and intuition, with each relying on an interplay of established rules and creative freedom to evoke meaning. Musical theory provides the scaffolding for harmony, melody, and rhythm, while tarot offers a symbolic framework for exploring the human experience. When these two worlds intersect, they create a rich tapestry of meaning, enabling musicians and listeners alike to deepen their understanding of music through the lens of tarot and vice versa.

The fundamental principles of musical theory, including scales, chords, and progressions, can be mapped into the symbolic language of tarot to explore the interplay between sound and meaning. Scales, for instance, serve as the foundation for melody, establishing the tonal framework within which music exists. Similarly, the Major Arcana establishes a symbolic framework that encompasses universal archetypes and human experiences. Each note in a scale and each card in the Major Arcana carries its own unique energy, yet they exist in relation to one another, forming a cohesive whole. This parallel invites a deeper exploration of how individual elements contribute to a greater narrative.

Consider the Major Arcana's Fool's Journey as an overarching structure that can be aligned with the development of a musical composition. The Fool, representing pure potential and the beginning of a journey, mirrors the tonic note of a scale, the starting point from which all other notes derive their context. In the same way that the tonic establishes the home base for a piece of music, the Fool establishes the thematic foundation for the tarot journey. As the journey unfolds through cards like the Magician, the High Priestess, and the Emperor, the interplay of major and minor chords in music can echo the evolving emotional and symbolic landscape. Major chords might align with the empowering energy of the Magician or the structural authority of the Emperor, while minor chords might capture the introspective mystery of the High Priestess.

Chord progressions, too, can reflect the narrative flow of a tarot spread. A common progression like I-IV-V-I, which creates a sense of tension and resolution, can be seen as analogous to the storytelling arc of a tarot reading. The initial tonic chord (I) establishes the theme, much like the central card in a spread. The shift to the subdominant (IV) introduces complexity or a new perspective, akin to the way tarot cards provide context or challenge. The dominant chord (V) builds tension, representing the moment of decision or climax in a narrative. Finally, the return to the tonic (I) resolves the tension, offering closure or insight, much like the conclusion of a tarot reading. This alignment emphasizes the shared emphasis on movement, resolution, and emotional storytelling in both music and tarot.

Modes in music provide another lens through which to explore tarot symbolism. Each mode carries its own distinct emotional and tonal qualities, much like each tarot card embodies a specific archetype or theme. The bright, uplifting energy of the Ionian mode (the major scale) might correspond to cards like the Sun or the Star, which evoke themes of joy and hope. The darker, more introspective energy of the Aeolian mode (the natural minor scale) might align with cards like the Moon or the Hermit, which delve into mystery and solitude. By associating specific modes with tarot cards, musicians can use the tonal palette of music to evoke the emotional and symbolic essence of a reading or a specific card.

Rhythm and tempo also play a significant role in aligning musical theory with tarot. The pacing of a musical piece can mirror the energy and movement of a tarot spread. A fast, driving tempo might reflect the dynamic, action-oriented energy of cards like the Chariot or the Knight of Swords. In contrast, a slow, meditative rhythm might capture the reflective, stillness-oriented qualities of the High Priestess or the Hanged Man. Changes in rhythm and tempo within a composition can mirror shifts in the narrative arc of a tarot reading, creating a dynamic interplay between sound and symbolism.

Harmonic tension and resolution, a cornerstone of musical theory, also align closely with the symbolic dynamics of tarot. Just as a dissonant chord creates a sense of unease that resolves into harmony, tarot often explores the tension between opposing forces, light and shadow, challenge and growth, chaos and order. Cards like the Devil and the Tower embody moments of dissonance, where the status quo is disrupted and tension arises. Their eventual resolution is mirrored in cards like the Start and the World, which bring a sense of healing and completion. Musicians can use these concepts to create compositions that mirror the emotional journey of a tarot reading, moving from tension to resolution in a way that resonates with the listener's own experiences.

The concept of intervals in musical theory provides yet another point of connection. Intervals, the distance between two notes, carry distinct emotional qualities, much like the relationships between tarot cards in a spread. A major third, often associated with brightness and positivity, might correspond to harmonious relationships between cards like the Empress and the Lovers. A minor seventh, with its more complex, unresolved quality, might reflect the tension between cards like the Moon and the Seven of Swords. By exploring these parallels, musicians can deepen their understanding of both musical intervals and tarot relationships, using one to inform the other.

Tarot's elemental associations, earth, air, fire, and water, also find resonance in musical theory. Each element corresponds to a specific suit in the tarot and carries distinct qualities that can be expressed through music. Earth, associated with the Pentacles, evokes grounding and stability, which might be reflected in steady rhythms and rich, low frequencies. Air, linked to Swords, suggests intellect and clarity, expressed through intricate melodies and bright, high-pitched tones. Fire, connected to Wands, embodies passion and energy, inspiring driving rhythms and bold dynamics. Water, aligned with the Cups, captures emotion and intuition, conveyed through flowing, lyrical lines and lush harmonies. By consciously incorporating these elemental qualities into their compositions, musicians can create pieces that resonate with the symbolic and emotional energy of the tarot.

The interplay between intuition and structure is another area where musical theory and tarot symbolism align. Both disciplines require a balance between technical skill and creative freedom. A musician might rely on theoretical knowledge to craft a piece of music, but the true magic happens when they allow intuition to guide their choices, bringing the music to life. Similarly, a tarot reader uses the structured meanings of the cards as a foundation but the depth of a reading comes from their intuitive ability to weave those meanings into a coherent and resonant story. This shared dynamic highlights the ways in which music and tarot both honor the interplay of intellect and emotion, discipline and inspiration.

Ultimately, aligning musical theory with tarot symbolism is an act of synthesis, where the logical and the intuitive meet to create something greater than the sum of their parts. Musicians who engage with tarot as a source of inspiration and reflection can deepen their connection to their craft, finding new ways to translate the symbolic language of the cards into sound. Similarly, tarot readers who incorporate musical theory into their work can enrich their readings, using music as a tool to evoke and explore the emotional and symbolic depths of the cards. In this convergence of systems, both music and tarot reveal their shared essence: a profound ability to explore, express, and transform the human experience.

Tarot as a Soundtrack

The process of crafting melodies inspired by tarot themes is a profound journey that bridges the symbolic language of the cards with the emotive power of music. Each tarot card carries its own unique energy, story, and emotional resonance, making it a fertile source of inspiration for musical composition. Translating these qualities into melody requires a deep engagement with both the archetypal significance of the cards and the creative potential of musical expression.

Melodies have an uncanny ability to communicate emotions that words often cannot. In tarot, the imagery and symbolism of the cards evoke specific feelings and ideas, which can serve as the foundation for a melodic narrative. For instance, the serene and luminous energy of the Star might inspire a melody characterized by rising intervals and flowing, legato phrasing. Conversely, the disruptive and chaotic essence of the Tower might translate into jagged, dissonant leaps or sudden rhythmic shifts. By tapping into the emotional core of a card, composers can create melodies that resonate deeply with listeners.

The Major Arcana, with its sequence of archetypal cards, provides a particularly rich source of inspiration for melody crafting. Each card represents a distinct stage in a journey of self-discovery, and its symbolic depth can inform the mood, tempo, and contour of a melody. The Fool, representing beginnings and unbridled potential, might inspire an open, playful melody with unexpected twists and turns, reflecting the card's sense of adventure. In contrast, the weighty and contemplative energy of the Hermit might call for a slow, introspective melody, marked by sustained tones and subtle harmonic shifts. These melodic choices allow the essence of the card to come to life in sound.

The suits of the Minor Arcana also offer unique melodic possibilities, each reflecting a specific elemental quality. Cups, associated with water and emotion, might inspire flowing, lyrical melodies that mirror the undulating movement of waves. Swords, tied to air and intellect, could evoke crisp, articulate melodies with rapid scalar passages or intricate counterpoint. The fiery energy of Wands might translate into bold, energetic themes with driving rhythms and sharp accents, while the grounded nature of the Pentacles might inspire steady, repetitive motifs that convey stability and strength. By aligning the musical character of a melody with the elemental attributes of a suit, composers can create pieces that embody the spirit of the tarot.

The narrative aspect of tarot can also guide the structure and development of a melody. Just as a reading unfolds a story, a melody can evolve to reflect a journey or transformation. A melody inspired by the Wheel of Fortune, for instance, might begin with a simple, repetitive motif that gradually expands and shifts, reflecting the card's themes of change and cyclical patterns. Similarly, a melody for Death could start with a somber, descending line that resolves into a brighter, ascending phrase, symbolizing the transition from endings to new beginnings. This narrative approach allows the melody to mirror the dynamic and transformative nature of the tarot.

Improvisation can play a vital role in connecting with tarot themes musically. Just as tarot readings rely on intuition to uncover layers of meaning, improvisation allows composers to explore melodic ideas in a free, instinctive manner. Drawing a card before sitting down to improvise can provide a thematic anchor, guiding emotional tone and direction of the music. For example, drawing the Moon might inspire an improvisation filled with mysterious, shifting harmonies and ethereal melodic lines, while the Sun could lead to a jubilant, radiant melody full of major key warmth. By allowing the card's energy to flow through the improvisation, composers can discover melodies that feel authentic and deeply connected to the tarot's symbolism.

The act of crafting melodies inspired by tarot themes is also a deeply personal process. Each composer brings their own experiences, emotions, and interpretations to the cards, resulting in melodies that are as unique as the individuals who create them. This personal connection allows the music to transcend mere representation, transforming it into a reflection of the composer's inner world and their relationship with the tarot. A melody inspired by the Lovers, for instance, might resonate differently depending on the composer's own experiences with connection and choice, resulting in a piece that feels intimate and authentic.

Collaboration between tarot readers and musicians can further enrich the melodic crafting process. A tarot reader's insights into the cards' meanings and energies can provide a deeper layer of inspiration for the musician, guiding the development of the melody and its emotional nuances. Conversely, the musician's interpretation of the card through melody can offer the tarot reader a new perspective, creating a dynamic exchange that deepens both their understanding of the card and their creative expression.

In performance, melodies inspired by tarot themes have the power to evoke profound emotional responses in listeners. By tapping into the universal archetypes of the tarot, these melodies resonate on a deep, subconscious level, connecting with the listener's own experiences and emotions. This connection creates a shared space where the boundaries between composer, performer, and audience dissolve, allowing the music to serve as a bridge to the collective human experience.

Daily Tarot Practices for Musicians

In the life of a musician, each day brings a blend of creative expression, technical refinement, emotional depth, and sometimes uncertainty. The world of music is as much about discipline as it is about inspiration, as much about introspection as it is about connection. Tarot, with its rich symbology and intuitive resonance, offers musicians a daily practice that bridges these elements, grounding their creative routines while opening new pathways of insight and inspiration.

Incorporating tarot into daily life as a musician begins with intention. Much like tuning an instrument before a performance, starting the day with tarot helps set a tone that aligns with both personal and artistic energies. The act of shuffling the cards and drawing one becomes a moment of presence, a pause before diving into the demands of practice, composition, or performance. It is a space where intuition and reflection meet, allowing the musician to tap into the flow of the day before it begins.

For a musician, every tarot draw carries potential meaning. The card selected in the morning can act as a thematic compass for the day's endeavors, offering guidance on how to approach creative tasks or navigate emotional landscapes. A card like the Star might suggest a focus on hope and inspiration, perhaps signaling a breakthrough in a project or a reminder to reconnect with the joy of music. On another day, drawing the Two of Pentacles might highlight the need for balance. Between creative work and rest, between technical discipline and emotional freedom. These small, reflective moments can help musicians stay attuned to their inner rhythms as they navigate the external demands of their craft.

Daily tarot practice can also deepen a musician's connection to their creative intuition. In music, intuition often guides improvisation, phrasing and interpretation. Similarly, tarot invites its practitioners to trust their instincts, to let their interpretations flow without overthinking. When a musician draws a card like the High Priestess, it may serve as a gentle nudge to listen to their inner voice, whether in deciding how to approach a difficult piece of music or determining the next steps in a creative project. This intertwining of tarot and musical intuition fosters a dynamic where both practices inform and enhance each other.

For those in the midst of creative work, a daily tarot draw can act as a source of inspiration. A musician working on a new composition might use the card they draw to influence the tone, mood, or structure of their piece. If the Chariot appears, the music might take on a driving, energetic quality, full of forward momentum. If the Moon emerges, the composition might lean into mystery, with shifting harmonies or unconventional forms. By engaging with the symbolic language of the cards, musicians can infuse their work with layers of meaning and emotion that might not have surfaced otherwise.

The practice of tarot also supports the emotional life of a musician, offering a space to process the complexities of their journey. Music is a deeply moving personal form of expression, but it often requires vulnerability and openness that can be challenging to maintain. A daily tarot draw provides a gentle framework for self-reflection, helping musicians navigate the highs and lows of their creative and personal lives. If a musician feels stuck, disheartened, or overwhelmed, a card like the Hermit might suggest a need for solitude and inner exploration, validating the choice to step back and recharge. On the other hand, a card like the Sun might remind them to celebrate their progress and embrace moments of joy and accomplishment.

For performers, daily tarot practice can prepare the mind and spirit for the demands of being on stage. Performing music is an act of vulnerability, where the musician becomes a conduit for expression, connecting deeply with their audience. Drawing a card like Strength before a performance can provide reassurance, reminding the musician of their resilience and the power of authenticity. Meditating on a card like the Lovers might emphasize the importance of connection, both with the audience and with the music itself. This daily ritual can act as a grounding force, helping musicians center themselves before stepping into the spotlight.

Beyond individual practice, tarot can enrich collaborative dynamics among musicians. If working in a group, band, or ensemble, incorporating tarot into daily or rehearsal routines can foster deeper understanding and shared vision. Drawing a card together at the start of a session can set a collective intention guiding the energy of the group as they work. A card like the Ace of Wands might inspire bold creativity, encouraging everyone to take risks and experiment. The Ten of Cups might emphasize harmony and shared joy, reminding the group of the emotional connection that brought them together in the first place.

Tarot also provides a sense of ritual and rhythm in a musician's life which can be especially grounding in a profession that often lacks structure. The unpredictable nature of creative inspiration, coupled with the irregular schedules of performances, rehearsals, and studio sessions, can make it challenging to maintain a consistent routine. A daily tarot practice offers a steady anchor, a simple yet meaningful ritual that remains constant amid the flux. This regular engagement with the cards fosters a sense of continuity, creating a sacred space where musicians can reconnect with their purpose and passion each day.

The Infinite Loop of Creation

Evolution as a musician is not a destination but a continuous journey. It involves refining technique, deepening emotional expression, exploring new creative horizons, and embracing personal and artistic growth. Tarot, with its rich symbology and capacity to illuminate the hidden, can be a profound companion in this ongoing process. Through its archetypes and the intuitive engagement it fosters, tarot becomes not just a tool for reflection, but a means of transformation; guiding musicians to explore, adapt, and expand their artistry.

To evolve as a musician requires a commitment to self-awareness. Tarot excels in this domain, acting as a mirror to the musician's inner world. Each card drawn reflects an aspect of the self or the current circumstances, providing an opportunity to pause and assess where one stands on their artistic path. For instance, encountering the Hanged Man might prompt a musician to reconsider their approach, encouraging them to view their work from a fresh perspective. Similarly, drawing the World can evoke a sense of completion and readiness to move to the next phase of growth. These reflective moments enable musicians to consciously engage with their evolution, recognizing patterns, strengths, and areas that call for change.

Tarot also invites musicians to embrace the cycles inherent in both life and creativity. Just as the seasons shift, so too do phases of inspiration, productivity, and rest. The Wheel of Fortune, for example, reminds musicians of the ebb and flow of creative energy. During times of stagnation, it reassures them that change is inevitable, encouraging patience and openness to the lessons of the moment. Conversely, during periods of great inspiration, the card can serve as a reminder to savor the flow and channel it effectively. By aligning with these natural rhythms, musicians can evolve in harmony with their own creative cycles, avoiding burnout and fostering sustainable growth.

Creativity thrives on risk and exploration, and tarot excels at nudging musicians out of their comfort zones. The cards often present themes or challenges that encourage experimentation. Drawing the Seven of Cups, with its imagery of choices and possibilities, might inspire a musician to explore unfamiliar genres or unconventional techniques. This act of stepping into the unknown is essential for evolution, as it breaks habitual patterns and opens doors to new forms of expression. Through tarot, musicians can safely explore these edges, guided by the symbolic language of the cards to embrace the unfamiliar with curiosity and courage.

Beyond individual growth, tarot fosters an understanding of the interconnectedness between the musician and the world. Music is not created in isolation; it is a dialogue between the artist and their environment. The cards often reflect this relationship, encouraging musicians to consider how their work interacts with and responds to the collective consciousness. The Star, for example, might remind a musician of their role as a beacon of hope and inspiration for others. The Six of Pentacles could prompt a reflection on the exchange of energy between artist and audience. This awareness deepens the musician's understanding of their place in the larger tapestry of artistic expression, fostering a sense of purpose that fuels continued evolution.

Embracing tarot as a guide also means developing a willingness to face challenges and confront fears. The path of a musician is often fraught with obstacles: creative blocks, self-doubt, and external pressures. Tarot provides a framework for engaging with these difficulties, transforming them into opportunities for growth. Encountering a card like the Tower might signify a moment of upheaval, but it also holds the promise of rebuilding on stronger foundations. By working through such moments with the cards as a guide, musicians learn to navigate challenges with resilience and grace, emerging from them more confident and capable.

A unique aspect of tarot is its ability to align the subconscious with conscious intention. Musicians often work from an intuitive space, but evolution requires bringing this intuition into dialogue with deliberate action. Drawing a card such as the Magician can act as a catalyst for this alignment, reminding the musician of their ability to channel inspiration into tangible results. It bridges the gap between vision and execution, encouraging a balance between dreaming and doing. This integration of intuition and discipline is vital for sustained artistic growth, allowing musicians to continually refine their craft while remaining open to the sparks of inspiration that guide them forward.

Collaboration is another area where tarot supports evolution. Music is often a shared experience, and tarot can illuminate dynamics within partnerships, bands, or ensembles. Through spreads that explore roles, communication, or collective vision, the cards foster understanding and cohesion among collaborators. A card like Justice might prompt a group to address imbalances, ensuring that every member's voice is heard and valued. As musicians learn to navigate these relationships with greater awareness, they grow not only as individuals but also as contributors to a larger creative whole.

The evolution of a musician is also deeply intertwined with their emotional and spiritual growth. Tarot's archetypes resonate with universal experiences, offering a lens through which musicians can explore their emotional landscape. Cards like the Hermit invite introspection, encouraging musicians to seek clarity about their motivations and desires. The Lovers might spark a reflection on the relationships that shape their work, whether with other artists, audiences, or themselves. These explorations deepen the musician's emotional reservoir, enriching their ability to convey authentic and profound expression through their music.

Ultimately, the continual evolution of a musician through tarot is an ongoing dance between reflection and action, intuition and intention. Each card drawn becomes a stepping stone on the journey, offering insight, challenge, or encouragement. The process is as much about embracing the unknown as it is about cultivating mastery, recognizing that true growth lies in the willingness to adapt, explore, and transform.

Through this practice, musicians can remain in a state of perpetual becoming, where every note played, every song written, and every performance given contributes to their unfolding story. Tarot, with its capacity to mirror the complexities of human experience, serves as a steadfast companion on this journey, a tool for deepening self-awareness, fostering creativity, and navigating the ever-changing landscape of artistic life. In this partnership, the musician and the cards evolve together, each day offering a new opportunity to grow, create, and connect.

Tarot Spreads: Crafting Creativity Through the Cards

In the intricate dance between tarot and music, spreads act as the choreographer, guiding movements and decisions with an invisible hand. Tarot spreads are the layouts through which meaning is distilled from the cards, each position serving as a vessel for insight. For musicians, these spreads become not just a tool for divination but a framework for creativity, offering a mirror to their artistic process and a map to navigate the uncharted territories of sound.

Imagine a single card pulled in isolation, a note sustained in the silence, waiting for the next. Now, envision multiple cards laid in a deliberate arrangement. Together, they form chords, harmonies, and rhythms, each card lending its voice to a greater symphony of interpretation. Tarot spreads, then, are the song structures of divination, providing the scaffolding for a story to unfold.

Consider the way a traditional three-card spread (past, present, future) might influence a songwriter. The first card, the past, could evoke memories of formative influences, the roots of a musician's style, or a pivotal moment in their journey. The present card might illuminate the emotional or thematic space they occupy now, perhaps pointing to a dissonance that needs resolution or a harmony ready to be embraced. The future card doesn't prescribe a fixed outcome but rather hints at where their music might evolve, urging them to consider the possibilities of growth and transformation.

For an improvising musician, a Celtic Cross spread could act as an elaborate blueprint. The central card represents the core theme or question, like the key of a piece or the foundational groove. Surrounding cards, those that cross, support, and oppose, layer additional textures and tensions, much like counter-melodies or syncopated rhythms. The outer ring of cards mirrors the musician's internal and external environment, reflecting influences, challenges, and aspirations that shape the creative process.

When a band or ensemble uses tarot spreads, the collaborative energy takes on new dimensions. Imagine each member interpreting a specific position in a spread, their instrument becoming the voice of that card. The Hierophant might inspire the bassist to create a grounding, structured rhythm, while the Star might lead the lead guitarist into a soaring, ethereal solo. The interplay between the cards becomes the interplay between the musicians, uniting them in a shared narrative crafted in real time.

Tarot spreads also invite exploration of unconventional song structures. A spread with a flowing, serpentine layout might inspire a piece with no chorus, just a continuous unfolding of melody and mood. A rigid, grid-like spread could suggest a piece grounded in repetitive motifs, exploring variation within structure. Each position in a spread can be assigned a musical parameter, tempo, key, dynamics, or tone color, allowing the cards to dictate not only thematic content but also technical execution.

Beyond song creation, spreads can guide a musician's personal growth. A spread exploring creative blocks might begin with a card representing the block itself, the Eight of Swords for example, signaling self-imposed limitation. Subsequent cards could reveal subconscious fears or external pressures contributing to the stagnation, while others suggest actionable steps to rekindle inspiration. Here, the spread becomes not just a reflection of the artist's current state but a roadmap toward liberation and renewal.

When used in performance, tarot spreads bring an element of spontaneity and ritual to the stage. Imagine a live show where the setlist is dictated by a spread drawn in real-time, each card determining the next song, style, or improvisational theme. This not only engages the audience with the mystery of the cards but also challenges the musician to adapt, innovate, and trust the flow.

Ultimately, tarot spreads are an invitation to embrace music as a dialogue with the unknown. Each card, like each note, carries infinite potential, waiting to be shaped by the hands of the artist. In this interplay between structure and intuition, tarot and music become indistinguishable, blending into a single, seamless expression of creativity.

Conclusion: Eternal Harmony of Tarot and Music

As we close this exploration of tarot and its connection to music, it's clear that these two art forms share a profound synergy, both rooted in intuition, symbolism, and the human desire for expression. Each serves as a mirror to the soul, reflecting back the stories, emotions, and truths that often lie just beneath the surface of conscious awareness. Together they form an extraordinary duet. A dynamic interplay of rhythm and meaning, sound and silence, logic and mystery.

Tarot is a language of archetypes and symbols, a map of human experience. Music, too, is a universal language, speaking directly to the heart without the need for translation. Both transcend cultural and temporal boundaries, inviting their participants into an endless dance of creation and discovery. Through their combination, musicians can find not just inspiration but a deeper understanding of themselves and their craft.

The tarot deck, with its seventy-eight cards, is much like a musical scale. Each card holds a distinct note, yet it is only when they are played in relation to one another that a melody emerges. A single card drawn from the deck can spark a theme, just as a single chord can set the tone for a piece of music. When the cards are spread out in patterns, they become akin to a composition, with each position offering its own contribution to the overall harmony. Musicians who allow the tarot to guide them often find their work infused with a new dimension of depth and resonance.

There is a certain courage in creating music from the tarot. To draw a card and respond to its message is to embrace uncertainty, to invite the unexpected. It is a process of surrender, where the musician becomes a vessel through which something larger speaks. This act of trust mirrors the leap of faith required when composing a piece or stepping onstage. Both tarot and music require vulnerability, a willingness to connect with the indescribable and translate it into something tangible.

At its core, this connection between tarot and music is about storytelling. Every song is a narrative, whether abstract or explicit, and every tarot reading is a tale unfolding in real time. When these two mediums intertwine, the resulting story gains layers of meaning, depth, and complexity. A simple progression of chords might suddenly resonate as the embodiment of the Magician's confidence or the Lovers' duality. A haunting melody might echo the introspection of the Hermit or the transformation heralded by Death. The archetypes of tarot breathe life into music, and music, in turn, gives voice to the silent wisdom of the cards.

For musicians, tarot offers not just a tool for creation but also a path for self-reflection and growth. It challenges the artist to confront their fears, honor their dreams, and remain present in the unfolding moment. Through its guidance, musicians can navigate the highs and lows of their journey with a deeper sense of purpose and clarity. It reminds them that creativity is not a straight line but a spiral, constantly looping back to familiar themes with new perspectives.

Performing musicians might find a unique kind of magic in integrating tarot into their live shows, where the act of drawing cards becomes a ritual shared with the audience. In these moments, the tarot and music combine to create a space of collective wonder and intimacy, where the boundaries between performer and listener dissolve. The music becomes a living, breathing entity, shaped not just by the artist's intent but by the energy of the room, the mystery of the cards, and the shared experience of all present.

In the end, both tarot and music teach us about harmony, not the kind that avoids dissonance, but the kind that embraces it, weaving even the most discordant notes into something beautiful and whole. They remind us that every moment, no matter how fleeting, is part of a larger composition. The tarot invites us to find meaning in the shuffle and placement of its cards, just as music invites us to find beauty in its patterns of sound and silence.

The dialogue between tarot and music is endless, an ever-unfolding symphony of inspiration and discovery. As you continue your journey with these two profound art forms, may you always listen to the whispers of intuition, follow the pull of creativity, and trust in the harmony that emerges when you allow yourself to fully engage with the unknown. In this meeting of worlds, where symbols become sounds and sounds become symbols, you may find the truest expression of yourself.